Perspectives on Strategy examines in depth five aspects of strategy. Strategic thought and behaviour are explored and explained from the perspectives of intellect, morality, culture, geography, and technology. Each perspective has attracted persisting controversy. *Perspectives on Strategy* is strongly complementary to the author's previous book, *The Strategy Bridge: Theory for Practice* (OUP, 2010). This new work takes a notably holistic view of strategic phenomena, which serves as a master framework within which detailed examination of strategic history and issues can usefully be pursued in the light of particular perspectives. Foundational for the argument in *Perspectives on Strategy* is the proposition that distinctive aspects of strategy (e.g. ethics, culture, inter alia) can only be appreciated properly when they are regarded in context. The author shares this view with T. E. Lawrence (of Arabia), who wrote of the 'whole house of war'. *Perspectives on Strategy* gratefully adapts Lawrence and writes about the 'whole house of strategy'. The book insists that the nature of strategy is best represented by a Venn diagram that shows overlapping perspectives. Thus, the subject of each chapter is shown as having meaning for, and in turn is influenced by, the subjects of the other chapters. For example, the book explores the importance of strategic ideas relative to the significance of the material weapons of war. The author poses the hardest of questions pertinent to each chosen perspective (e.g. do ideas matter more than muscle? In practice how robust is the ethical code with which warfare is waged? Is geography destiny, as some theorists have claimed? Do technically superior weapons win wars?) *Perspectives on Strategy* demonstrates that it is possible to look closely at strategic matters from limited but arguably powerful perspectives, without being captured by them. This book asks and answers the most challenging and rewarding questions that can be posed in order to reveal the persisting universal nature, but ever changing character, of strategy.

Perspectives on Strategy

COLIN S. GRAY

OXFORD
UNIVERSITY PRESS

OXFORD
UNIVERSITY PRESS

Great Clarendon Street, Oxford, OX2 6DP,
United Kingdom

Oxford University Press is a department of the University of Oxford.
It furthers the University's objective of excellence in research, scholarship,
and education by publishing worldwide. Oxford is a registered trade mark of
Oxford University Press in the UK and in certain other countries

First published 2013
First published in paperback 2016

Published in the United States of America by Oxford University Press
198 Madison Avenue, New York, NY 10016, United States of America

British Library Cataloguing in Publication Data
Data available

Library of Congress Cataloging in Publication Data
Data available

ISBN 978-0-19-967427-5 (Hbk.)
ISBN 978-0-19-877871-4 (Pbk.)

To T J, truly unique

Preface

Perspectives on Strategy is a companion though stand-alone work to my earlier book, *The Strategy Bridge*. In the Preface to *Bridge* I speculated that I might find it desirable to write a *Bridge: The Missing Chapters*. The topics treated in *Perspectives* are not those 'missing' from *Bridge*, because they would not have fitted there. *Perspectives* is a complementary, hence companion, work that rests vitally upon the general theory of strategy that *Bridge* presented and explained. The logical connection between the two books is both necessary and easy to explain. *Perspectives* is able to explore deeply five particular dimensions of strategy—conceptual, ethical, cultural, geographical, and technological—because it is the legatee of a firm theoretical foundation: it has no need to revisit the nature of strategy and its general theory, because they have already been covered at length in *Bridge*. The five topics in *Perspectives* were all treated in *Bridge*, but only *en passant* as elements in a very large composite picture. As a benign consequence, *Perspectives* is able to seek depth of analysis by a sustained focus on a handful of large subjects.

The five perspective chapters owe their design to somewhat different approaches, adopted hopefully to yield the kind of tailored examination likely to be most productive. The chapters on concepts, ethics, and culture, are each treated conceptually, even philosophically, though with illustration in detail. The chapter on geography is oriented to show the relevance of its topic to strategic issues of deterrence; while the chapter that explores strategy in technological perspective examines the relative importance of the tools of war as compared with the other factors that contribute to military and strategic effectiveness. In the same way that I intend *Perspectives* to be positively complementary to *Bridge*, it is my aspiration that the different approaches taken to the five perspectives are mutually enriching.

Perspectives has much to say that is controversial, but it is not prescriptive for policy or strategy. The book has no hidden agenda directly relevant to contemporary issues of public policy. The mission of *Perspectives* is strictly one of education to help readers comprehend better what they need to understand in order to cope well enough with the practical demands they must meet. There is a place for vigorous policy advocacy, but these pages are not one of them.

My authorial debts are many and heavy. Above all others I wish to thank my academic home and employer, the University of Reading, whose scholarly environment has been encouraging and vitally supportive. Geoffrey Sloan, Dale Walton, Patrick Porter, and Beatrice Heuser comprise a lively and doughty mini-legion of stimulating colleagues. In addition I wish to register my gratitude for the friendship and support offered over some years by Philip Giddings: the chapter here on strategy's 'moral maze' may well cause him some unease.

Next, the support I have received from my university colleagues has been augmented over the years by the confidence shown in me by The Earhart Foundation and its Trustees of Ann Arbor, Michigan. I wish to thank the Foundation, and especially its President, Ingrid Gregg, for their warm support for this book. As usual, the project took longer and resulted in a larger work than had been anticipated. That said, I hope that they are suitably gratified by the final result.

By way of specific intellectual and other academic debts, I must cite the connection between Chapter 2 on the ethical perspective and the extensive effort now long underway at the University of Reading on its Liberal Way of War Programme, funded by The Leverhulme Foundation and led at the University by Professor Alan Cromartie. My chapter was written for this book, but in common with some other elements in this project, in writing it I have drawn nourishment from the research environment around me. Important sources of academic calories for the scholar are friends, including graduate students and colleagues, who are repositories of particular expertise or inspiring stimuli. Among my students, I am grateful to Jeannie Johnson, whose enthusiasm for cultural topography though not reflected faithfully in my Chapter 3, nonetheless had some impact on these pages, I hope for net positive effect. In addition, I must thank my good friend Lt. Colonel Frank G. Hoffman, USMC (ret.), who continues to be a stimulating controversialist with whom frequently, though not always, I am in agreement. He rode to my rescue promptly and effectively when asked.

I am grateful to the National Institute for Public Policy and its President, Dr Keith Payne, for permission to use a revised version of a study for them as Chapter 4 in this book. The National Institute's version is published as 'Geopolitics and Deterrence', in *Comparative Strategy*, 31 (July–September 2012).

My more personal debts are all too typically heavy. My professional typist and friend Barbara Watts has succeeded in reading my handwritten manuscript, even when I could not. Yet again, this work is more than marginally a joint production by a team of two. As for my family, human and other(s), Valerie and Tonia have enabled, I cannot quite say encouraged, this mission to be undertaken and performed. Words alone do not suffice to express my gratitude.

Colin S. Gray

Wokingham
June 2012

Contents

Tables and Figures

Strategy without tactics is the slowest route to victory. Tactics without strategy is the noise before defeat.

Anon. (often falsely attributed to Sun Tzu)

Introduction: Master Narrative

Strategic concepts and theories may march divided through cyberspace these days, but they apply as a whole to a single unique though ever familiar historical context. In aspiration at least, it was a hallmark of Napoleon's intended way of warfare for his army corps to march divided, but then to combine in order to fight united. It is a purpose of this book to demonstrate that strategic history is intellectually coherent, even if strategists and strategic performances frequently are not. Whatever the chaos, friction, and contingency, and notwithstanding the complexity of all the working parts that mysteriously generate a single course of events, there is always only one stream of history. There is a single actual and therefore objectively sovereign run of events, even when it readily reveals neither discernible pattern nor purposeful strategic intent. Of course, contemporary records, participants reminiscing in tranquillity, historians, and other scholars, interpret events differently. That unavoidable fact granted, still it is important to understand that there is always a true unity to the apparent diversity in the strategic historical reality that was the past. Often there are competing narratives, each claiming to explain what a particular episode was really about. The past becomes history, actually rival histories, and it is explained by the theories that are the stories told by historians. It is necessary for a good story to have a plot keyed to a favoured destination. Once decided upon with the advantage of hindsight, the plot enables one confidently to assign meaning to, and possibly justify, the steps taken en route to journey's end. The truth can be embarrassing if it might be explained and characterized by the adapted maxim that 'if you do not know where you are going, any road will take you there, and that was the road that we took'. Another maxim holds that 'you may not be interested in strategy, but strategy is interested in you'. The line between banality and potent insight can be faint, but in the case of these two maxims insight just wins, though admittedly not by a comfortable margin. The first maxim translates as meaning that all relevant behaviour, purposeful or not, has a strategic effect upon the course of events on an uncharted and possibly unchartable voyage. The second claims that the strategic effect of behaviour is unavoidable. In common with breathing for living species, so strategy also is an ineradicable function that is a condition of life for human beings.

The simplest ideas are not always the easiest to grasp, and neither need they be the correct ones. However, strategy is a simple subject in its essential logic, but alas it is one that lends itself to what can become an intellectually disabling granularity in treatment; especially when no effort is expended to promote the thought that detail only has meaning in context. It is a central part of the mission here to attempt to recover a fuller appreciation of the unity of strategic phenomena, without as a consequence incurring crippling transaction costs. Familiarity with such a word as strategy works to obscure the widespread truth that frequently it is unhelpfully defined, misunderstood, and therefore is misused. This sad condition has unfortunate practical consequences, because strategy refers to a function that is literally as vital to security and general well-being as it is unavoidable. Everyone behaves strategically much of the time. But everyone does not always behave competently, let alone consciously and purposefully, as a functional strategist. Moreover, even high competence in strategy provides no guarantee of success. The core reason is because strategy is, by its nature, a competitive project. To do well enough as a strategist means passing a dynamic examination set and marked by antagonistic competing strategists. There is some substantial comfort in this historical reality. It means that a strategist need not be superior as such in order to win. Rather, he need only be sufficiently superior to his adversaries on the day: they may well all be less than premier strategists by some objective standard.

The lead mission of *Perspectives on Strategy* is to show that strategy is an inclusive rather than an exclusive realm of thought and behaviour, while demonstrating convincingly that the different perspectives in which strategic matters can be viewed need to be recognized as sources both of constraint and opportunity. For example, one could argue that although Adolf Hitler proposed, the Russian winter of 1941–2 disposed. This familiar climatic historical judgement is not implausible. Nonetheless, it is rather more persuasive to argue as does historian Geoffrey P. Megargee that '[t]he weather did not defeat the Germans: their failure to plan for it did'.[1] After all, winter happens annually.

In this work I adhere to the same definitions of strategy per se, grand strategy, and military strategy, that I employed and explained in my book *The Strategy Bridge*. It is regrettable to be repetitive, but these definitions need to be repeated, since they are vital to the sense in the entire work.

1. *Strategy* (content neutral): The direction and use made of means by chosen ways in order to achieve desired ends.

2. *Grand strategy*: The direction and use made of any and all among the total assets of a security community for the purposes of policy as decided by politics.

3. *Military strategy*: The direction and use made of force and the threat of force for the purposes of policy as decided by politics.[2]

If this trinity of definitions of strategy strikes some readers as pedantic and academic in its pejorative sense, then so be it. Meaningful debate requires that we know what it is that we are talking about, and that mandates definition. The substantive issues that attract strategic argument provide all of the intellectual challenge that renders strategy such a fascinating field of enquiry and dispute. Unintended confusion caused by linguistic indiscipline is self-inflicted damage. Although strictly it is true to claim that definitions are only discretionary, they can be neither right nor wrong save with respect to accepted common usage, nonetheless it is necessary to recognize that some definitions, as well as casual usage, confuse and hinder understanding. Strategy is a concept that attracts misuse. All behaviour is tactical in the doing, but strategic in its meaning, whether the meaning is assessed to be great or small.

Strategy does not have to refer to military matters, but that is the default reality throughout this book. The context of discussion will make clear whether or not the strategy under examination is military. If my master narrative is designed to show the inclusive unity of strategy, so, ironically, the text demonstrates that inclusivity by highlighting the distinguishing singularity of each of the dimensions of strategy that offer a distinctive perspective.[3] The pervasive differences between the many parts of the strategist's domain provide a stark contrast with their essential unity in meaning and consequence. The general theory of strategy yields all the explanation needed of why it is that apparently widely disparate military and other activities in combination have coherent meaning for defence and security. This is not a mystery. Rather is it proof of strategic theory doing its duty of sorting out what needs to be arranged tidily, and making sense of it. Far from being merely the intellectual plaything of armchair strategists, the theory of strategy is the necessary enabler of the strategic understanding required if tactical behaviour is to be done for a higher purpose. Just as tactics require strategy if they are not to be pointless, so strategy depends on, indeed is, theory. The conceptual perspective on strategy refers to the brain of the project.

Strategy as a subject is subordinate to the far more inclusive subject of security. In its turn security can be regarded as a sub-field of politics.[4] The ambitious but still limited mandate of this work is so to examine strategy that the diversity within the field is explained in ways that do not imperil grasp of the entire enterprise. The tension between forces pressing for fission and those for fusion has been an eternal and universal feature of strategic discourse. Newcomers to strategic debate can be bewildered by references to nuclear strategy or, today, cyber strategy, when more accurately they should meet mention only of strategy for nuclear and cyber weapons. The former usage appears to refer to nuclear strategy and cyber strategy as if they are twin-headed concepts with integrity: they seem to privilege the adjectival modifier over the noun. The latter plainly favours the noun, strategy, over the qualifying adjectives, nuclear and cyber. Unwary entrants into strategic debate might well believe that nuclear strategy, air strategy, space strategy, cyber strategy, and the rest are each distinct species. Moreover, so obvious are the differences among the material and derivative tactical features of these military ideas that the case for uniqueness would seem to make itself. The general theory of strategy has no difficulty equipping novices to enhance their resistance to categorical confusion. That theory states that there is strategy, singular and overall, and there are strategies, notably plural and ever subject to change. In theory though by no means necessarily in practice, strategies for land power, air power, and sea power should be mutually supportive. It is an episodic but recurring reality that new and new-seeming ideas and capabilities threaten the authority of settled strategic 'cultural thoughtways'.[5] This is no bad thing, because undue stability in authority promotes intellectual laziness and some loss of ability to innovate or react effectively to innovation by others. However, if a security community is not well educated in strategy, it is perpetually in danger of capture by the prophets of perilously partial and misleading concepts.

It can be difficult to appraise the hottest strategic prospect of the moment in a suitably prudent perspective, which is to say with an open mind but in a sceptical spirit. The purveyors of apparently compelling concepts and machines are near certain to insist upon embedding their arguments and products in the perspective that they themselves have chosen to emphasize and provide. The mutually reinforcing and validating strategic concept and context offer a package deal that insists on the value of hammers because all problems are claimed to be, or at least can be treated as, nails. Strategic reductionism, in this case the insistence that all challenges are reducible to tasks with which one's favoured idea or instrument is well able to cope, is a familiar feature of strategic argument. It would be a mistake to dismiss out of hand claims for multi-task effectiveness as pure fantasy. When scaled back from fantasy to mere overstatement, ambitious assertions of anticipated strategic effectiveness may well have merit. So uncertain is the strategist's domain for action that it is not always self-evident which of the possible roads to Tokyo, or should it be Berlin, one ought to favour most.

The batting order is not of critical importance for the chapter subjects here. The master narrative of argument is more cumulative than sequential.[6] A master narrative of strategy that denies sequentiality might make for some reader discomfort. Strategy has to modelled and understood in terms of a Venn diagram. While strategy has a temporal dimension and context and needs to be examined chronologically, nonetheless all of its dimensions are permanently live on the field of play. This means that although *Perspectives* must deconstruct and dissect in order to employ the tools of particular perspectives; care has to be exercised lest some approximation to a law of the instrument creeps in like a virus to infect the argument. For example, Chapter 4 adopts a geographical perspective on strategy, employing the strategic concept of deterrence as an aid to focus in the analysis. That chapter only provides a geographical perspective, it does not advance a geographical theory or explanation of strategy. Geography is important, which is why it is on this select team of perspectives, but it is not competing to be elected Chosen Theory. We already have the Chosen Theory; it is the general theory of strategy within whose broad tent geography and the other perspective subjects of this book are to coexist and cooperate to mutual advantage. Before proceeding further, it is advisable to check in briefly with the greatest strategic theorist of them all, Carl von Clausewitz. The Prussian insists strongly, though in terms that leave him room for discretion, upon the necessity for a holistic view. He opens *On War* with these words

> I propose to consider first the various elements of the subject, next various parts or sections, and finally the whole in its internal structure. In other words, I shall proceed from the simple to the complex. But in war more than in any other subject we must begin by looking at the nature of the whole: for here more than elsewhere the part and the whole must always be thought of together.[7]

Notwithstanding their common-sense plausibility, there is no denying the intellectual agility in the words just quoted. Clausewitz stops short of self-contradiction, but not by much. Elsewhere, he beats the drum again for holistic understanding when he warns that the 'elements of strategy' (identified by him as allowing for classification in the following five 'types': 'moral, physical, mathematical, geographical, and statistical') require comprehensive assay. He warns that

> It would however be disastrous to try to develop our understanding of strategy by analysing these factors [the famous five named above: CSG] in isolation, since they are usually interconnected in each military action in manifold and intricate ways. A dreary analytical labyrinth would result, a nightmare in which one tried in vain to bridge the gulf between this abstract basis and the facts of life. Heaven protect the theorist from such an undertaking! For our part, we shall continue to examine the picture as a whole, and take our analysis no further than is necessary to elucidate the idea we wish to convey, which will always have its origins in the impressions made by the sum total of the phenomena of war, rather than in speculative study.[8]

The holistic theme returns forcefully when Clausewitz explains that '[s]ubordinating the political point of view to the military would be absurd, for it is policy that creates war'.[9] He should be hard to misunderstand.

> If we recall the nature of actual war, if we remember the argument in Chapter 3 above—that the probable character and general shape of any war should mainly be assessed in the light of political factors and conditions—and that war should often (indeed one might say normally) be conceived as an organic whole whose parts cannot be separated, so that each individual act contributes to the whole and

itself originates in the central concept, then it will be perfectly clear and certain that the supreme standpoint for the conduct of war, the point of view that determines its main lines of action, can only be that of policy.[10]

Everything of strategic significance must occur within the same bounds of time and space. However, such essential and objective simultaneity cannot be understood quite literally by scholars. Just because many factors matter at the same time, fortunately it is not usually necessary that literally they be addressed simultaneously. Although many factors are not pure with completely impermeable boundaries, nonetheless they will have a 'grammar' of their own attributable to their own nature.[11] To illustrate, politics, geography, culture, and technology all interpenetrate as reciprocal sources of influence, but that obvious fact does not reduce to relative unimportance their distinctive natures. The function that is strategy has integrity when regarded as a whole project, but then so also to a lesser degree do the several distinctive parts of the whole (e.g. politics, operations, and tactics). The challenge to the scholar is to honour the full story of strategy, while not losing the grip needed on the separate parts of which often unharmoniously it is composed. The more common malady, though, is that which might be expressed in some old fashioned social science jargon as sub-system dominance. Such dominance takes the form of heavily reductionist theories that assert that 'strategy most essentially is about...' (geography, culture, technology, economics, or anything else that has captured the scholar's affection).

Two perspectives rule themselves out for distinctive adoption here because they are too imperial to be disciplined should they be assigned to a premier league all to themselves: they are the human and the political. Human nature and politics invade and occupy these pages pervasively, but the very ubiquity and potent elasticity of these mighty two would detract from overall explanation and understanding were they to be released unharnessed to other perspectives. Because strategy has to be understood as a Venn diagram there is some arbitrariness in the chapter order. The chapters are themed by perspective in order to ensure depth and breadth to the whole enquiry. However, each perspective derives some of its meaning from other perspectives that provide essential contexts. Because the master narrative must rule, this book both opens and closes with treatment of 'the whole house of strategy'.[12] Both ends of the work affirm the wholeness of the subject of strategy. The chapters provide perspectives on strategy, not distinctive theories of strategy. Readers are not invited to rank-order their preferences as if there could be conceptual, ethical, cultural, geographical, or technological approaches to strategy, considered as alternatives.

Perspectives opens five windows upon strategy. The story arc of the book is less important in its precise trajectory than in its total content, which is advanced more with a sense of cumulative layering than of sequential revelation.

Chapter 1 examines the conceptual apparatus invented, refined, and periodically mislaid, by means of which people for millennia have striven to impose some intellectual order on a chaotic strategic world. Next, Chapter 2 considers strategy in ethical perspective. Strategic theorists typically are uncomfortable with the moral dimension to their subject; not infrequently they suspect that this dimension has the potential to paralyse and disable strategy's practitioners. Strategic expediency can be morally troublesome.

Chapter 3 explores the strongly contested cultural perspective on strategy. In common with morality, many people are certain that culture is important for strategy, but they are deeply uncertain as to how much and how often this is so. The scholarly debate over strategy and culture has moved on radically over the past decade. Culturalists came in from the cold and as they became fashionable they overreached, as happens in the dynamics of controversy, and were duly challenged by the return of the critical tide by sceptics. This betrays both the healthy rhythm of debate, as well as the flow and contraflow of real-world events. Strategy is a practical subject and the theories produced by its theorists reflect the worries of the period. There was geography before there was strategy. It is a common assertion that geography is the most fundamental of the factors that influence and shape strategy. Chapter 4 looks at strategy in geographical perspective in a way intended to facilitate identification of the input from geographical matters. In order to do this the chapter focuses on the meaning of geographical phenomena for the relevance and functioning of strategies intended to promote deterrence. By thus linking a major, indeed the hegemonic, modern strategic concept, one that has material referents in military forces *inter alia*, and to the geophysical context for its possible application, the analysis seeks to impose some discipline on what can be undergoverned scholarly terrain.

The technological perspective is the lens for Chapter 5. There is general agreement not only that technology is important, but also that that importance often is attributable to reasons that reach far beyond machinery. Ideas and qualities of human character, as well as geographical and temporal contexts, can all trump apparent advantages in technology, but not reliably so in ways that one can always explain with high confidence.

Perspectives closes with a chapter designed to ensure that every perspective receives due notice, and that the master narrative comprising inclusivity, cohesion, and unity, has not been mislaid.

Perspectives builds upon and from my earlier work, *The Strategy Bridge*, but it can stand alone. *Strategy Bridge* presented a new version of the general theory of strategy and examined the subject in broad terms. By way of contrast, *Perspectives* moves on to examine strategy using the foci of five principal perspectives to shed light. Scholarly controversy swirls around arguments pertaining to each of these.

A story arc more cumulative than sequential in character has the potential to be controversial. Although the order of presentation of perspectives may be somewhat discretionary, I have had no serious doubt that this book should proceed from the conceptual, through the ethical and the cultural, to the geographical and the technological. While respecting other possible navigational choices, I am satisfied that the route followed in these chapters is right enough. The intention here is not to score points in current debate, but rather to help move strategy debate on. We must begin with the brain of the strategist and recognize that when strategic theorists are in professional difficulty, so too will be their societies. The twenty-first century already has recorded a severe strategic intellectual crisis that one can characterize fairly as nothing less than concept failure.[13] With this potent fuel now burning and shining light on intellectual chaos, the mission can launch in quest of better understanding—'to boldly go . . .', untroubled by Victorian grammatical prejudice that I share.

NOTES

1. Geoffrey P. Megargee, *War of Annihilation: Combat and Genocide on the Eastern Front, 1941* (Lanham, MD: Rowman & Littlefield, 2006), 103.
2. Colin S. Gray, *The Strategy Bridge: Theory for Practice* (Oxford: Oxford University Press, 2010), 18.
3. Colin S. Gray, *Modern Strategy* (Oxford: Oxford University Press, 1999), 23–44.
4. See Ken Booth, *Theory of World Security* (Cambridge: Cambridge University Press, 2007).
5. Ken Booth, *Strategy and Ethnocentrism* (London: Croom Helm, 1979).
6. J. C. Wylie, *Military Strategy: A General Theory of Power Control* (1967; Annapolis, MD: Naval Institute Press, 1989), ch. 3, offers an exemplary brief discussion of the differences between cumulative and sequential strategies, while also specifying the limitations as well as the attractions of this binary construct.
7. Carl von Clausewitz, *On War*, trans. Michael Howard and Peter Paret (1832–4; Princeton, NJ: Princeton University Press, 1976), 75 (emphasis in the original).
8. Clausewitz, *On War*, 183.
9. Clausewitz, *On War*, 607.
10. Clausewitz, *On War* (emphasis in the original).
11. Clausewitz, *On War*, 605.
12. An adapted borrowing from T. E. Lawrence with his 'whole house of war'. *Seven Pillars of Wisdom: A Triumph* (New York: Anchor Books, 1991), 191.
13. I pursue this thought in my *Categorical Confusion? The Strategic Implications of Recognizing Challenges Either as Irregular or Traditional* (Carlisle, PA: Strategic Studies Institute, US Army War College, February 2012).

1

Concepts: Mind and Muscle

Even if we break down war into its various activities, we will find that the difficulties are not uniform throughout. The more physical the activity the less the difficulties will be. The more the activity becomes intellectual and turns into motives which exercise a determining influence on the commander's will, the more the difficulties will increase. Thus it is easier to use theory to organize, plan, and conduct an engagement than it is to use it in determining the engagement's purpose. Combat is conducted with physical weapons, and although the intellect does play a part, material factors will dominate. But when one comes to the *effect* of the engagement, where material successes turn into motives for further action, the intellect alone is decisive. In brief, *tactics* will present far fewer difficulties to the theorist than will *strategy*.

Carl von Clausewitz[1]

1.1 STRATEGY AND INTELLECT

Strategic theory and the concepts that are its building blocks have only one purpose: to enhance understanding, to educate for action. In order to be fit for that purpose the strategic theory of the day needs to do two things. It has to keep faith with the unchanging general theory of strategy, while also it must be adaptable to the transient character of the historical context. Theorists have a policing function and duty. They should discipline contemporary strategic thought so that fads and fashions are detected and revealed to be only such, rather than the revelation of eternal value that often is claimed. It is commonplace but useful to think of fighting power, the core potential fuel for strategic effectiveness, as having three ingredients: the intellectual, the material, and the moral. As is unavoidable with super-reductionist trinities, this one risks explaining too little as the price for aspiring to explain too much. Nonetheless, the trinitarian formula highlights appropriately the importance of the intellectual contribution to strategic history. From time to time there is an intellectual crisis when strategic thinkers seem manifestly unequal to the challenges of the day. Authors of strategic theory are apt to forget that fine-sounding concepts alone achieve nothing, much as excellent intelligence that is not actionable tends not to be useful. This conceptual perspective on strategy distinguishes between understanding strategy in general and doing it in a specific context. It is always necessary to be able to do both. This is not to ignore the enduring reality that the ability to invent and implement strategies fit for particular current circumstances is ever likely to be imperfect. Just as logistics typically is more demanding a command responsibility than is strategic conception, so conception for a specific purpose is more likely to be a serious challenge than is a sound grasp of the basics of strategy's general theory. The latter is vital for the former, but it falls in the necessary class of understanding, not the sufficient.

The conceptual perspective accommodates the whole house of strategy, but its domain is limited to the identification, understanding, and explanation of strategic phenomena.[2] To comprehend a problem is not synonymous with understanding how to solve it, while even the achievement of such understanding does not mean that one is able to solve it. In the winter of 1940–1, RAF Fighter Command fully understood its problem in attempting to defend against the Luftwaffe's Night Blitz. The RAF recognized that there was no practicable solution until reliable airborne radar and the aircraft to carry it were ready in suitable numbers, and that could not be done in the winter of 1940–1.[3] This was not a classic case of concept failure, but rather one of priorities and their consequences in sequenced achievement. Fighter Command's overwhelming first priority was the ground-based radar system to detect and help counter daylight attack. British science, technology, and industrial production achieved a near miracle with the Chain Home and Chain Home Low radar stations that were ready for the enemy by the summer of 1940. They could not be partnered by an airborne system in the same time frame, given the practical limits on resources, including the availability of appropriate two-seat air defence fighters. The tactical success of British daylight air defence in the summer of 1940 was the enabling expression of strategic conceptual excellence. The RAF's victory in the Battle of Britain was achieved only because the concept was executed tactically and directed operationally well enough. One needs to be ever alert to the error of undue exclusivity of assigning too much weight to the possibly brilliant inspiration, too little to the implementation, in considering historical strategies.

The conceptual perspective on strategy does not seek to diminish the weight attached to tactical matters, but it insists that as a general rule intellect does and should rule over muscle.[4] There is a great deal of literature as well as visual media material that focuses on the human dimension of lethal conflict. Not infrequently it is claimed that war is really all about the experience of the soldier, or the brutality of it all, and so forth. The 'face of battle' and the experience of war reach us emotionally and morally in ways that discourse on strategy tends not to.[5] Unfortunately, the cost of reaching emotions and touching moral nerves is usually borne by some notable loss of understanding of the events in question. For example, the justly acclaimed 2010 television series, *The Pacific*, was utterly convincing and appropriately literally awful in the human reality of violence presented. But, the men and their violent deeds were presented in no historical or strategic context whatsoever. When the military violence that is tactical behaviour of all kinds is presented as entertainment with no endeavour to explain the purpose behind the action, it approximates a form of pornography. *The Pacific* did offer some modest measure of domestic social context for the young American soldiers, including their forward staging in and through Australia. That social context, however, offered no help to a viewer who would like to know why the American marines were required to fight as the series shows in convincing detail.

The conceptual perspective on strategy, and indeed strategy itself, often is overwhelmed by tactics that become self-referential. One reinforces success in that one does what one can do either because one can, or because one must do it. Military careers tend to appeal to people who are inclined to privilege 'doing it' over 'thinking about why one might do it'. The descriptors theorist and academic, as well as the adjectival use of arm-chair, are familiar features in pejorative professional military characterization of strategic thinkers and writers. Military anti-intellectualism is as old as military history itself, is thoroughly understandable, and often is well targeted. It is scarcely surprising that the person whose life is on the line should be sceptical of the authority, especially the moral legitimacy, of any advice he is given by a person who is not so endangered. There are severe limits to the practicality of this principle, but it has always been a necessity for effective leadership that the leader should 'be there', known and preferably seen to share some of the risks with the troops that he strives to lead as well as command.[6]

The apparent tacticization of strategy is an ever present danger in historical practice, because there is some sense in Charles F. Callwell's claim that '[s]trategy is not, however, the final arbiter in war. The battle-field decides.'[7] Belligerents fight in ways and for objectives that lend themselves to strategic conceptual explanation, certainly to ex post facto rationalization. But, because the enemy usually cannot be denied a vote on the acceptability of the contemporary trajectory of the course of events, and also because chance is all too active, the narrative of warfare is more likely to reflect operational opportunity that is exposed by the verdict of battlefield engagement. So essential is the tactical enabler of strategy that the role and contribution of the latter is apt to escape notice. Given that today strategic history is publicly accessible primarily as visual entertainment that presents war as violent tactical behaviour bereft of more than cursory strategic contextualization, it is unsurprising that the conceptual perspective typically is missing from the frame. After all, it is

hard to photograph a concept directly, unlike its plausibly inferable consequences (e.g. German soldiers freezing at Stalingrad in winter 1941–2;
or American soldiers freezing at the Chosin Reservoir in North Korea in
December 1950).

The material, including human physical, and the moral narratives of warfare are so compelling that the conceptual narrative usually is in peril of being
slighted. To borrow gratefully from American historian Brian Linn, though to
expand upon his usage, there is a 'heroic' tradition among the possible
approaches to military behaviour that in practice encourages disdain for the
conceptual perspective.[8] Superficially, though plausibly, strategy can seem a
luxury of little value to the unfortunates who must get the military job done.
Those people indeed do strategy in their tactical behaviour, for without such
behaviour there can be no strategy. However, it does not follow that tactics has
no need of strategic direction, that in practice it can provide its own guidance
and, in effect, substitute for and therefore function strategically. Despite the
popularity of the thesis, it is a categorical error on a major scale to believe that
strategy can be 'tacticized'. Strategy and tactics are different in nature and
cannot mate to produce a hybrid offspring.

1.2 FROM THE GENERAL TO THE PARTICULAR

Because strategy is a practical art, an education in its general mysteries can
only be of limited value. This does not mean that the general theory of strategy
is strictly of academic interest, understood pejoratively. Rather the point is that
general wisdom requires application for particular contexts in ways appropriate to the circumstances. The general theory is exactly that, general[9]: its writ is
eternal and universal. From Athens in the fifth century BC and before, to
Afghanistan and after in the twenty-first century, the general theory of strategy
is authoritative (see Table 1.1).

But the necessary price paid for this authority, indeed the condition for its
rule, is a lack of specificity. The theory educates the aspiring strategist in how
to think and what to think about, but only generically by category of concern.
The general theory helps educate those who are educable, but its economical
dicta provide no answers to strategists' pressing contemporary questions. The
theory warns that strategy is difficult, but it does not specify what that means
for a particular time or place. Furthermore, even if the practising strategist has
succeeded in using his education to help select a promising strategy, he must
also turn in a command performance for strategic execution that requires
abilities beyond the intellectual. When presented as in Table 1.1, the general
theory of strategy may have the appearance of a statement of the obvious,
presented pedantically in the style of a check-list. The fact that theory should

Table 1.1 The General Theory of Strategy in 22 Dicta

Nature and character of strategy

1. Grand strategy is the direction and use made of any or all of the assets of a security community, including its military instrument, for the purposes of policy as decided by politics.
2. Military strategy is the direction and use made of force and the threat of force for the purposes of policy as decided by politics.
3. Strategy is the only bridge built and held to connect policy purposefully with the military and other instruments of power and influence.
4. Strategy serves politics instrumentally by generating net strategic effect.
5. Strategy is adversarial; it functions in both peace and war, and it always seeks a measure of control over enemies (and often over allies and neutrals, also).
6. Strategy usually requires deception, very frequently is ironic, and occasionally is paradoxical.
7. Strategy is pervasively human.
8. The meaning and character of strategies are driven, though not dictated and wholly determined, by their contexts, all of which are constantly in play and can realistically be understood to constitute just one compounded super-context.
9. Strategy has a permanent nature, while strategies (usually plans, formal or informal, expressing contingent operational intentions) have a variable character, driven but not mandated by their unique and changing contexts, the needs of which are expressed in the decisions of individuals.

Making strategy

10. Strategy typically is made by a process of dialogue and negotiation.
11. Strategy is a value charged zone of ideas and behaviour.
12. Historically specific strategies often are driven, and always are shaped, by culture and personality, while strategy in general theory is not.

Executing strategy

13. The strategy bridge must be held by competent strategists.
14. Strategy is more difficult to devise and execute than are policy, operations, and tactics: friction of all kinds comprise phenomena inseparable from the making and execution of strategies.
15. The structure of the strategy function is best explained as comprising political ends, chosen ways, and enabling means (especially, but not exclusively, military) and the whole endeavour is informed, shaped, and may even be driven by, the reigning assumptions, both those that are recognized and those that are not.
16. Strategy can be expressed in strategies that are: direct or indirect; sequential or cumulative; attritional or manoeuvrist-annihilating; persisting or raiding (more or less expeditionary); or a complex combination of these nominal alternatives.
17. All strategies are shaped by their particular geographical contexts, but strategy itself is not.
18. Strategy is an unchanging, indeed unchangeable, human activity in thought and behaviour, set in a variably dynamic technological context.
19. Unlike strategy, all strategies are temporal.
20. Strategy is logistical.
21. Strategic theory is the fundamental source of military doctrine, while doctrine is a notable enabler of, and guide for, strategies.

Consequences of strategy

22. All military behaviour is tactical in execution, but must have operational and strategic effect, intended and otherwise.

be uncontentious in its dicta has not prevented it being ignored in major respects throughout history. The theory is a trans-historical and trans-cultural summary of what should be close to intuitive understanding.

A strategist who has drunk deeply at the well of the classics on strategy should be incapable of forgetting that his military mission has a political purpose, that his enemy will ensure that any war is a project shared among all belligerents, and that friction, including the products of chance, is a certainty. Unfortunately what ought to be the refreshing waters of Sun Tzu, Thucydides, and Clausewitz have limited practical value. Brian Linn has been impressed by '[t]his failure of military intellectuals to agree on a concept of war [in the 1990s and 2000s]', as they have debated the latest 'buzzwords', among which he cites 'asymmetric conflict, fourth-generation warfare, shock and awe, [and] full spectrum dominance . . .'[10] But, it is misleading to identify concept failure as being partially responsible for intellectual confusion. Strategy's general theory has more utility as a source of guidance for history's strategies than appears possible at first glance.

When viewed in conceptual perspective, modern strategic history frequently has recorded lively debate among military (today defence) intellectuals. The evidence of intense debate of recent years about the nature, by which they mean only the character, of modern war and warfare can be identified as concept failure. As Linn claims, assuredly there is a lack of contemporary consensus over the most appropriate concepts. But, is this phenomenon truly a confusion of incompetent strategists who severally and collectively are responsible for concept failure? Does it make sense to talk of concept failure? Presumably the alternative condition to concept failure would be concept success. In this happy latter case, contemporary strategists would have gone to their inventory of concepts and located the one or more most fit for current strategic purpose. Or, possibly, strategic theorists would have discovered a new concept that seemed to fit the recent context comfortably.

For a heretical thought it might be argued that modern defence intellectuals have been guilty of categorical reification. After the fashion of Victorian botanists and entomologists, modern theorists are never happier than when they can locate, capture, and classify by name a new species of conflict (or warfare). The intention is worthy and usually is not without all merit. The problem is that while this kind of conceptual perspective is fun and sometimes profitable for expert theorists, it can be seriously misleading to the tactical agents of strategy who tend not to be sufficiently well versed in strategic theory to distinguish foam from substance. Clausewitz contributed to confusion when he wrote in a famous passage about the importance of 'establishing by that test [of fit with policy] the kind of war on which they are embarking; neither mistaking it for, nor trying to turn it into, something alien to its nature'.[11] Ignoring Clausewitz's confusing use of war's 'nature' here, when he means character, he fuels the illusion that particular wars are of a definite, identifiable, and therefore stable kind. If to this belief one adds the proposition that wars in a particular era can usefully be comprehended collectively—let alone super-collectively, as in such heroically inclusive categories as early-modern war, modern war, or post-modern war—then the conceptual perspective can be applied in quest of the right idea that best captures the historical reality of the period.

The problem is not with theory per se. Theory is only about explanation and is essential for data to be transformed into information, and for that information to be transformed into candidate knowledge. Theory is not and cannot be the issue. Indeed, it is the very utility of theory that makes it so dangerous to misunderstand and misuse. In common with the case of the purported lessons of history writ large, so the sub-species that is strategic history lends itself to competitive theorization. It is an unusual concept of war for which no apparently plausible empirical evidence can be mustered. Because strategic history is so richly and diversely endowed a permanent field of experience, it is always probable that any and every family of concepts and sub-concepts will make some sense and probably have some validity. If strategic debate pertains to future conflict, either imagination or authority will have to act as conceptual policemen, because empirical evidence certainly cannot fulfil that function. Conceptual authority is required in the real world of defence and security, because plans must be developed and sometimes implementing action taken. These behaviours need to be tolerably congruent with the conflicts to which they are applied, and that therefore mandate an effort at understanding. The provision of explanation for understanding is the function of theory.

Michael Howard once wrote that wars in all periods have more in common with each other than they do with non-war phenomena in their own particular period, though I am less confident that a similar claim can be sustained for the commonalities among all armies in all periods.[12] This is why there can be a general theory of military strategy that is universally and eternally valid. Two of the levels of theory that can exist below the general are the domain (or geographically) specific but still general, and the strategy specific. This means, for one example, that below the general theory of strategy there is a general theory of (specific to) air power, and also that theories of air power in historical application are conceptualized and deployed to craft particular strategies.[13] The air component to a joint plan will reflect the relative strengths of air power *inter alia*, and those strengths will be more, or less, relevant to the particular challenges of the day. Also, the potential contribution of air power will vary over time and between strategic contexts. Thus there is a simple hierarchy that reveals the structure of the conceptual perspective on strategy. With a single major exception, that of strategy for nuclear weapons (and for other weapons of mass destruction [WMD] also), in principle the strategy realm comprises reasonably well-ordered space. Because of the importance of this claim, Table 1.2 should minimize the possibility of misunderstanding.

Table 1.2 Good Conceptual Order

From the general to the particular there is hierarchy.
1. The general theory of (military) strategy.
2. The general theory of military power for particular geographical domains: land power, sea power, air power, space power, cyber power—and arguably for nuclear weapons/WMD.*
3. The particular theory of application, when relevant, for each kind of military power, in individual historical cases as expressed in plans that are strategies.**

* There is no disputing that nuclear weapons can be and have been held to be a category of military power different from the five with a necessary geographical association. This difference is discussed in the main text below. Although cyber power and particularly cyberspace today typically are discussed as though they have geophysical properties analogous to the land, air, sea, and Earth-orbital space, it is nonetheless important not to forget that the cyber domain is a wholly constructed artificial one.
** Two admirably terse definitions of strategy serve helpfully to lay emphasis on this level of strategic phenomena. J. C. Wylie advises that strategy is '[a] plan of action designed in order to achieve some end; a purpose together with a system of measures for its accomplishment'.[14] The second half of that sentence is probably redundant. Also, with superb economy Carl H. Builder recommends that *'[a] strategy is a concept for relating means to ends'*.[15]

Reference to the specific general theories of strategy has to be qualified by the caveat, 'in principle', because none of the geographically keyed bodies of strategic theory enjoys high authority today. Ironically perhaps, land power is too important to be confinable within meaningful intellectual boundaries. There is no ignoring the fact that it cannot be regarded simply as another one of war and strategy's distinctive environments. Sea power, air power, space power, and now cyber power, all have to find strategic expression in consequences on the ground as land power. So many and so important can be the contributions of, say, sea and air power to the fortunes of land power, that theory tends not to succeed in providing useful explanation of the latter's structure and dynamics. Even land-locked battlespace these days typically witnesses belligerent action that requires reliable access to, through, and from the world's four great commons: the sea, the air, Earth-orbital space, and cyberspace.[16] Studies of land warfare still appear, but their conceptual integrity is as uncertain as is their logistical feasibility.[17] The general theory of land warfare as such has all but ceased to exist. What has happened is that the increasing complexity of the jointness of armed conflict has resulted in the theory of land warfare being elided into the general theory of warfare. Because of his Prussian continentalist outlook as well as his determination to address the basics of his subject, it is only a modest exaggeration to argue that we have a fairly sound general theory of land warfare in the impressive and arguably authoritative pages of Carl von Clausewitz's *On War*. In the Prussian's two-environments world of the early nineteenth century, he manages to make only a couple of insubstantial references to the sea.[18] For all intents and purposes, *On War* is a theory of war on land. The complete absence of a maritime dimension to *On War* is not remotely invalidating of the book's mission, but nonetheless it is modestly troubling. The reasons for this absence are not hard to surmise, but still it would be useful had Clausewitz offered some brief explanation.

The four geographical environments other than the continental are neither more nor less geophysically distinctive than is the land. However, the vital difference is that the land is unique in strategic importance. All human conflict must have some territorial reference, because that is the sole environment where we humans can live. Even though the land is the environment most influenced by others, it is always in a league of its own in strategic significance.

Although technological change has characterized warfare in all geographies, it is an error to attempt to connect relative maturity to strategic theory for a particular geography to the maturity of its machines of war and war support. To explain: strategic theory often changes in good part because theorists confuse temporary apparent facts, verified or only assumed, with a permanent condition. Also, in addition to honest intellectual error the strategic realm has always attracted theorists with political, economic, and cultural-ideological agendas. This has meant that strategic theorists often have not been scholars seeking truth, rather have they been advocates for particular military and political causes who sought to advance recognition of a truth already discovered but in need of marketing to credulous customers. Such theorists have usually been able to construct the theory that purports to explain why what they believe is correct.

Modest understatement of the favoured case for particular kinds of military power is not a characteristic often found among strategic theorists. The nature of the marketplace for strategic ideas and their associated artefacts commands overstatement. In modern times, each of the newly exploited geographies of conflict—the air, Earth-orbital space, and cyberspace—has attracted imperial claims for superior relative potency. Contemporary insistence that cybernauts will determine future strategic success or failure is only the most recent example of a standard stamp of assertion masquerading as argument. Given that the strategic effectiveness of the machine most exciting today is being estimated (i.e. guessed) for the unknown, unknowable, and therefore largely unforeseeable future, claims for anticipated contingent strategic disaster can be hard to refute or prove. It is a challenge to identify anything that can serve as credible evidence for a future that by definition cannot now exist. Defence planners have this (non-)existential problem. It is difficult to persuade sceptical people that one knows enough to make expensive decisions now about a subject—future strategic need—about which actually one can know little for certain.[19] Much that sparkles in a dazzling PowerPoint presentation on the subject of 'international security in the twenty-first century' will transpire to have been costume jewellery rather than authentic gems. There is always someone who does guess correctly in anticipating future challenges. The trouble is that there is no thoroughly reliable way of knowing at the time how to identify that person.

A prime merit of competent general theory is that it evades the unsolvable problem of absent foreknowledge without sacrificing its intellectual integrity, though naturally at the cost of eschewing specific advice. For example, planning for the use of the air component to a joint campaign requires detailed understanding of current air power; what it can do, what it cannot, and how the particular enemy of today might be able to thwart it. But, behind the rationale for the strategy expressed in today's plan for air power there lies air power's general theory. Table 1.3 is this author's understanding of that theory. What the theory should do is help understanding of the nature of the air instrument of strategy; properly drafted, it will not need major revision as the world changes. However, what do need constant revision are the plans expressing strategies for the threat or use of air power in particular contexts. New technologies and changing ideas about legitimate military employment, for example, should not be able to invalidate the general theory of air power. When competently developed and carefully expressed, the theory should be subject only to marginal improvement by clearer contemporary phrasing, not to radical overhaul to accommodate new revelations.

It takes time for security communities to come to terms with abrupt seeming or even with cumulatively radical military change. It is one thing to notice and then implement military and highly military relevant innovation (e.g. the railway and the telegraph in the nineteenth century), it is quite another to understand their strategic meaning. Today, the specific general theories that explain the several kinds of military power differ in their maturity. Sea power theory is in fair condition for reason of Geoffrey Till's comprehensive reassessment,[20] while the theory of air power has been notably poor and misleading until recently.[21] The theory of space power remains a project still much in need of conceptual good order.[22] Finally, the theory of cyber power is ungoverned intellectual space, though early steps are being made to fill the vacuum.[23] Strategic anxiety has a way of propelling the creative imagination. A sure sign of conceptual uncertainty is the absence of discipline over spelling. For example, writings on cyber reveal uncertainty as to whether the subject is 'cyber power', 'cyber-power', or 'cyberpower'. The jury is still out. In times not long past, military literature referred to 'air-power', 'air power', and also to 'airpower'.

It is arguable how much empirical evidence is necessary before reliable environment and even weapon specific general theory can be composed. The relational precedence between technology and strategic theory is contested by scholars. While there was much highly imaginative speculation about air power before the first purpose-built military aircraft took to the sky in 1908, action not theory was in the cockpit from 1914 to 1918. Following the extensive evidence from trial by battle, air power was able to soar on wings of aspiration to any strategic destination favoured by its theorist advocates. It is plausible to suggest that by 1918 most of what needed to be checked

Table 1.3 The General Theory of Air Power

1. Air power theory is subordinate to the general theory of strategy.
2. Air power theory helps educate air power strategists: it is theory for practice.
3. Air power theory educates those who write air power doctrine and serves as a filter against dangerous intellectual viruses.
4. Air power is the ability to do something strategically useful in the air.
5. Air power is aircraft and air forces, not only Air Force.
6. Air power requires a dedicated Air Force, though not all air power needs to be Air Force.
7. Warfare is joint, but physical geography is not—the air domain is different.
8. Air power in its very nature has fundamental, enduring though variable, attributes that individually are unique, especially when they are more or less compounded synergistically for performance.
9. Air power has persisting characteristic strengths and limitations.
10. The strategic value of air power is situational, but is never zero.
11. Control of the air is the fundamental enabler for all of air power's many contributions to strategic effect.
12. Superior air power enables control of vital strategic 'commons'.
13. Control of the air is either essential or highly desirable, and it differs qualitatively from control of the ground.
14. The air is one and so is air power.
15. Air power has strategic effect, but it is not inherently strategic.
16. All air power has strategic value in every kind of conflict.
17. Air power both supports and is supported by land power and sea power (and space power and cyber power).
18. By its nature air power encourages operational and strategic perspectives, a fact with mixed consequences for good and ill.
19. Air power is not inherently an offensive instrument; rather does it have both offensive and defensive value.
20. The history of air power is a single strategic narrative, and a single general theory has authority over all of it—past, present, and future.
21. Strategy for air power is not all about targeting—Douhet was wrong.
22. Air power has revolutionized tactics, operations, and strategies, but not the nature of strategy, war, or warfare.
23. Air power is uniquely capable of waging geographically parallel operations of war, but this valuable ability does not necessarily confer decisive strategic advantage.
24. Aerial bombardment 'works', though not necessarily as the sole military instrument that decides a war's outcome.
25. The high relative (to land power) degree of technology dependency that is in the nature of air power, poses characteristic dangers as well as provides characteristic advantages.
26. Air power, space power, and cyber power are strongly complementary, but they are not essentially a unity.
27. One character of air force(s) does not suit all countries in all circumstances.

This theory is presented and explained fully in Colin S. Gray, *Airpower for Strategic Effect* (Maxwell Air Force Base, AL: Air University Press, 2012), ch. 9.

empirically, albeit arguably, about the strategic promise and meaning of air power was visible to those with eyes to see and assess it. However, one has to recognize the comfort of hindsight. It is sensible to bypass as a secondary matter the interesting question of how long it takes for scholars and practitioners of strategy to understand the strengths and limitations of radically new technology. What is certain is that in the past century strategists have had no choice other than to make what sense they could of air power, space power, cyber power (indeed all aspects of the electromagnetic spectrum [EMS], going back to the electric telegraph in 1837 and then the telephone in 1876). In addition, worthy of special mention, there has been the class of weaponry that kick-started modern strategic studies with three startling explosions in 1945, two of them delivered in anger. The nuclear age arrived largely unanticipated, unheralded, and not understood.

1.3 NUCLEAR WEAPONS AND STRATEGY

In modern times, at least, it has been usual for a radically new weapon technology to be anticipated in speculative literature, some of it explicitly fictional and intended to entertain as much as to inform. Furthermore, new military capabilities typically arrive in primitive guise beset by problems that inhibit high performance in action. They emerge and then mature by trial and error over a period of years or even decades. For example, the machine gun that contributed so greatly to the dominance of the defence from 1914 to 1918, had its useful origins in the 1860s, was invented more or less in its final form in 1885–6 by Hiram Maxim, and has been improved technically until the present day.[24] The strategic implications of the machine gun were not fully appreciated for thirty years. By 1916–17, it was appreciated as a team player along with artillery and, in due course, radically revised infantry tactics, as well as close ground-supporting aircraft.

A conceptual perspective on atomic weapons reveals a narrative very different to that for the machine gun. Atomic fission was achieved as a scientific breakthrough in January 1939, was not understood to have serious near-term practicable weapon potential until 1940, and was not known conclusively to be weaponizable until July 1945.[25] In 1945 the atomic bomb was employed to coerce Imperial Japan into surrender. There was extant no strategic literature on the threat, use, or probable consequences of atomic bombs. American (and British) policymakers and strategists had motive, opportunity, and indeed the need, to invent strategy for the use of atomic weapons in the summer of 1945. Notwithstanding scientific speculation and limited laboratory advances in atomic physics in the preceding decades, the authors of books on military subjects were thoroughly unaware that the weaponization of the atom was a practicable proposition in the near term. Modern strategic studies has an intellectual ancestry extending over millennia, but in 1945 there was no conceptual perspective whatsoever available specifically on atomic weapons. Given that for its first decade and beyond the atomic bomb could only be delivered over long distances by large aircraft, air power thinking dominated US nuclear strategy.

The first question the conceptual perspective has to address regarding atomic, then thermonuclear, weapons (henceforth generically nuclear weapons), is whether or not these weapons are indeed such, or whether they are something else. Are nuclear weapons weapons and can they be accommodated conceptually with some comfort within the domain of strategy? Nearly seven decades of thought and behaviour, albeit behaviour short of military action, have yielded a shaky consensus, with many dissenters, upon the proposition that nuclear weapons are weapons and that they do fall within the domain of strategy. Notwithstanding a relatively brief American conceptual and material infatuation with nuclear weapons in the 1950s and early 1960s, the dominant view has been that these weapons differ significantly from other weapons. This view emphasizing nuclear singularity has long retained practical authority in the West.[26] But, singular weapons or not, the awkward truth was and remains that major powers, to remain such, had no prudent choice other than to acquire them. Objectively existential facts demand that the logical structure of strategy cannot be withheld from nuclear weapons. It is scarcely possible for a nuclear-arming state to avoid performing the strategic function expressed in the mantra of ends, ways, and means, even if this eternal trinity is framed by the assumption that these are not weapons for use. The probable fact that nuclear weapons in use would prove self-defeating on several scores—physical damage suffered, political interests harmed, moral values affronted, and so forth—does not remove them from the strategic domain. Many strategic choices for the (tactical) employment of weapons of all kinds have proved ill advised. What nuclear weapons have achieved is a dramatic raising of the stakes. The inherent risks and costs of war flagged emphatically in the general theory of strategy are raised to a level that sane, sober, and careful statesmen should find intolerable. However, there appears to have been great and even decisive value in the strategic effect of nuclear menace short of military use. The proposition that nuclear weapons prospectively are so destructive that they are really political, not military, weapons is simply logical nonsense. All weapons are political in purpose, but military in (tactical) employment.

It is important to recognize the potency of circumstance. Since no security community acquires nuclear weapons by accident, or once having acquired them could afford to treat them with an utterly benign and total neglect, these devices of arguable necessity have to be treated strategically. Polities need to be strongly motivated for them to be willing to pay the high costs of nuclear acquisition. It follows that they are all but certain to have specific security concerns that will be reflected in the technical and tactical detail of their evolving nuclear force postures. Whatever the propelling political motivation, once a state acquires these weapons it is obliged by that fact to treat them within the conceptual framework of defence policy and strategy. They may be devices of last resort that politicians can scarcely imagine ever using, but their servant nuclear armed forces are obliged by necessity to train for war, albeit nuclear war. The human race is trapped strategically by its own technical ingenuity in the context of essentially permanent, if usually controllable, rivalry. Regarded politically, people should not have been trusted with the weaponization of nuclear fusion. However, it is no use blaming the scientists, the technologists, the military, or even ourselves as citizens (and policy-makers). We are what we are, and nuclear weapons arrived, indeed were force-marched into hasty action in 1945, well before the human race was ready for them. The weapons once invented under acute pressure of immediate anxiety (and then expediency) in the Second World War, required military mastering for strategic appreciation and for political understanding, all of which took time. Meanwhile, as the Cold War decades rolled on, rival nuclear arsenals and force postures had to be developed, deployed, commanded, and exploited in peace for deterrence and experimentally as occasional threats for attempted coercion. Plans were drafted and practised for the war that must never be waged.

With millennia of experience upon which to draw for strategic education, and with two of the greatest conflicts in history conducted well within living memory, one might think that the challenge to understanding presented by nuclear weapons would have been relatively easy to meet. The problem was to know what, if any, pre-nuclear historical experience was relevant to the nuclear era.[27] For most of the first decade of the nuclear age it was just about plausible to argue that atomic weapons simply added a new dimension of fairly prompt destructive potential to the grand narrative of modern industrial-age mass warfare *après* the templates of 1914–18 and 1939–45.[28] As late as the 1940s a Third World War thus would be a yet more awful version of the already terrible historical experience of the century to date.[29] Most of the argument between theorists over the character—or was it the nature?—of modern great power war was settled by the scientists, technologists, and engineers when they were able to produce the true 'super' hydrogen fusion bomb (ignited by a fission trigger) in the early 1950s. Weapon energy yields now could leap from the modestly horrific kiloton range to the monstrously immodest megaton zone, and they could do so with no theoretical limit. The hydrogen bomb was different from the atomic bomb. Quantity can have a quality all its own, as the saying goes, accurately. Military planners and prospective 'war-fighters'—to resort anachronistically to the contemporary jargon of Americans in the post-Cold War world—could consider atomic warfare within an intellectual framework that one might term Second World War-plus. The arrival of hydrogen bombs by the mid-1950s cancelled that framework conclusively. Unfortunately for strategic theorists, they had to attempt to make strategic sense of a military context that seemed to preclude the probability, perhaps even the possibility, of the achievement of strategic advantage. A nuclear armed enemy certainly could be defeated by reasonable definition, but what would be the value of that if such a success could not prevent one's own near simultaneous or subsequent defeat? The most mighty of the strategist's questions here intruded yet again, 'so what?'

The intellectual products of the huge efforts expended on the conceptual perspective upon nuclear weapons were, and remain, deeply problematic. This author was raised on nuclear lore and behaviour, a body of assumptions, assertions, arguments, theories, attitudes, and practices that incontestably proved compatible with a peaceful outcome to the Cold War. It might appear churlish to attempt to argue with success. Self-evidently, the conceptualizers for the nuclear age performed well enough. Nonetheless, it is sensible to question assertions of particular intellectual cause and its claimed effect. What follows should not be read as criticism of the defence intellectuals who founded and developed modern strategic studies, but rather as a sceptical, though ironically admiring, look in the rear-view mirror of historical hind-sight at the performance of those who provided the conceptual perspective on strategy for nuclear weapons.[30]

A body of strategic theory was invented and then refined, keyed to a dominant concept of stable mutual deterrence that served adequately to enable policymakers and strategists to make sense of their strategic context. The apparent strategic fact that the superpowers were caught by technology in a military context that precluded meaningful military victory was obvious to most people by the mid-1960s, but could never prudently be assumed by responsible military establishments to be a reliable permanent truth. We know today that the strategic terms of engagement in the 1960s and 1970s were robust against feasible technical change. However, that condition of stalemate could not be assumed at the time: it was only prudent for both sides to compete energetically in nuclear weapons and their delivery vehicles. Such effort offered the win–win outcomes either of (unlikely) meaningful advantage, or at least of high assurance that the adversary could not secure any strategically menacing superiority.

Western strategic thinking about nuclear weapons was intensely rational as well as notably ahistorical and often anti-historical, disdainful of the possible relevance of strategic experience prior to 6 August 1945. The logic of mutual nuclear deterrence and the generally comforting calculations of the requirements of deterrence stability were overconfident expressions of faith in the permanent authority of cool and calculating prudent people. Those people would prudently command and securely control vast untried machines of war in the face of whatever friction and contingency might throw at them. To call this project a gamble is indeed appropriate.[31]

From the earliest years of the nuclear era strategists as theorists and as planners have sought to cope with the unavoidable practicalities of contingency action plans. Since nuclear arsenals undoubtedly are here to stay, how should these weapons be used in war? Even after nearly seventy years the conceptual perspective on this class of weapon cannot provide a thoroughly convincing answer. That is a scholar's self-indulgent judgement. The practical matter is that throughout the nuclear period, politicians, officials, and soldiers have been obliged to make practical choices concerning contingent nuclear employment options, whether or not those action plans for use deserved to have confidence placed in them. The obvious fact that there has rarely been a fully satisfactory answer determinable, does not serve as an excuse for evading the issue. Intellectually mastered or not, nuclear weapons have figured in war plans since the 1940s.

Defence communities learn from history what they want to learn. More often than not they learn from the particular interpretations found in some historians' stories what is believed to serve best the interests of institutions or bodies of opinion. Unfortunately for the potency of the usual argument from claimed analogy, there was general agreement among those theorizing about strategy that strategic history ended (and began again, differently) in 1945. The nuclear era might be a post-strategic age, strictly impossible though that would be, but nuclear weapon technology was assumed to have caused a break-point in strategic time. This Revolution in Military Affairs (RMA) was effected by technology and was married to the air power of the new armed service that was the US Air Force. The RMA prompted an intellectual context wherein theory for the new era devolved upon a small number of gifted physical and social scientists to whom the rejection of pre-1945 experience came naturally.[32] To be polite, nuclear-age strategic theorizing in its early decades was an effort undisturbed or challenged by potential evidence that pre-dated Hiroshima. The conceptual foundations of nuclear oriented and related strategic theory were constructed with a near total absence of historical perspective. Relevant history was born abruptly by surprise in 1945.

The lack of historical perspective meant necessarily that an empirical basis for new strategic theory also was absent. For understandable reasons, the conceptual perspective on contemporary strategic challenges was restricted to '(limited) war in the nuclear age'.[33] Since it was assumed that everything that really mattered had changed in 1945, the assumption that the relevant evidential base for strategic conceptualization could only postdate the Second World War seemed eminently reasonable; indeed, it was not contested seriously by scholars for many years. The near total absence of pre-1945 historical reference in nuclear weapon strategic theorization, added to the agreeable fact that there was no nuclear battle action as decade succeeded decade, has created

a situation wherein the relevant strategic theory happily is thoroughly speculative, though less happily rests with possibly unwarranted confidence upon
contestable assumptions.

Whether or not the early theorists of the nuclear age as well as most of their
successors merit criticism for largely ignoring the pre-1945 historical record,
there can be little doubt that their speculative products are distinctly imperfectly verified by anything worthy of the label of positive evidence from
experience. The real problem with the strategic thinking for nuclear related
issues that theory could address is the fact that its fragility is hugely underappreciated. The logic of mutual deterrence is easy to understand, but the fact
that there has been no nuclear use since 1945 may be more attributable to luck
than to wisdom in theory and skill in practice. The conceptual perspective on
nuclear weapons typically has remained comfortably focused on the prevention and early containment of nuclear war. Despite the unarguable existential
peril of large-scale nuclear use in a world that shows no practical enthusiasm
for strategically meaningful nuclear disarmament (regrettably for excellent
pragmatic reasons, one must add), the conceptual perspective on nuclear
weapons continues to risk misleading its dependants by assuming an authority
for which it lacks reliable evidence. What is deplorable is not the absence of
well evidenced theory for policy and strategy, but rather the assumption that
no bad news on nuclear use amounts to the good news that the theory of stable
deterrence must be correct.

The richly human as well as political and cultural history of strategic
behaviour is not much in evidence in the library of strategic theory on and
about nuclear weapons. In the same way that the Cold War, including its novel
nuclear dimension, needs to be better integrated into the whole grand narrative of history, so theory for and about nuclear weapons is much in need of
fuller reconciliation with the dicta of strategy's general theory.[34] Those who
specialize in providing the conceptual perspective have yet to recognize
adequately the need for this historical mission to be attempted. Prominent
among the reasons why strategy for nuclear weapons needs to benefit more
from strategy's general theory is the insistence in the latter that strategy's
adversarial nature and context and its vulnerability to friction of many kinds
must never be forgotten. Strategy's adversarial nature and its liability to
harassment by friction should not simply be noted and then in practice
ignored, because assumed to be of little consequence. Although strategy for
nuclear weapons was developed for half a century with a particular dominant
adversary in mind, it is still quite surprising when one is obliged to reflect
upon how little Western officials, soldiers, and scholars really knew about the
enemy of those decades in nuclear regard. It was a persisting fact during the
Cold War that no matter how confident Western defence communities were
in their unilateral conceptual mastery of evolving nuclear circumstances, they
could never be confident that they enjoyed a reliable grasp of and grip upon

Soviet nuclear reasoning. Of course, many Western officials and theorists were certain that they understood Soviet nuclear thinking. In truth there was considerable doubt over Soviet assumptions and planned intentions regarding the use of nuclear weapons. Strategic history records many cases of states misunderstanding their adversaries' concepts and plans, but often there has been time to learn and adjust to unanticipated revelations. A problem with conceptual error and derivative mistakes in the assumptions informing plans with a nuclear dimension is that probably there would be no time to adapt to unanticipated and unexpected epiphanies.

The strategic conceptual perspective on nuclear weapons can never be assessed prudently save with reference to the possible behaviour of a self-willed Other, the enemy. Moreover, that enemy's nuclear style is unlikely to be readable in advance reliably, either from strictly material assessment or from the contingent menaces in declaratory policy and strategy. The much contested cultural perspective cannot prudently be ignored and is, in consequence, discussed at some length in Chapter 3.[35] The cultural perspective on strategy comprises a sub-set of influences inside the perilously big tent of the conceptual perspective. However, honesty compels one to admit that a no less potent claim can be made for the intellect in conceptual action as a sub-set inside the tent of culture.

From the earliest years of the nuclear age a powerful strand in the conceptual perspective on nuclear weapons in effect has denied that they can be thought about strategically at all. This is by no means an entirely foolish attitude to adopt.[36] One can acknowledge that nuclear weapons exist and cannot be disinvented. Furthermore one can recognize that nuclear disarmament is uninteresting because it could not be policed and enforced when states would be motivated to build, or rebuild, nuclear arsenals. An astrategic view appreciates that although nuclear weapons may have some welcome deterrent merit occasionally, that virtue would only be of existential strategic value. It follows that even though it is probably unavoidable to go through the motions of strategic reasoning, and to appear to exercise some care in the material provision for a nuclear force posture of modest size, hardly any of the strategic detail of the pertinent ways and means really matters. The strategic value of nuclear weapons is merely existential: 'they exist, therefore we assume that they will deter whomever and whatever might need deterring and is deterrable'. Details of warheads, means of delivery, basing and deployment modes, number of delivery vehicles, targeting plans, and so forth, are assumed, though of course not declared, to be irrelevant to the real world of prospectively terrified all too human politicians. And who could blame them?

The attitude just outlined and somewhat caricatured is reasonable on a number of grounds, not totally excluding the strategic. However, reasonable and plausible or not, assuredly it is not responsible, unless one assumes that strategic thought about (and planning for) the 'unthinkable' might have the potential to lower desirable barriers against nuclear use.[37] Strategic theorists long have had to contend with the charge that their careful thought about dangerous subjects is itself a source of danger. This is foolishly anti-intellectual, but it cannot be denied that familiarity with the theory that is nuclear strategy can lead under-recognized to some over-familiarity, and even to the apparent neglect of ethical safeguards and moral sensibility. That said, there has been no practicable alternative to the provision of conceptual guidance for the new class of weapons that exploded with no strategic, intellectual, or moral notice upon the astonished world in 1945.

The focus here has been upon an extreme case of strategic conceptual challenge and response. The nuclear example of the difficulties in achieving conceptual mastery of strategy is especially rich, despite the fact that there is no reliable evidence that can be deployed in aid of discrimination between wise or foolish strategic ideas. Historical hindsight is an immense advantage, but does it reveal which ideas about nuclear strategy—the assumptions, ends, ways, and means—were more, as opposed to less, sound? The answer is a resounding 'no'. The strategic context of the early Cold War decades saw an impressive conceptual response to what was generally agreed to be the overwhelming challenge of the era; the need to understand the meaning of nuclear weapons for statecraft and strategy. Much has been deduced about the consequences of the nuclear revolution for peace, crisis, and war, but the historical record since 1945 has settled few of the controversies. Scholars do not know for certain whether or not nuclear weapons deterred. They do not know for certain whether or not anyone has needed to be deterred by nuclear anxieties. And assuredly they do not know how nuclear warfare would have proceeded and to what outcome. This essential ignorance does not mean that we are unable to make heavily favoured best guesses, but they are only guesses. The conceptual perspective upon strategy for nuclear weapons mercifully has no empirical base in actions beyond the initial awful demonstration with two entry-level atomic bombs that wrought havoc in Hiroshima and Nagasaki. How challenging is it to master intellectually a whole class of weaponry when there are no certain empirical referents? Materially and conceptually the understanding of air power, as well as much misunderstanding, was massively accelerated by the experience of war from 1914 to 1918. Space power continues to lack for a convincing strategic conceptual framework, despite its half-century plus of evolution.

The latest strategic conceptual challenge, that posed by cyber power, is being met with far more expedition than was space power, because cyber 'warfare' already is a notable, if constrained, reality. Governments are wrestling conceptually and politically with the conundrum posed by hostile action, not merely with potential menace, in the EMS. Is cyber warfare war? Whether or not it is so treated today, how ought it to be regarded for the future? Electrons that are maliciously chosen and directed can have deadly physical consequences, even though they lack the material reality of traditional land power, sea power, air power, and even space power. The burgeoning strategic debate about the meaning and implications of cyber power generically is analogous to the intellectual challenge posed by nuclear weapons in the 1940s and 1950s.

1.4 FAITH, HOPE, AND ASSUMPTIONS

Concept failure refers to the phenomenon of strategic theory found wanting as a guide to strategic practice. For example, in the 1930s and into the 1940s the US Army Air Corps, and later Forces (USAAC/USAAF), adopted, promoted, and implemented in action the strategic theory of victory by unescorted high-altitude daylight precision bombing.[38] For its time and place, largely over Germany in 1943–5, the master concept simply was unsound. The general theory of strategy for air power does not and cannot condemn this idea. Instead, the theory maintains that the strategic effect generated by such a use of air power is highly situational. There can be many reasons why some strategic concepts fail to meet the pragmatic needs of strategists at particular times. As often as not, the principal cause of failure will be faulty operational military direction, doctrine, and tactical execution of strategic ideas that appeared sound enough in principle.

A frequently neglected foundation of strategy is the role played by the assumptions of strategists. T. X. Hammes, an important contemporary theorist, with reference to Eliot Cohen as heavyweight support, claims that

> He [Eliot Cohen] starts with the requirement to make assumptions about the environment and the problem. Once the strategist has stated his assumptions, then he can consider the ends (goals), ways (the how) and means (resources) triangle. However, Cohen states an effective strategy must also include prioritization of goals, sequencing of actions (since a state will rarely have sufficient resources to pursue all its goals simultaneously) and finally, a theory of victory ('How does this end?').[39]

Hammes (and Cohen) are correct; the great chain of strategic logic expressed in the words quoted is made of precious metal. But, there are traps for the incautious that can limit the value of that logic, particularly with respect to the requirement for according assumptions an explicit and even a formal role in the strategy-making process.

Consideration of the conceptual perspective on strategy might seduce one into recommending recognition of the role of assumptions as an intellectual key that should open many doors to understanding. However, two difficulties with assumptions are fundamental and beyond reliable alleviation. First, argument for privileging the role of assumptions readily is revealed to be perilously close to tautological. Sound assumptions should promote the prospects for sound strategy. But, how does one test for the soundness of assumptions? The answer presumably has to be through empirical verification, though the record of success or failure is likely to be inconclusive as evidence because of the phenomenon of redundant causation, as well as the laws of physics that deny us knowledge of events that are yet to occur. Strategy may succeed despite being founded upon faulty assumptions, just as poor strategy may succeed because the troops perform well tactically, despite their strategic disadvantages, or because the enemy underperforms.

Second, it is an easy matter to slip innocently into abuse of the meaning of assumptions. By definition, an assumption is something that currently is not known for certain to be true, but nonetheless is taken for granted (assumed to be true). It may be knowable, though it is not known at present. However, more often than not assumptions are made about subjects that literally cannot be known today because they lie in the future. Thus there is a severe definitional limitation to the strategic value in the scrutiny of assumption. No methodology can reveal what is unknowable, though it should be helpful to identify assumptions as such, which is to say as 'known but assumed unknowns'. Since strategic assumptions typically refer to anticipated features of future strategic history, there has to be a measure of uncertainty irreducible save by the passage of time and events. This translates as meaning that it would be nonsensical to try to insist that a strategy-making process should strive to 'get its assumptions right'. The working assumptions of strategists must always by definition be more or less problematic. This claim was registered uncompromisingly by Clausewitz, though in different words, when he identifies uncertainty as constituting a permanent feature of the 'climate' of war, and when he argues incontestably that 'war is the realm of chance'.[40]

The practical problem is how, even whether, the strategist can improve his assumptions. The logical fact that a superior performance in assumption identification and utilization should ensure strategic success, alerts us to the tautological difficulty. Because strategic assumptions by definition are factually unproven, though not necessarily unsupported, the challenge to strategy reform can no more lie with assumptions per se than with strategy per se. A security community that performs poorly with strategy is unlikely to be one capable of achieving substantial reform by improving its strategic assumptions. On the same reasoning, it is improbable that a strategically challenged leadership would be able to correct its deficiencies in assumptions. The one weakness implies the other. To suggest otherwise would be to commit an error characteristic of the creative authors of 'virtual history', wherein historical actors are postulated to behave in ways of which they were systemically incapable. For example, it is interesting to speculate about Hitler's mistakes in his strategic misconduct of the Second World War. The problem with such analysis is that it is deeply misleading to refer to strategic behaviour that was always very probable because of the nature of the individuals and institutions involved.

Although the conceptual perspective on strategy, in common with strategy's general theory, needs to recognize the practical significance of assumptions, there is small reason to anticipate that such recognition can enable much improvement in strategic performance. All aspects of practical strategy, from initial conceptualization, through planning, on ultimately to tactical implementation, have to rest upon assumptions, which is to say upon beliefs about causal relationships as yet unverified by events. The core reality of historical strategy, strategic thought, and military intention, is all speculative theory, which is the world of assumptions prior to validation or refutation by action.

Because they tend to be future oriented, and because the future is an unattainable foreign country, the assumptions of the strategist should not be accorded any more authority than one allows to hope resting upon a faith that currently is unverifiable. This reasoning does not challenge the importance of assumptions in the conceptual perspective on strategy, but it does suggest that

Table 1.4 Assumption Troubles

Assumptions are hugely important to the strategist. However, recognition of that importance is of less practical utility than one might think. The following list summarizes this theorist's methodological troubles with assumptions.

1. Some beliefs are so popular and uncontentious that they escape notice as the contestable assumptions that they are.
2. If assumptions are believed to be facts they are likely to evade examination in an assumptions audit.
3. Because assumptions must be unproven, though not necessarily unprovable, in order to be classed as assumptions, there is always going to be some uncertainty as to their reliability. There are unbreakable limits to what can be known with certainty at any one time.
4. Many assumptions of high importance for defence planning and strategy making must always be unprovable because they pertain to a future that is never reached: tomorrow never comes. By definition, assumptions about the future cannot be proven. No research methodology yet invented enables time travel.
5. By definition, sounder assumptions must be desirable and may be useful, but their identification is neither a necessary nor a sufficient condition for strategic success.
6. Strategic assumptions should not be considered a variable independent of the policy- and strategy-making process. A weakness in the working assumptions, whether or not they are recognized explicitly as such, is virtually certain to cohabit with other strategic conceptual weaknesses that will be systemic.
7. It is probably a serious mistake to believe that one can submit a strategy to an assumptions test in the expectation that it can be improved by an assumptions repair job. Many strategic assumptions are not really selected from a catalogue of offerings, but rather have cultural roots and are anchored in particular geopolitical and historical contexts.

it points to what would be a gold mine if only it could be exploited usefully. The more deadly of assumptions for the strategist are likely to be those of which either he is unaware or that are highly resistant to correction. Concept failure typically does reflect some assumption failure, but such recognition does not advance the cause of better strategy very far. It is necessary to penetrate deeper into the conditions and causes of strategic behaviour. It is appropriate to think of assumptions as providing a significant context for strategy making and execution. But, the common-sense claim that this context must enjoy authority as provider of an independent variable for the education of strategists is not a safe one. In practice, assumptions often are discovered and articulated under pressure in response to the perceived necessity of debate. Assumption discovery and generation is a process always apt to be corrupted by the explicit or implicit pressure to validate strategic choices already made. After all, once one has decided what should be done, it is no great intellectual feat to find the assumptions that provide legitimation. Table 1.4 summarizes most of the concerns expressed here.

1.5 STRATEGY IS TIMELESS, BUT STRATEGIES AND STRATEGISTS ARE NOT

There is more to strategy than can be seen strictly in conceptual perspective. After all, theory achieves nothing without practice. That logical point granted, this perspective should provide understanding relevant to the whole house of strategy. It identifies the structure of strategy in all its aspects and is the arsenal of ideas for the governance of otherwise chaotic strategic space. At the apex of the conceptual perspective towers general theory on the strategy function. The general theory is the principal fortress of distilled knowledge on strategy.[41] The sheer variety in human strategic history can be a potent source of needless confusion, as also can be the differences in language between diverse polities and cultures over time and in contrasting geographies. It is perhaps paradoxical that the rich variation in the details of human strategic affairs has coexisted with seemingly eternal and universal prosecution of the strategy function, whatever the contemporary local terminology used to contemplate its practice. To claim thus inclusively for the strategy function is not to 'ride roughshod' over the wealth of historical variation, as one historian has charged.[42] Empirically appraised, security communities have always performed the strategy function, whether or not they had a contemporary term approximating modern usage of the word strategy. The logic in, as well as the historical evidential support for, this argument could hardly be more compelling.

For reasons of politics inclusively and tolerantly understood, men have always been obliged by necessity to identify a concept or concepts to guide the use of their means, particularly their military means. Political and strategic conceptual choices reflect the extant assumptions, not all of which express favourable news. Security communities of every character must function strategically in order to survive and prosper. Strategy is not an option, let alone a conceptual invention of modern times. Many communities have not performed the strategy function well enough and have suffered severely as a consequence. But even this logic may mislead the unwary, should they neglect strategy's competitive nature. It is not necessary to be excellent in the practice of strategy, but it is certainly advisable to be better than the enemy of the day. For a conceptually disturbing thought, one might speculate that an enemy inferior in strategy may find more than adequate compensation elsewhere for that deficiency. However, when soundly assembled the general theory of strategy, with its high inclusivity, is able to cope with apparently disabling 'what ifs . . .' Should any of the dicta in the general theory be falsifiable either empirically or logically, they would not belong in the theory in their current form, if at all.

The conceptual perspective on strategy is of timeless relevance because strategy understood as performance of the strategy function itself is timeless. In the late 2000s the American and other allied forces that had intervened in Afghanistan lacked a credible strategy for success in their war against a complex enemy known collectively, but loosely and not entirely accurately, as The Taliban. In the 1340s, England's King Edward III required, found, and pursued a strategy to bring his French foe, Philip VI, to battle in circumstances where he could be defeated. Edward's strategic concept to achieve this result was the reliable agency of a bloody and fiery *chevauchée* (cavalry raid) across northern France that Philip could not ignore.[43] Edward was reasoning and acting strategically. The political goal was the crown of France, the military means was a largely professional army of modest size deployed tactically to best advantage, and the raiding style in campaigning enticed the French into seeking a battle that they were unlikely to win: this comprised a sound theory of victory, a strategy for success. By way of contrast, the United States and its NATO allies in Afghanistan in the 2000s did not operate with a strategic understanding of their practicable choices and limitations at all comparable to the superior English strategic performance in 1346 in the Crécy campaign. However, the strategy function was needed equally in the two cases, and competitive strategic effect was generated in both of them, though in the needful quantity only in the 1346 example. A strategic conceptual perspective applied equally to both cases.

The timelessness of strategy as a challenge inherent in the human security condition is not matched by a like timeless quality to the thoughts and behaviour of historically contextualized strategists. Those who must practise strategy by devising and commanding contextually adapted strategies are always, without exception, the products of their particular time, place, and circumstances. No strategic theorist or practitioner performs outside of his time, though certainly he may speak to later generations should they choose to read him, assuming that his words survive and can be recovered. There is a timeless reality to the strategy function that finds detailed historical expression in ever changing thought and action. Another way of stating this fundamental proposition is with the claim that strategy has an eternal and universal nature, but a highly variable character. The greater among the theorists of strategy are those authors who have exposed the enduring truths of the subject most clearly and perceptively. Regarded thus, Clausewitz can be appreciated necessarily as a man of his time, but also as the one who has understood and explained most persuasively to generations of variably faithful readers the unchanging nature of war and strategy.[44]

Clausewitz is justly revered as a theorist not because one can argue that he unravelled once and for all time the mysteries of war, but rather because his explanation is by far the most persuasive extant. For all its superiority over other explanations of the phenomena of war, that by Clausewitz is only a particular empirically based theory of an ever shifting historical reality of practice. But, that shifting historical reality of strategic practice is a contemporary expression accommodated within the single conceptual category we understand as the strategic. Explanation of strategy should begin, but not end, with Clausewitz.[45] Endeavours to comprehend strategy should command that we move forward with, not from, his achievements. Clausewitz does not provide a complete strategic education, but this is not a potent criticism. He is either plainly correct or arguably correct enough on most of the major concerns of the strategist, present and prospectively future.

Provided Clausewitz is read carefully with as much empathy and respect for his historical context of composition as one can muster, and so long as one is not paralysed into thoroughly uncritical adulation by the authority conferred by his reputation, *On War* can only be a positive intellectual force. There are important matters that Clausewitz does not treat very well, but so what? We can be unashamedly grateful that the conceptual perspective on strategy contains a work as theoretically powerful in its explanation as *On War*. This is not to slight other notable contributors to strategy's general theory.[46] Each in his way has added to our ability to govern the intellectual space of strategy. Much of Clausewitz's strategic wisdom has value that should prove timeless, but necessarily it was written in a way, and even with a content, plainly attributable to its historical context of creation.[47] Clausewitz's genius as a theorist sometimes sufficed to offset what could have been serious error. For example, his silent assumption that policymaking was a distinctly elite activity finds much useful compensation in his trinitarian theory of war, with its allocation of high significance to the people and popular enthusiasm in its many possible forms. Clausewitz understood and explained war and strategy better than did those who preceded or succeeded him. But, unsurprisingly and indeed necessarily, his was a conceptual accomplishment that left work to be done by others. Clausewitz's writing requires some interpretation and even amendment, as well as clear restatement in our contemporary language, if it is to yield high value for the twenty-first century.

The theory in *On War* needs translation when effort is made to shift levels from the general and abstract to the specific and contemporary practical. Ideally, *On War* should be able pre-eminently to help educate the contemporary strategist to cope with the challenges of, say, menaces in the Earth-orbital space and cyber realms. Unambiguously, Clausewitz did not seek to advise strategists directly.[48] Nonetheless, uncritical borrowing of such potent seeming ideas from *On War* as the 'culminating point of victory', and the 'centre of gravity' has no small potential to mislead the incautious.[49] Strategic ideas matter for strategic performance.

NOTES

1. Carl von Clausewitz, *On War*, trans. Michael Howard and Peter Paret (1832–4; Princeton, NJ: Princeton University Press, 1976), 140–1 (emphasis in the original).
2. My 'whole house of strategy' is adapted and borrowed from Lawrence's 'whole house of war'. *Seven Pillars of Wisdom: A Triumph* (New York: Anchor Books, 1991), 191.
3. See David Zimmerman, *Britain's Shield: Radar and the Defeat of the Luftwaffe* (Stroud: Sutton Publishing, 2001), ch. 13.
4. A particularly firm determination to demonstrate the historical merit in this generally sound if not always obviously correct, belief is John A. Lynn, *Battle: A History of Combat and Culture* (Boulder, CO: Westview Press, 2003).
5. See John Keegan's classic study, *The Face of Battle* (London: Jonathan Cape, 1976).
6. This issue is central to John Keegan, *The Mask of Command* (New York: Viking Penguin, 1987) and is discussed in Colin S. Gray, *The Strategy Bridge: Theory for Practice* (Oxford: Oxford University Press, 2010), ch. 6.
7. Charles E. Callwell, *Small Wars: A Tactical Textbook for Imperial Soldiers*, 3rd edn. (1906; London: Greenhill Books, 1990), 90.
8. Brian McAllister Linn, *The Echo of Battle: The Army's Way of War* (Cambridge, MA: Harvard University Press, 2007), 6–7. Linn traces the influence of three traditions in US military culture: the guardian, the heroic, and the managerial. The three are not thoroughly exclusive and all have endured, even as their relative fortunes have fluctuated.
9. See Gray, *The Strategy Bridge*, ch. 1.
10. Linn, *The Echo of Battle*, 2.
11. Clausewitz, *On War*, 88.

12. Michael Howard, *The Causes of Wars and Other Essays* (London: Counterpoint, 1983), 214.

13. I present my version of the general theory of air power in *Airpower for Strategic Effect* (Maxwell Air Force Base, AL: Air University Press, 2012), ch. 9. The theory is presented in summary form in Table 1.3.

14. J. C. Wylie, *Military Strategy: A General Theory of Power Control* (1967; Annapolis, MD: Naval Institute Press, 1989), 14.

15. Carl H. Builder, *The Masks of War: American Styles in Strategy and Analysis* (Baltimore, MD: Johns Hopkins University Press, 1989), 49.

16. Alfred Thayer Mahan advised memorably that '[A] first and most obvious light in which the sea presents itself from the political and social point of view is that of a great highway; or better, perhaps, of a wide common, over which men may pass in all directions, but on which some well-worn paths show that controlling reasons have led them to choose certain lines of travel rather than others.' *The Influence of Sea Power upon History, 1660–1783* (1890; London: Methuen, 1965), 25. A fine application of the 'commons' concept is in Barry R. Posen, 'Command of the Commons: The Military Foundation of U.S. Hegemony', *International Security*, 28 (Summer 2003), 5–46.

17. See David E. Johnson, *Learning Large Lessons: The Evolving Roles of Ground Power and Air Power in the Post-Cold War Era, MG–405–AF* (Santa Monica, CA: RAND, 2006). Also see Colin S. Gray, *Understanding Airpower: Bonfire of the Fallacies*, Research Paper 2009-3 (Maxwell Air Force Base, AL: Air Force Research Institute, March 2009), 31–5.

18. Clausewitz, *On War*, 220, 634.

19. This permanent reality for defence planning is discussed in Colin S. Gray, 'Strategic Thoughts for Defence Planners', *Survival*, 52 (June–July 2010), 159–78.

20. Geoffrey Till, *Seapower: A Guide to the Twenty-First Century*, 2nd edn. (Abingdon: Routledge, 2009).

21. Two somewhat contrasting reviews of air power are Martin van Creveld, *The Age of Airpower* (New York: Public Affairs, 2011), and Gray, *Airpower for Strategic Effect*. By far the best book on air power history is John Andreas Olsen, ed., *A History of Air Warfare* (Dulles, VA: Potomac Books, 2010).

22. Some years ago I wrote an essay about space power that registered serious dissatisfaction with the contemporary state of the relevant theory: 'The Influence of Space Power upon History', *Comparative Strategy*, 15 (October–December 1996), 293–308. The condition of space power theory today shows considerably improvement, but much remains to be done. Certainly there is as yet no market-leading magisterial work of space power theory. However, worthy steps along the way to such an accomplishment can be recorded in the publication of these works: Jim Oberg, *Space Power Theory* (Washington, DC: Government Printing Office, 1999); Michael V. Smith, 'Ten Propositions Regarding Spacepower', thesis (Maxwell Air Force Base, AL: School of Advanced Air and Space Studies, Air University, June 2001); Everett C. Dolman, *Astropolitik: Classical Geopolitics in the Space Age* (London: Frank Cass, 2002); and Charles D. Lutes and Peter L. Hays, eds., *Toward a Theory of Spacepower: Selected Essays* (Washington, DC: National Defense University Press, 2011).

23. See David J. Lonsdale, *The Nature of War in the Information Age: Clausewitzian Future* (London: Frank Cass, 2004); Martin C. Libicki, *Conquest in Cyberspace: National Security and Information Warfare* (Cambridge: Cambridge University Press, 2007); Franklin D. Kramer, Stuart H. Starr, and Larry K. Wentz, eds., *Cyberpower and National Security* (Dulles, VA: Potomac Books, 2009); John B. Sheldon, 'Deciphering Cyberpower: Strategic Purpose in Peace and War', *Strategic Studies Quarterly*, 5 (Summer 2011), 95–112; and David J. Betz and Tim Stevens, *Cyberspace and the State: Toward a Strategy for Cyber-Power* (Abingdon: Routledge for the International Institute for Strategic Studies, 2011). Bearing in mind the salience of Raymond Aron's judgement that '[t]roubled times encourage meditation' (*Peace and War: A Theory of International Relations*, Garden City, NY: Doubleday, 1966), it is unsurprising that cyber focused strategic worries manifested themselves in an exciting literature as the twenty-first century advanced into its second decade. See Richard A. Clarke and Robert K. Knake, *Cyber War: The Next Threat to National Security and What to Do About It* (New York: HarperCollins, 2010); James P. Farwell and Rafal Rohozinski, 'Stuxnet and the Future of Cyber War', *Survival*, 53 (February–March 2011), 41–60; and Chris C. Demchak and Peter Dombrowski, 'Rise of a Cybered Westphalian Age', *Strategic Studies Quarterly*, 5 (Spring 2011), 32–61.
24. C. J. Chivers, *The Gun: The AK-47 and the Evolution of War* (London: Allen Lane, 2010), esp. chs. 1–4. Also, Anthony Smith, *Machine Gun: The Story of the Men and the Weapons that Changed the Face of War* (London: Judy Piatkus, 2002), is a pacey popular but informative narrative.
25. From an enormous literature, see Gerard J. DeGroot, *The Bomb: A Life* (London: Jonathan Cape, 2004); and Jeremy Bernstein, *Nuclear Weapons: What You Need to Know* (Cambridge: Cambridge University Press, 2008). See also Colin S. Gray, *Modern Strategy* (Oxford: Oxford University Press, 1999), chs. 11–12; id., 'The Nuclear Age and the Cold War', in John Andreas Olsen and Gray, eds., *The Practice of Strategy: From Alexander the Great to the Present* (Oxford: Oxford University Press, 2011), 237–59; Lawrence Freedman, *The Evolution of Nuclear Strategy*, 3rd edn. (Basingstoke: Palgrave Macmillan, 2003); and Beatrice Heuser, *The Evolution of Strategy: Thinking War from Antiquity to the Present* (Cambridge: Cambridge University Press, 2010), Part V.
26. The immodest official American enthusiasm in the 1950s for nuclear weapons in all forms of warfare is described critically in Linn, *The Echo of Battle*, ch. 6.
27. My own early attempt to deal with the issue of continuity and discontinuity after 1945 was offered in 'Across the Nuclear Divide—Strategic Studies, Past and Present', *International Security*, 2 (Summer 1977), 24–46.
28. Nuclear arsenals (almost entirely atomic, not thermonuclear) climbed from two for the United States and zero for the Soviet Union late in 1945, to 2,422 for the United States and 200 for the Soviet Union (and 14 for Britain) in 1955. Unclassified figures are to be found in Robert S. Norris and Hans M. Kristensen, 'Global Nuclear Weapon Inventories, 1945–2010', *Bulletin of the Atomic Scientists*, 66 (July/August 2010), 77–83.

29. See David Alan Rosenberg, 'The Origins of Overkill: Nuclear Weapons and American Strategy', *International Security*, 7 (Spring 1983), 3–71; and Stephen T. Ross, *American War Plans, 1945–1950* (London: Frank Cass, 1996).

30. See Colin S. Gray, *Strategic Studies and Public Policy: The American Experience* (Lexington, KY: University Press of Kentucky, 1982); and Freedman, *The Evolution of Nuclear Strategy*.

31. See the robust critique of American nuclear theory, policy, and strategy in Keith B. Payne, *The Great American Gamble: The Theory and Practice of Deterrence from Cold War to the Twenty-First Century* (Fairfax, VA: National Institute Press, 2008).

32. Bernard Brodie, *War and Politics* (New York: Macmillan, 1973), chs. 9–10. See also Fred Kaplan, *The Wizards of Armageddon* (New York: Simon & Schuster, 1983); John Baylis and John Garnett, eds., *Makers of Nuclear Strategy* (New York: St. Martin's Press, 1991); and Alex Arbella, *Soldiers of Reason: The RAND Corporation and the Rise of the American Empire* (Orlando, FL: Harcourt, 2008).

33. Morton H. Halperin, *Limited War in the Nuclear Age* (New York: Wiley, 1963) is an authoritative period piece.

34. Scholarship on the Cold War marches on, but inevitably still lacks much historical perspective, both for assessment of that episode as well as for its place in the whole narrative of modern history. The leading edge of recent historical consideration is well represented by Gordon S. Barrass, *The Great Cold War: A Journey Through the Hall of Mirrors* (Stanford, CA: Stanford University Press, 2009), and the near monumental trilogy that is Melvyn P. Leffler and Odd Arne Westad, eds., *The Cambridge History of the Cold War*, 3 vols. (Cambridge: Cambridge University Press, 2010).

35. The 'cultural turn' in American strategic thought and attempted behaviour in the 2000s was a belated response to evident strategic failure in the field in Iraq and Afghanistan. That granted, the modern strategic studies community had been debating the merit in cultural analysis since the mid-1970s. See my *Nuclear Strategy and National Style* (Lanham, MD: University Press of America, 1986), which, though plainly a period piece, did seek to address some important strategic issues from a perspective that had some, admittedly arguable, validity beyond its time of writing.

36. See Lawrence Freedman, 'Has Strategy Reached a Dead-End?' *Futures*, 11 (April 1979), 122–31. Freedman began this article with the following robust claims: 'For the moment strategy has effectively come to a dead-end. In future any radical departures in strategic thought will be prompted more by political change than innovation in weapon systems. Thus the tasks of strategic studies will lie more in the realm of political science than in traditional military science.' 122.

37. Compare the contrasting approaches to deterrence and possible nuclear use in Herman Kahn, *On Thermonuclear War* (Princeton, NJ: Princeton University Press 1960) and id., *Thinking About the Unthinkable* (New York: Horizon Press, 1960), with Thomas C. Schelling, *The Strategy of Conflict* (New York: Oxford University Press, 1960) and id., *Arms and Influence* (New Haven, CT: Yale University Press, 1966). In *The Great American Gamble*, Payne argues convincingly that the intellectual history of American policy and strategy for nuclear

weapons can be understood with heavy reference to the sharply contrasting schools of thought led by Kahn and Schelling. The conceptual legatees of those frontier theorists of the 1950s and 1960s are alive and active to this day.

38. See Peter R. Faber, 'Interwar US Army Aviation and the Air Corps Tactical School: Incubators of American Airpower', in Phillip S. Meilinger, ed., *The Paths of Heaven: The Evolution of Airpower Theory* (Maxwell Air Force Base, AL: Air University Press, 1997), 183–238; and Tami Davis Biddle, *Rhetoric and Reality in Air Warfare: The Evolution of British and American Ideas about Strategic Bombing, 1914–1945* (Princeton, NJ: Princeton University Press, 2002), ch. 3.

39. T. X. Hammes, 'Assumptions—A Fatal Oversight', *Infinity Journal*, 1 (winter 2010), 4. Hammes is the author of the conceptually challenging book, *The Sling and The Stone: On War in the 21st Century* (St. Paul, MI: Zenith Press, 2004).

40. Clausewitz, *On War*, 101, 104.

41. With gratitude I have borrowed the concept of a fortress of knowledge from Daniel J. Boorstin (then the Librarian of Congress), who said that '[w]e must never forget that our libraries are our fortresses of knowledge'. *Gresham's Law: Knowledge or Information?* (Washington, DC: Library of Congress, 1980), 4. Boorstin presciently invoked the logic of Sir Thomas Gresham (1519–79), and applied it to the claim that information drives out knowledge.

42. Hew Strachan, 'Strategy in the Twenty-First Century', in Strachan and Sybille Scheipers, eds., *The Changing Character of War* (Oxford: Oxford University Press, 2011), 506. The complete sentence reads as follows: 'Gray rides roughshod over change across time and assumes that there can be a concept of strategy, and a practice derived from it, for epochs and civilizations which had no word for it.' Strachan's charge is answered in Gray, *The Strategy Bridge*, Appendix C; id., 'Conclusion', in Gray and Olsen, eds., *The Practice of Strategy*, 287–300; Beatrice Heuser, 'Strategy Before the Word: Ancient Wisdom for the Modern World', *The RUSI Journal*, 155 (February/March 2010), 36–42; ead., *The Evolution of Strategy*, ch. 1; and ead., *The Strategy Makers: Thoughts on War and Society from Machiavelli to Clausewitz* (Santa Barbara, CA: Praeger, 2010), ch. 1.

43. See Lynn, *Battle*, 87–8.

44. See the analysis and appreciation in Hew Strachan, *Clausewitz's On War: A Biography* (New York: Atlantic Monthly Press, 2007).

45. For a full explanation of this judgement, see Colin S. Gray, *Schools for Strategy: Teaching Strategy for 21st Century Conflict* (Carlisle, PA: Strategic Studies Institute, US Army War College, 2009).

46. My candidates for the hall of fame of great strategic thinkers is provided and briefly justified in *The Strategy Bridge*, 264–6.

47. For Clausewitz's intellectual and cultural historical context, see Peter Paret, *Clausewitz and the State* (New York: Oxford University Press, 1976); Azar Gat, *The Origins of Military Thought: From the Enlightenment to Clausewitz* (Oxford: Clarendon Press, 1989); Lynn, *Battle*, ch. 6; Strachan, *Clausewitz's On War*; and Heuser, *The Evolution of Strategy*.

48. Clausewitz, *On War*, 141.

49. Clausewitz, *On War*, 528, 595–6n.

2

Ethics: Strategy's Moral Maze

What distinguishes justifiable war from the blank check is the fundamental notion that in the justifiable war tradition, one needs a warrant before one has a right to destroy one's neighbors and their culture. Military activity is never beyond debate, automatically acceptable, or self-justified. It needs to be supported with moral justifications in each particular case. Going to war always must bear the burden of proof. The point needs to be made in our time as much as in any earlier time. For many who operate at least implicitly from the blank check perspective, the value of the nation is not debatable, the authority of national government is not subject to critique, and the moral value of their leaders is such that no questions are to be put to them when they command.

John Howard Yoder[1]

2.1 STRATEGY AND ETHICS

Ethics is a perspective upon strategy that only rarely attracts disciplined attention from scholars able to do full justice to the complexity and dilemmas of the subject. It is argued here that both ends of the spectrum of possible attitudes towards ethics and strategy are seriously in error. On the one hand it is misleading, though not technically incorrect, to regard and approach strategic practice as an exercise in applied morality, strategic ethics one could say. On the other hand, it is foolish to argue, let alone assume, that purposeful strategic behaviour is chosen and pursued for pragmatic reasons utterly bereft of moral content. War and its warfare and the strategy that should guide it is not applied morality, neither is it 'lawfare', and nor is it purely expedient pragmatism.[2] For easily understandable reasons the perspective of this chapter invites confused analysis and prescriptive dicta in unusual measure.

Morality and its direct product, ethics, attract rigidities in opinion that this author finds unhelpful. Morality and ethics, stripped bare of scholarly flourishes, are simply about right conduct, and by logical contrast, wrong conduct.

More accurately stated, morality and ethics are about what is believed to be right or wrong conduct. A code of ethics identifies and prescribes proper as opposed to improper behaviour. Such a code gives expression to moral beliefs, with actions and even thoughts classifiable on one or the other side of the line that distinguishes what is morally permissible from what is not. Ethically expressed moral argument and assertion can hardly help but fuel attitudes and judgements unfriendly to nuance, unforgiving of claims for exceptional circumstances, and intolerant of ambiguity. When an ethical code drives a neatly binary audit of behaviour into the categories only of good and evil, compromise is apt to be unavailable for statecraft. For example, it is easier to compromise politically when the issue of the day is regarded as one where only more, or less, territory is at stake, rather than when the territory in dispute is valued as a matter of principle and therefore of claimed right.

Ethics and the moral beliefs that fuel them matter because strategic history tells us that human actors are all but hard-wired to think in moral terms, and that history primarily is thoroughly human. Moreover, the brain is relatively more important than is muscle. Difficult beyond the point of being metrically resolvable, epistemological questions lurk to entrap us in an entangling web of complications. Boldly, we will proceed on the basis of a reductionist syllogism: strategy is a pervasively human endeavour, human beings cannot function in a moral vacuum, therefore all strategy must have a moral dimension. Defin- itions are vital. Judgements of right or wrong behaviour have to rely on the moral authority behind an ethical code. The ethical code that a society endorses and polices exists for the purpose of educating its members as to what is acceptable or right behaviour and what is not. This is active morality, or morality in prescribed practice. This author has no wish to argue with those who insist that an extra-human authority is the source of the moral authority expressed in the relevant ethical code. At this stage of the argument it is necessary only to acknowledge the eternal and ubiquitous presence of moral beliefs and feelings, and their presence in ethical codes.[3]

An ethical code issues to each of its human subjects moral guidance manifested in laws, rules, principles, and norms which, when followed by and large, should enable a person knowingly to engage in right rather than wrong conduct, at least with reference to the moral standard extant in his or her society. When considering strategy it is not usual for scholars to devote much attention explicitly to its ethical dimension. Quite often the literature relevant to strategy that does treat moral issues seriously is not blessed with a useful empathy for the human strategic estate. It was noted earlier that disputes purportedly about principles, which is to say about right and wrong, notoriously are resistant to political compromise. Similarly, those who feel obliged to make moral judgements about issues in statecraft and strategy, understandably if unhelpfully are wont to privilege the clear ruling of a moral compass that is not well enough designed or employed to offer helpfully practicable navigational guidance on behaviour—deliberately to misuse the metaphor.[4] Empirically we know for certain that security communities always have needed to perform the strategy function. Also, we know for certain that those communities always have needed to discover and enforce an ethical code. The challenge is to comprehend how communities reconcile the moral beliefs expressed in their ethics, with the strategic behaviour that is all but mandated by the nature of politics, which eternally and universally principally is about relations of power.

Morality and its ethics are not metaphorically parachuted in to complicate the lives of pragmatic people who are attempting, often against heavy odds, to perform the strategy function well enough. Instead, morality, supported and enforced by its ethics, is always a player in strategic history. This discussion strives to identify, explain, and justify the answers to fundamental questions about the relevance of morality and its implementation as ethics for strategy. The questions are the following:

1. Why do ethics matter to the strategist?
2. Where do ethics come from?
3. How do we know what is right and what is wrong?
4. Are strategy and morality incompatible?
5. What sense is there in the concept of moral advantage, and can it yield strategic advantage?

These questions are not thoroughly discrete, but it is useful to address them individually, tolerating the overlaps, in order to ensure that the most vital matters are considered explicitly. The intention here is not prescriptive, rather is it strictly to assist understanding of the structure of the morality/ethics–strategy relationship. What follows has no substantive moral and ethical content. Readers should be able to engage with and use my explanation and analysis, regardless of the particular encompassed moral ground that informs and inspires their chosen ethical code. I realize that many people are not comfortable addressing morality and ethics in relation to strategy. Professional, certainly personal moral, comfort tends to be advanced if strategy and morality are kept apart in separate categories. An important reason why the serious literature on strategy and morality is so slim is because strategy professionals, military and civilian, believe that close interrogation of this relationship may yield conclusions that would be embarrassing and unacceptable, though hard to ignore or deny. The subject of strategy and morality can be difficult to discuss because for many people it engages unavoidably with fundamental matters of faith. Whether the faith be secular (but functionally quasi-religious) or explicitly religious, appeal to its believed authority is apt to be a challenge to reasonableness in debate. Anyone who strives rigorously to probe the mysteries of nuclear deterrence theory and practice soon realizes that rational behaviour may yet be utterly unreasonable.

For a hideous classic example of perverse rationality, the Holocaust was a rational project for Nazi Germany, given the particular values in the secular religion of the Nazi state.[5] It made no strategic sense for German war-making, but that is not a relevant criterion. Unreasonable behaviour by rational statesmen is a persisting problem in strategic history. The popular theory of rational choice is logically powerful, until one recognizes that choices are deemed rational only with reference to the ethical code and the values behind it of the actors in question. The awesome and awful implications of this point have been so grim for governments in the nuclear age that by and large they have elected to ignore it, because they cannot comfortably acknowledge let alone refute it.[6]

2.2 MORALITY, ETHICS, AND SURVIVAL (OR, WHY DO ETHICS MATTER?)

It is possible to write a strategic history dominated by the ethical perspective.[7] There is always an ethical dimension to thought and behaviour. All communities, including the proto-international one, require rules to live by. A condition of true and literal anarchy cannot long endure, because a set of rules eventually will be imposed by the most cunning and probably the physically stronger player(s). The ethic of 'might is right' may seem quintessentially immoral and unethical to the liberal conscience, but it is nonetheless an ethic.[8] Thucydides' notoriously brutal Melian dialogue reveals the ethical code of an asserted concept of political order based upon superior power.[9] People only behave unethically when they knowingly do wrong according to a code of moral conduct they accept as legitimate and authoritative for them. This line of reasoning ventures into perilous moral terrain very rapidly. For the moment, though, it suffices simply to register the claim that all people (and other species, also), in all communities find it necessary to have an ethical code as a guide to behaviour. Some elements of the code will be mandatory and policed by severe sanctions, others will only be strongly advisory if not quite discretionary.

Analogy can be treacherous, but it has its advantages. In Britain there is a formal, published *Highway Code* that specifies both mandatory and enforced rules as well as expected norms of good driving practice. In civil as in military affairs there are minor as well as major offences. Rules of the road have been found necessary because unregulated highways would be unsafe for all users. A world of interacting polities that sought to persist and prosper in the absence of rules for strategic behaviour would soon be a world wherein nothing and nobody would be safe. It is worth recalling a typical pattern of political revolution: grievance *inter alia* feeds popular enthusiasm for radical change; the change becomes too dynamic and non-linear for stable, let alone effective, governance; a condition of impending or actual chaos then is exploited opportunistically by the strongest player in the 'game of thrones', the one who promises and delivers the political order of the iron fist. By and large, people can be personally safe enough even under tyrannical rule, provided they understand and are sufficiently obedient to the ethical code extant, either imposed in the absence of popular consent or otherwise.

Because rules distinguishing right from wrong behaviour are so important for stable political life, it is unsurprising that their claimed moral content and quality is invoked. To illustrate: we ought not to cause harm deliberately to civilians assumed to be innocent, not only because the laws of war so demand and the military's explicit and written 'rules of engagement' (code of conduct) so command. In addition, a moral sanction is claimed. It is deemed morally wrong to harm innocent civilians, not merely unlawful and contrary to military discipline. Ethics and morality are by no means synonymous, even though an ethical code certainly expresses moral judgement, since it must divide acceptable from unacceptable acts, which is to say right from wrong.

Communities require ethical codes, formal or informal, because their survival requires predictability in behaviour. People and institutions need to know what is required as well or what is expected of them, in order for them to conform in the interest of what the Chinese value so highly, harmony and balance.[10] There is a universal and eternal ethic of (political) power active in human affairs, which is why our history has a permanent strategic dimension. This ethic obliges people to compete for relative personal and other advantage. However, most of strategic history reveals the authoritative operation of what one may fairly term strategic ethics. There have been exceptions to this rule, or ethic, but belligerents recognize that the conduct of war quite literally *à l'outrance*, total war in all senses of that contested concept, is not strategically prudent.[11] All strategic behaviour at all times and by all people, and however that behaviour was described in the linguistic conceptual usage of the period, has had locally and therefore contextually valid ethical content. Every society needs an ethical code to live or die by. From gangsters in fairly well organized crime, through guerrilla forces, to states great and small, ethical conduct is important and unethical behaviour can license and provoke severe punishment. A leading historian has written damningly of Napoleon's foreign policy as a 'criminal enterprise'.[12] Hitler was not, as the distinguished British historian A. J. P. Taylor claimed, merely an ordinary European statesman, but rather was a rogue who had behaved so contrary to the norms of the contemporary code of acceptable state behaviour, that he and major elements in his government were judged criminal.[13] Not only was Hitler's foreign policy regarded and eventually treated as having been a 'criminal enterprise', but the Nazi regime itself was so categorized.

It is understandable and probably desirable, certainly useful, for ethics and morality effectively to be merged in many people's minds. The inclination to obey rules prescribed for acceptable behaviour can be helpfully reinforced by the sanction of moral rebuke. I doubt strongly whether medicine, psychology, and anthropology combined can determine reliably the roots of the near ubiquitous human desire to behave correctly, which is to say in conformity with authoritative local norms for good enough practice. Empirically, though not entirely convincingly in theory, it would appear to be an enduring fact that people prefer to behave correctly, that is to say morally. Also, people typically assign positive moral value to whatever the ethical code of their place and time prescribes for them. This is an uncomfortable thought, because it should mean that morally correct enough action, assayed in historical context, needs to be judged in relation to its period. An even more uncomfortable thought is that the desirable relationship between morality and ethics that privileges the authority of the former as inspiration for the latter, can all too readily in practice be reversed. Instead of morality educating and determining ethics, not infrequently it is the case that expedient ethics, or rules, seem to acquire a moral weight that they do not deserve. That which is apparently convenient not to do—to take prisoners while conducting a special operation, for example—easily may be translated into the 'working' judgement that it is right (enough) to kill rather than to hold prisoners of war.

We must conduct strategy with constant reference to what Michael Walzer has termed collectively the 'war convention', comprising the amply populated arsenal of laws, rules, and norms that today are widely held to be authoritative guides to strategically proper and improper behaviour.[14] However, if we seek to back-fit anachronistically major features of the contemporary 'war convention' onto the actors in periods past, we are certain both to weigh historical figures unjustly and, more important, to misunderstand them and the causes and consequences of their actions.[15]

Given that military strategy requires the threat or actual infliction of harm, it cannot help but engage moral feelings and judgements. Intra-species killing, or murder, generally does not come naturally or easily, if one may so express the matter.[16] This is a well and reliably known fact, not merely a theorist's hopeful assumption. Armies work hard in order to overcome the aversion to killing/murder that is early pre-programmed into their initially civilian soldier recruits and only candidate warriors. Plainly this aversion, though widespread and powerful, is neither universal nor unbreakable.[17] The eternal phenomena of murder and warfare attest to the fragility of the inhibitions that discourage, but do not preclude, intra-species killing.

A nettle that must be grasped is the enduring historical reality of authoritative ethical codes that have demonstrated the capacity to license as morally justifiable acts of brutality literally on an industrial scale, genocide in effect.[18] There can be no sensible argument over either the relevance of ethics, or the eternal historical reality of morally founded ethical judgements. Rather does the challenge to the contemporary scholar lie in his or her ability or otherwise to tolerate a moral relativity in historical judgement. It can be difficult to employ strategic history as a library full of potential evidence for strategic education, if one declines to accept as legitimate for their time and place the deeds and alleged misdeeds of more or less distant events. Moral standards and their derivative ethics have differed over time and from place to place.

Ethical order fuelled by and calibrated to fit contemporary moral feelings and judgements is apt to be prejudicial to fair and accurate assessment of yesterday's strategists. The assumption that a particular ethical code has universal and eternal authority is a fatally flawed conviction. Nonetheless, it is a conviction that can be detected in some strategic historical commentary, and it is a frequently misleading contributor to contemporary strategic writings that employ historical examples as claimed analogies for today. Scholars of strategy in the twenty-first century are encultured to be alert to military behaviour that now is defined as criminal misbehaviour. National and international law and contemporary social values provide a formidable body of rules for ethical guidance that is claimed to rest upon morally authoritative principles. At least, that is the appearance of the current ethical context for the use of force. However, a number of caveats important for this discussion require recognition and explanation. At this juncture it is useful simply to state baldly five broad caveats that serve constructively to harass undue certainty in the treatment of strategy in ethical perspective.

1. Ethical codes have differed over time.

2. Ethical codes can differ between societies even at the same time.

3. Ethical codes tend to be general, while they need to be interpreted for specific cases.

4. An ethical code in practice may be set aside under the pressure of extraordinary necessity (not mere convenience). Ethics can accommodate this practice by providing for a rare 'opt out', so long as some penance is imposed even for authoritatively condoned misbehaviour.

5. Ironically, the existence of an ethical code and its manifestation in formal legal guise can provide justification for immoral behaviour, thanks to the play of discretion in the interpretation of rules and norms.

These five empirically based claims are not intended to challenge the roles and importance of ethics, let alone of morality; quite the contrary. A major problem with the ethical perspective on strategy is not that it is irrelevant in what it reveals, but rather that it demonstrates a lethal lack of moral discipline inherent in the concept of ethics and its practical application. For this particular narrative, it is necessary to investigate the basis upon which strategic ethics, which is to say operational morality, rests. What we have argued thus far is only that an ethical code is unavoidable, as indeed are moral feelings (about right and wrong). Unfortunately, also we need to consider the argument that almost any behaviour will be judged moral if the extant ethical code and norms so signify. I am treading on treacherous ground, because I could appear to be trying to argue that immoral conduct can be ethical. As usually is the case with claimed paradoxes, the contradiction is only apparent.[19] Whatever behaviour is judged acceptable and proper by the authoritative ethical code must also be viewed as ethical and, most likely, as moral also. To deny this chain of logic one has to deny authority to the ethical code in question. In practice it is hard to avoid doing this, even though it is seriously unhistorical. For the most obvious of examples, former Reichsführer Hermann Goering embarrassed his accusers at Nuremberg by all too accurately challenging the legality of part of his indictment. For a specific: If a behaviour was not a crime when allegedly it was committed, how could its performance be judged criminal (e.g. planning to wage aggressive war, with legally ambitious reference to the Kellogg–Briand Treaty of 1928)?

When we claim that 'times change' (for the better, it is assumed) for ethics and therefore presumably for their foundational morality, it is necessary not to accept that near truism with uncritical enthusiasm. Most, though certainly not all, of the atrocities in times past were indeed atrocious, but not in a legal sense or in their own contemporary terms. As something of a historical de-contextualizer, it is well to remind ourselves that in this age of warfare as 'lawfare' and generally of high sensitivity to strategic ethics, the nuclear menace rather makes a mockery of the near global popularity of the ethical perspective. If the liberal democracy that is the United States of America, a country nothing if not legalistic in its public culture and vocally committed to high moral principles, could reconcile those principles with the strategic concept of assured destruction as a desirable intellectual guide for its (declared) nuclear strategy, what value can there be in strategic ethics? Two logically alternative positions can be taken vis-à-vis nuclear strategy.[20]

Either such strategy must be paradoxically contradictory when blessed or even just tolerated by ethics, or it is not. If it is not paradoxical, one must have located a way in which to view it that is ethically acceptable. This way cannot include hopes for extreme and improbably reciprocated restraint in nuclear use, because hope that is unreasonable is neither a prudent basis for strategy nor a safe foundation upon which to rest morally propelled ethical judgement. Moral argument continues to beset and occasionally harass noticeably the nuclear facts of strategic life in some countries, but it has not posed a disabling challenge to modern strategists. This is simply an empirical claim. Perhaps it should have been strategically, and as a consequence morally and politically disabling, but that is another matter. When we examine more or less well recovered historically distant strategic atrocities, we should not forget that although our contemporary nuclear age has witnessed the practice thus far only of virtual contingent atrocity with weapons of mass destruction, a move from the virtual to the real would qualify for award of the title, 'mankind's greatest crime'.

Matters of principle are not readily permissive of management by political compromise, as was noted already.[21] In practice, flexibility in ethics, one can hardly say flexible ethics, often gives the appearance of an absence of ethics. If societies and political systems like those of the United States and Britain have been able to plan, albeit only contingently, to take military action that must result in the killing (murder?) most probably of millions of people who could hardly be other than 'innocent' (or at most only nominally complicit), is there any practicable reality to the concept of strategic ethics? If it could be judged ethical and presumably moral to kill those millions, then what would be unethical and immoral? The alleged high crimes of a Ratko Mladich pale into insignificance when compared with the scale of (legal) atrocity that much strategy for nuclear use contingently has intended.

Contrary to appearance, perhaps, I am not passing moral judgement on strategy for nuclear weapons. Rather is it my purpose to suggest that there is far more continuity in willingness to do massive harm in the practice of strategic ethics than the apparent, certainly the officially endorsed and proclaimed, ethical code of our day asserts.

2.3 MORAL COMPASS AND MORAL AUTHORITY (OR, WHERE DO ETHICS COME FROM?)

It would be agreeable were one not obliged by the evidence of gruesome behaviour to explore in a disciplined way the licensing moral authority for strategic ethics. Notwithstanding the importance of ethics for strategy, it is a subject that attracts relatively little careful attention. The reasons for this are not hard to identify and explain. People doing tactics at the sharp implementing end of strategy require rules to live, and sometimes to die, by. What they do not need is a permanent seminar on the appropriateness of their rules of engagement. It is challenging enough to interpret the rules that they have, sometimes in unanticipated situations of the direst peril, without venturing into the often murky waters that spawned the current rules. Some strategic judgements that could be explained with moral content typically are not so explained, because they are driven so much by customary cultural norms of proper (ethical) behaviour that their rightness is assumed to be self-evident and in no need of reinforcement by explicitly moral reference. Unfortunately, the proposition that customary moral truths provide a mighty barrier against atrocity is not as well evidenced as one would like. Rather casual citing of such attractive concepts as, for example, 'the ordinary human moral sensitivities', or 'the decent opinion of Mankind', alas are far too casual. Mankind is not thoroughly globalized in a full common understanding of the meaning and practical implications (the theory and practice) of the Universal Declaration of Human Rights. And, 'ordinary human moral sensitivities' are in practice and malpractice often quite different both from society to society as well as from situation to situation.

No one in his own mind behaves unethically and therefore immorally. Literally nothing is beyond moral justification. This is why the specifics of the ethical code that identifies right from wrong conduct are so important. If the code in practice is infinitely permissive, then it should be revealed as an emperor with no clothes. But, such is not the case; at least it is not when the matter is regarded functionally in strategic terms. Regardless of the deeds that it licenses as right and proper, an ethical code is still an ethical code. Those who perform the hard duty of, say, 'ethnic cleansing', may take much comfort from the fact that they are doing right by their *Volk*, possibly in addition to taking pride in an unpleasant, indeed revolting, but necessary job done well enough in obedience to orders apparently legitimately designed morally and politically, and correctly delivered. This is not to deny that some of the people who commit atrocity do so because they enjoy it. Every army has potential psychopaths in its ranks who need only the opportunity to reveal their darker side.

It would be pleasing to be able to laager one's moral concerns for protection with some form of barrier defence impenetrable by foes, no matter how clever and ruthless. It may seem that Mankind has done just this with much of the deontological approach to nuclear ethics.[22] The deontologist seeks to foreclose on moral debate by proclaiming an ethical code based on moral absolutes. To the more rigorous deontologist right and wrong behaviours are clearly flagged and are unforgiving of exceptions. Hypothetical argument of the 'what if . . .' rarity is not permitted to erode the solid front of unambiguous moral duty expressed in ethics. Thou may and probably should do right, but emphatically thou must not do wrong. And wrong may be explained in excruciating detail, as also may be the punishment that would follow for the miscreant. Since people require some certainties to aid predictability in their lives, and many crave certainty resting on unarguable authority as a way of coping with what otherwise would be unduly confusing challenges, the appeal of the absolute view of moral guidance for ethics taken by the deontologists is obvious.

A personal benefit of ethical absolutism is that one can simply refer an emerging or suddenly erupting moral issue to the ethical play-book in order to find the unchallengeably right answer. There is much to be said for an absolute ethics. Assuredly it is easier to administer than is the principal alternative of consequentialism. By analogy, 'thou shalt not kill' is as clear and apparently beyond possibility of misunderstanding as is 'no smoking' and 'no alcohol'. 'Some smoking' and 'moderate alcohol' require constant and careful policing, but zero is easy to understand and administer. For a practical hypothetical strategic analogy, 'zero nuclear weapons' must be far easier a disarmament regime to monitor, and for which to verify compliance, than would 'some nuclear weapons' prohibitions.[23]

The core of the consequentialist perspective on ethical prohibition is best illustrated by saying that it appends the qualification 'unless...' to the negative command. With only the rarest of exceptions Mankind, and assuredly Strategic Mankind, is and has always in practice adhered to an ethical code keyed to the assessment of anticipated consequences. Strategy is all about consequences. Deeds and misdeeds are tactical, but their meaning is strategic and is the realm of consequences.[24] But, in ethical perspective what are the implications of judging military ways and means according to their achievements? Never forgetting that warfare is violence, which inherently is harmful, how should one handle the task of comparing the good secured, or at least intended, with the transaction cost of the pain instrumentally inflicted? Do morally worthy political ends of policy justify any and every beastly act committed in pursuit of virtuous goals? These are not mere scholastic matters, instead they relate to the whole of the human strategy project, at all times and everywhere. Ubiquitous and powerful though consequential logic certainly is, it is not completely satisfactory as a base for moral judgement.

It is sensible to claim that all people and communities behave ethically and probably morally in their own evaluation. Even when the local ethical code consciously is broken, there is likely to be an escape clause that allows apparently deviant action in order for exceptional dangers to be met or fleeting opportunities exploited (with a right intent, of course). Plainly and worryingly, this discussion is close to saying that practical strategic ethics can and do translate as an expedient morality that permits any kind of action. This is an authentic paradox, one facilitated by confusion of thought. The paradox lies in the fact that an ethical code that in practical application makes a mockery of moral standards is indeed truly such a code and need not reveal widespread hypocrisy. The historical reality is that individuals, but especially security communities, fail to recognize that their moral judgements are moderated for good enough practice by an ethical code that in action is permissive. This is just the way that things are. Moreover, there are overwhelming reasons why strategic behaviour long will continue to evade inconvenient control by potentially disabling moral injunctions in the form of administrative ethics with serious bite.

If an ethical code is presumed to have moral authority behind its commands and advice, whence does that authority itself derive? The moral judgements that inspire the set of standards for an ethical code provide each of its human and institutional subjects with a convenient moral compass (to misuse the metaphor again). But, who or what manufactures authoritative moral judgements? One needs to be careful of tautology. Presumably, action judged unethical is so assessed because it is believed to be immoral. However, it is likely to be found or assumed to be immoral because the authoritative ethical code so indicates.

The intention here is only to explore the basis for the ethical rulings that flow from moral judgements, not to advance a particular set of standards. The subject of morality and ethics is, at least certainly should be, unavoidable in strategic discourse.[25] Whatever the local standards for acceptable behaviour may be, on the evidence available people think if not reason morally and their moral beliefs have more or less effect on their ethical behaviour. Mercifully only a few deviant individuals are innocent of any moral beliefs and feeling, meaning that they do not recognize any moral impulse or code of ethics beyond the immediate rationality of apparently expedient conduct (e.g. whatever secures gain for me now is right enough). However, at a stretch, even such rogue behaviour might be said to recognize a quasi-moral rule. The rule could be held to license that which may be done for advantage, while it would forbid conduct likely to result in more pain than gain. This is applied morality via an ethic with a wholly self-serving and short-horizon moral metric. It may seem incorrect as well as inadvisable to dignify a rule of naked advantage and disadvantage by classifying it as moral, but strict logic compels one to do so. A state or a person in pursuit of expedient advantage is unlikely to prosper in the longer term, but it is hard to deny the logic by which such pursuit and its ethical code of practice should be accorded moral status. The code in question defines acceptable and unacceptable behaviour tautly with reference to anticipated benefits balanced rationally against expected costs, and it can rest logically on the sincere belief that it is a good thing to seek advantage. If this is the local standard, one is obliged to recognize that in its indication of what is right and what is wrong conduct it meets the minimum definition for an ethical code. Assuming the licensed behaviour is believed to be right as well as permitted, the minimum standard for the moral function is met also.

Moral claims and arguments, both explicit and more often implicit, are pervasive in strategic debate. For reasons that social and physical scientists have difficulty explaining conclusively, all human beings (save for a few deviants) generate and accept or reject particular moral judgements. It is human to believe that right and wrong comprise a meaningful opposed pair. It is logically necessary to affirm both concepts in the pair, while recognition of this distinction is essential to human survival and prosperity. But, although moral judgement per se is eternal and universal, its content is not; due appreciation of this empirical refinement often is missed. Furthermore, it is in some measure ironic that a variety of sources of moral authority for ethics are compatible with a commonality of standards of licensed and proscribed behaviour. Although some licensing authorities may seem more potent than others, the injunctions can be the same. Whether sanctions be spiritual or secular, what matters is their effectiveness in influencing behaviour. It is irrelevant for strategic conduct whether the pertinent moral guidance is assumed ultimately to have been designed in Heaven, or whether it is known to have been invented and manufactured terrestrially and therefore rather more locally. What matters is that moral guidance exists and has some traction over choices in behaviour.

The subject here is not, and cannot be, morality and ethics per se. One need not just assume the ubiquity of ethical codes. Rather can one claim as an abundantly evidenced fact that all societies do, indeed, require ethics. Human social and political life would be insupportable in the absence of rules and norms for behaviour: if we have moral rights, then also we must have matching moral duties. All too often, though, strategic behaviour is judged immoral because contrary to some ethical code, when more accurately it is only guilty of reflecting a different code or divergent interpretation of a shared one. We are so habituated to thinking ethnocentrically according to our moral values and their ethical expression, that behaviour by others contrary to our preferred norms of acceptable conduct almost reflexively attracts condemnation as immoral and therefore wrongful.[26] The moral indignation behind ethical audit can have serious strategic consequences. If Clausewitz is correct in his fundamental claim that '*[w]ar is thus an act of force to compel our enemy to do our will*', the fuel of moral sentiment registers high among the factors that drive the course of history; in the form of 'hatred' it was, after all, the first of the Prussian's three elements in his theory of war.[27]

Moralists and ethicists of many persuasions have speculated about the proper issuing authority for the moral compass. What follows here is not a bold venture in moral philosophy. Rather is it a modest critical review of some of the major claims for exclusive manufacturing rights for this necessary fabled instrument. Only five claims to manufacture will be considered, though the number could be much larger were one to adopt a more inclusive view. The authorities favoured for discussion are: religion (and the just war tradition); natural law (or reason); politics; strategic situation; and culture. Deliberately, these candidates for the moral throne are not listed and considered in rank order, ascending or descending. There can be no conclusively correct answer to the fundamental question of the source(s) of moral authority for ethics. It is a matter sometimes of choice, more often of custom and tradition, and not infrequently of situation. The discussion proceeds without intended authorial prejudice or implied preference. However, by way of a working proposition I suggest that none of these candidate authorities merit classification as inherently more weighty or true than the others. That said, there is no doubt that some putative moral authorities serve better the goals of comfort and convenience than do others.

2.3.1 Religion

Ethics, including strategic ethics, may be treated as a branch of theology. It is apparently expedient as a way of precluding enervating debate to believe that right and wrong behaviour are absolutely, eternally, and ubiquitously identified and distinguished by a divine authority that literally or functionally is regarded as a Supreme Being (or Force or some equivalent phenomenon).[28] The ultimate source of moral authority, and therefore of the rightful ethical code, thus is by definition Supreme and beyond argument and dispute. The divine authority from above and beyond often is expressed and sometimes explained through parables that illustrate to educate and instruct. When divine rulings on right and wrong are required, usually they need to be locatable in interpretations of the sacred will and word. Religion and its priests, official and unofficial but customary, provide ethical guidance as to morally acceptable behaviour by interpreting the divine intention.

Religion and its functional parallels in such seriously flawed secular guises as Nazism and communism should serve the strategist well by providing useful certainties.[29] Unfortunately, whatever the assessed benefits of religious authority, history reveals that religion occurs in many forms and with considerable differences in content. Moreover, the adherents of distinctive religious persuasions have a long and bloody record of arguing by the sword for the Right as they know and therefore hold it to be. Religion often may seem to be an independent variable in strategic history, but more careful and somewhat sceptical enquiry is apt to reveal that religious motivation often is fuelled by plainly non-spiritual concerns and sentiments. This is not to be generically cynical about the role of religion; it is not by any means to dismiss it on the basis of crudely functional assumptions. Just because religious belief is socially, and sometimes arguably strategically, useful, it does not follow that the belief must be false. The important matter of what is true and what is not has no relevance to strategic affairs, since such issues literally cannot be resolved; with religion necessarily one is strictly in the realm where faith is sovereign. But, what does have great relevance for the course of strategic history is the substance of popular belief about acceptable as opposed to unacceptable behaviour. An ethics claimed to rest upon the authority of divinely inspired morality is often lacking self-evident prescriptive content for the particulars of unique contexts. Of course, Holy Writ can descend from the general to much lower levels of specific applicability, but even then the divinely inspired rules of engagement likely will require interpretation for concrete cases.

It is an uncomfortable historical reality that, true or false, and who can claim which, with authority based on incontestable evidence, religion can be a potent motivator of strategically relevant behaviour. People may fight about and with religion (on their side, of course), as if trial by military combat can serve as agency to settle theological argument between rival systems of faith.

When ideas of right and wrong are ascribed to a supreme spiritual or secular, but functionally sacred, authority, combat is always likely to be especially tenacious. Compromise is difficult to justify when one's course is heavily invested with asserted moral value.

It might seem most appropriate to consider the just war tradition at this point in the text as a key to understanding the code of strategic ethics that derives most significantly from Christian morality.[30] The just war tradition, though unquestionably pervasively theological, is most usefully analysed in a framework that allows for, but does not strictly require, theological sanction. Just war thinking is so important that it needs to be decoupled from distinctively Christian morality in order for its historical significance and continuing global relevance to be fully appreciated. To that end, discussion of just war doctrine is deferred to the next section. For a related matter, it would be appropriate to consider the religious dimension to, and indeed the entirety of the ethical perspective on, strategy, under the permissive umbrella of culture. That approach has been rejected in the interest of highlighting the enduring pertinence of morality and ethics for a subject that typically chooses not to engage with such a controversial issue-area. Moral judgement is so subjective that politicians wield it in potent assertion of high sounding rectitude. But, those same politicians typically are disinclined even to attempt to justify their behaviour by citing candidate evidence in their support. To be empathetic, it should be acknowledged that moral arithmetic suffers severely from a currency conversion problem. If a policymaker seeks to make strategic decisions that will result in the doing of more good than harm, what serves well enough as the unit of account, and how reliably can the course of future strategic history be anticipated? It is easy to understand why practical people do not linger long over such conundrums.

2.3.2 Natural Law (or Reason)

An ethical code may claim authority from a postulated natural law, most probably one deemed capable of discovery through the power of a near reified Reason.[31] It is probably useful to explain that strategic behaviour is influenced by belief and the effect of that belief upon motivation for action. Since an ethical code has always been a necessity for human survival and prosperity, historically the relevant issues are only 'which moral beliefs and derivative ethics', and 'how strictly are they obeyed and policed, and by whom'? The source of moral authority is not important. What matters is its social-cultural, political, and strategic presence, and its specific content. All political power has to be supported by an applicable and applied ethical code, though there can be occasional exceptions.

When the state defines the right arbitrarily in ways unrelated to one's behaviour, then there is no operating ethical code to guide one for personal safety. Notwithstanding the existence of functionally sacred texts and seemingly unmistakable principles for the guidance of prudent behaviour, purposeful choice of obviously rightful conduct could not guarantee a person's security in Stalin's Soviet Union in the late 1930s. Ethical conformity cannot save one when the state itself is the terrorist. When pain and death are inflicted almost at random as exemplary punishment meted out to induce fear, ethical compliance ceases to function as protection. The principle of 'objective criminality', if one were Jewish in Nazi controlled Europe for a leading case, should mean that the objective innocence of being non-Jewish translates as personal safety.[32] One can rephrase the idea of objective criminality as categorical guilt. Right is whatever the political authority claims it to be now, and one's guilt need rest upon no basis other than the malevolent whim of those with the power to enforce their will. Natural law becomes the law of the jungle, and the only ethic governing official, or even unobstructed private political violence, is that of superior strength by the king or kings of that jungle. It should not be supposed that arbitrary state terrorism in its internal misgovernance is necessarily astrategic. On the contrary, it is only much of the individual human targeting that is arbitrary not the terrorism itself. Such terrorism can make strategic sense. A potentially politically restless public—and which public is beyond restlessness?—may be rendered so insecure and fearful that it is cowed into reflexive political compliance with political authority, and as a result is disabled from active opposition, organized or otherwise. Of course, such official terrorism does have the potential to brew revolutionary anger, but it would be a seriously mistaken judgement to deny that violent repression, including arbitrary terrorism, has a distinguished history of some political success. Repression can work. Not for ever, but sometimes for long enough to attract politicians who are not overly risk-averse and can calculate that the longer-term hazards of the strategy are more than balanced by its anticipated near-term benefits.

Alas, there are serious problems with Reason as an authoritative source of moral authority for ethics. Most obviously, appeals to Reason can have difficulty finding the unchallengeably correct address for their needful communication with final authority. Where and with whom or what does Reason reside? Most of us have decided that it is convenient and prudent, perhaps simply expedient *faute de mieux*, to claim that Reason lives within that reified concept of The World Community, and that that Community is best represented in the United Nations as the institution most representative of all humankind. Undeniably, all members of humankind tend to think rationally, as they must, obliged as they are to strive to match their ends with suitable ways and means. But, frequently people can be simultaneously rational yet unreasonable in the estimation of others. At one time there was a quaint idea that much international strife could be prevented by the spread of a common language (recall Esperanto).[33] Unfortunately, the problems of international security typically have little to do with values in dispute because of linguistic miscommunication. The language of high moral principle that expresses and asserts the allegedly common beliefs and orientation of all Mankind are thoroughly devalued by their subordination to interpretation that is inherently political. For example, declarations of human rights, no matter how solemn, are empty rights, if indeed they are to be regarded as rights at all, if the reliable duty and ability to enforce them is not also present. A right without a matching duty is not only practicably without meaning, actually it has the potential to do harm if it encourages expectations and actions that have no realistic basis in supporting strength. Assertion of human rights requires an enabling strategic narrative.

Law and Reason (natural or other) have at worst only a spurious authority, and at best a fragile one, if they are regarded in isolation from politics and its strategies. It is popular to treat law and morality (with dependent derivative ethics) as independent variables (maybe as invariables), floating as it were outside, but above and definitely authoritatively over the crude deeds and misdeeds of politicians and soldiers. The sense in this insistence upon legal and ethical rules for the moral governance of strategic affairs is close to unchallengeable. However, those who for strong and worthy reasons insist upon the absolute primacy of legal and ethical codes, both formal and less so, are apt to mislead themselves as well as others. Humankind is not short of law or ethics; rather is there a shortfall in the non-trivial region of common interpretation, application, and therefore effective deterrence and enforcement. Some governments today wax lyrical as well or tediously repetitive in their referencing of the aspirational notion of a 'rules-based international community'. But, one has to ask: which rules; whose rules; what do the rules assert; who decides which reading of the rules are the most authoritative in particular cases; and who or what enforces the rules that an international ordering process and authority makes? These are not questions of minor importance.

Common words do not always have meaning common to all Mankind, especially given the inherent variations in nuance between languages (e.g. control and *contrôle*).[34] Were all men saints then they would need neither a legal framework nor an explicit ethical code. The unavoidable trouble has always been that every legal system, ethical code, and exercise of Reason has to function within a political context. Law is politics and, to hazard a truly dangerous thought, so too are the morals that supposedly identify the behavioural standards expressed as ethics. These claims may be too bitter a compound pill for some among us to swallow. However, the overriding purpose here is to add fuel for clear understanding of the ethical perspective on strategy and its basis in moral authority. This mission requires acceptance of some uncomfortable facts pertaining to the primacy of politics over, indeed in good part as, morality and its applied ethics.

2.3.3 Politics

One can argue that moral guidance constructs an ethical code that advises with a moral authority derived from politics. To state the matter directly, morality is political and ethics are politics (one may go so far as to claim that morality and ethics are merely politics).[35] This formulation can appear shocking, at least at first sight. If one is prepared to approve or condone Harold Lasswell's classic functional definition of politics as the process that is about 'who gets what, when, how', and adds to it the important consequential element, 'and what they do with it', secure enough grip should be achievable on the core of the subject.[36]

To explain the moral foundation to contemporary strategic ethics (whenever and wherever that happens to be), it suffices to backtrack along the trail of causation from normative nostrums at the sharp end, reversing through explicit formal rules of engagement, to military law, back to national and international law, to moral sentiments, yet further back to culture, and ultimately to the fount of human rulings on acceptable social behaviour— politics. There is usually a discretionary element at every stage in the great chain of ethics just specified and simplified. Also, some of the stages overlap and mutually infuse. In practice, politics rules on culture, but naturally culture provides high octane fuel for politics. While grasping the need to recognize the validity of many caveats, still there is high merit in taking seriously the chain of causation identified here. The moral choice behind ethical prescription reflects cultural assumptions, though it may distort in the reflection because those assumptions and preferences are always politically mediated. This may be a little too discretionary a process for some readers, but as the barest bones of the structure of a theory that can explain the causal dynamics of strategic ethics, it seems to be fit enough for purpose.

Explanation of the issue area of moral authority cannot help but have difficulty navigating among major categories whose contents and relations are matters of methodological choice and belief, not evidence. Morality, ethics, politics, culture, law, norms and customs, and religion, can be discussed separately, but they are not discrete subjects. For convenient handling, this book investigates strategic phenomena in the light cast from their exploration in five perspectives. However, it is ironic that this study has as a meta-theme the necessity for holistic understanding of strategy.

Politicians may claim that politics is about values, not about power, but even if uttered sincerely this assertion must mislead. A political process cannot decide who has the moral edge in argument. Politics decides whose values will be advanced, not whose values are right, unless, of course, a society chooses to believe that political heft is synonymous with moral weight. It can be argued that values and interests converge, then merge, and finally are truly synonymous. This nonsensical sleight-of-concept(s) was perpetrated most egregiously by Prime Minister Tony Blair, in his Chicago speech on 22 April 1999, in the immediate context of Serbian brutality in Kosovo. Hoisted on the petard of his high moral purpose and propelled by asserted righteousness, he enunciated what some have called 'The Blair Doctrine'.

> Now [in contrast to the years of the Cold War] our actions are guided by a more subtle blend of mutual self-interest and moral purpose in defending the values we cherish. *In the end values and interests merge.* If we can establish and spread the value of liberty, the rule of law, human rights and an open society then that is in our interests too. The spread of our values makes us safer.[37]

The Prime Minister was no doubt sincere and well intentioned. Unfortunately, those attributes have limited traction for advantage in, let alone as, applied strategy. They are not to be despised, though, because firm self-belief is a major source of spiritual and perhaps moral strength, and was properly emphasized by Clausewitz in the powerful but content-neutral concept of 'will'.[38] Will can be key to strategic advantage or disadvantage, just as it can be applied for good or ill. While in principle it is highly desirable for a politician and strategist, it is perilously abstract and naked of implied specific content regarding purpose. Will is only of high value to a security community when it is devoted to the achievement of prudent and useful policy goals. Also, will needs a strategy, it is not equipped by nature with GPS. Energy and moral strength are apt to have dangerous consequences when they are not harnessed to workable methods and adequate means. One should remember Sun Tzu's caveat about courageousness in generals: such men are likely to be dangerous, while a combination of stupidity and courage is a 'calamity'.[39]

As a rule it is prudent to be sceptical of strategic argument framed in moral terms, and sometimes it is wholly appropriate to claim detection of cynicism. In at least two major respects the eponymous 'Blair Doctrine' is confused and confusing, although its prophet almost certainly was blissfully unaware of the fact. Notwithstanding the specification of some realistic seeming tests for applicability in particular cases, the relationship between values and interests was not clearly explained. Should values lead in the determination of interests? If the two categories merge to become a single category of 'values-interests' (though not of valued interests), how can one assess whether or not the merger has continuing integrity for the political episode at issue? The logical confusion is caused by the collapsing of values into politics and policy. In practice, if they become one and the same, values vanish and are subsumed in and subordinate to the necessities of political practice attempted through strategy.

Among the troubles with the moral and ethical assay of political behaviour, which by definition includes strategic behaviour, is the near universal fact that people behave morally in their own estimation. Apparent deviation from the extant authoritative ethical code typically is excused and justified with reference to ethically condonable and therefore moral necessity. Far more often than not in strategic history, misdeeds only contestably are identifiable as such. Monstrous brutality, for a rousing pejorative label, is locally excusable and is excused not as a legitimate deviation, but deviation nonetheless, from what authoritatively is coded as rightful usual practice. Instead, allegedly compelled by grim circumstances, the misdeeds are recoded and rebranded as properly moral conduct when the ethical code is rightly comprehended and applied. Frequently, morality is alive, though not well, in the form of a code that is interpreted on the basis of the principle that a particular person or institution is the sole authority on what is right and what is wrong. The applied morality in ethics can descend into mere political will, which may be all too personal and arbitrary. For example, in effect the Führer is the authoritative fount of moral judgement. What he decides is right and must be so, because he is never wrong. The Party can be substituted for the 'Führer'. The legitimating authority behind the power to decide on right and wrong can be anything or anybody that a community is willing to believe in, or at least prudently pretend that it does. One is in the realm of faith and the sacred, whether the historical case is formally spiritual, secular, or a potent hybrid mix of the two. The subject is authority, not some objective plausibility to authority's basis. All that is truly authentic is the fact of public consent to a particular claim to authority, not any purportedly objective quality to the authority itself. Leaders, including moral leaders, can only be such if they are able to attract and secure compliant followers. If people are willing to believe that a particular individual is the contemporary agent of the divine, or in quasi-religious but nominally secular guise is the properly licensed (by History, Destiny, or whatever) interpreter of the Correct Theory of History, then a community's domestic moral and ethical challenges are easily met. Simply consult political authority, which is conveniently merged with moral authority.

As in physics with its futile quest for ever more fundamental sub-atomic particles, so the hunt for the true source of moral authority is doomed to failure: by way of analogical contrast, it is not to be compared with the search for the source of the Nile in the nineteenth century.[40] The worthy pursuit of an ever purer ethical code via the authority of a moral truth which identifies it, soon is confounded by the elusiveness endemic to the prime-mover problem. Whomever or whatever the moral authority is assumed to be, there is always the logical option available to enquire into and challenge the authority of the asserted authorizer. It has to follow on this reasoning that identification of the source(s) of the moral authority commanded in practice by ethics is highly discretionary and cannot be revealed by any methodological sophistication in research effort. Although authority is definable as legitimated power, there is plausibility in the uncomfortable thought that power is in some measure self-legitimating. It is morally awkward to be obliged to recognize the possible paradox that the moral authority behind political power may well flow non-trivially in circular fashion from that power itself. Readers must decide whether this is merely an irony or actually is the disturbing contradiction of a paradox.

Charles Guthrie and Michael Quinlan are empirically correct though somewhat misleading when they register the following pre-emptive claims in the opening sentences of their important book on just war:

> Moral accountability is a central part of what it means to be a human being. Every human activity must be open to moral examination, to questions about what it is right or wrong to do. That applies even—perhaps especially—to extreme activities like armed conflict, where some of the normal ethical rules, like not killing, have to be overridden.[41]

Guthrie and Quinlan emphatically are right in asserting that 'moral accountability is a central part of what it means to be human'. In support of those authors I approve the syllogism that holds that strategy is human, humans think morally, therefore there is and has to be an important moral perspective on strategy. This argument is solid because all that it claims is that because strategy is a thoroughly human endeavour, which is self-evidently true at all levels of the project, humans doing strategy cannot help but accommodate, or acknowledge but then ignore, moral considerations. This is empirical theory, not deduction. It is regrettable that the claims and arguments just made probably inadvertently conceal at least as much as they explain. The fact that human beings think, indeed are programmed by nature or nurture to think, in moral terms assuredly is true, but has limited policing value over strategic (mis)behaviour. How can this be? The reason is that the moral and ethical police force of the 'war convention' and its agents have demonstrated beyond plausible question that they are under-instructed and under-armed to tackle the heroic mission of shaping a moral character to combat. The mission is as desirable and even necessary of performance as it needs prudently to be recognized as impossible. After all, the subject of this chapter can be summarized in the eminently contestable concept of moral combat, followed by a much needed question mark.[42] When war and its warfare are considered strategically, a huge shadow of potential contradiction is a permanent menace to ethical practice guided other than by expediency.[43]

Clausewitz asserted that war is really only armed politics, but also he argued persuasively that the core and possibly defining feature of war is violence.[44] War may be owned, in the sense of sponsored, by politics, but the violence of politically motivated force has a grammar which can drive a logic of its own.[45] Warfare can serve yet more warfare because its dynamics may shift it beyond meaningful control by policy and its politics. The grip of policy upon the conduct of war in its warfare can lose both power and authority. Military success in the warfare may become the practical purpose of the whole bloody effort, in effect regardless of the politics of war causation. Indeed, the dynamic demands of warfare have a way of reshaping the policy and politics that triggered the violence initially. Clausewitz's theory of war is generally convincing, but it states a normative understanding that necessarily is only aspirational. The great Prussian certainly understood this. Confusion arises when the explicit and implicit caveats in *On War* concerning the challenge to policy reason posed by the very nature of war are ignored. Clausewitz's claim for the supremacy of policy, regarded perhaps contestably as reason, is best regarded as normative, not empirical, social scientific theory. There can be no doubt that war must always have political meaning, and it is sensible to insist that politics as reason in policy ought to be authoritative in providing guidance for military effort. However, *On War* does not argue that politics as policy in actuality has to be dominant over public sentiment or over the conduct of war by the army and its commander. The interactive dynamics of the warfare in war usually threaten the practical authority of the licensing policy and its politics.

The empirical merit in the claim that morality and its ethics are really only politics in normative dress is not a recognition that many strategic theorists are willing to make, at least not explicitly in polite society. Unfortunately, perhaps, the case for equating morality and its ethics with politics is a strong one. The relevant chain of reasoning proceeds as follows:

- Strategic behaviour always has a moral context as a source of guidance for ethical behaviour, because all people require and acknowledge moral compass that distinguishes acceptable (right) from unacceptable (wrong) acts.

- All human beings are morally encultured, though by no means always by or to a common standard yielding similarly calibrated moral compass.

- In historical practice every ethical code expresses a particular moral worldview and both are products of, and are policed by, political power. Relations of power, whatever the source of the influence, are definable most plausibly as political. Wherever one looks for the moral authority behind ethics, one is obliged to conclude that the search reveals political influence.

The reasoning immediately above typically meets with resistance because it seems almost self-evidently incorrect. How can the great truths about right and wrong that flow from morality and are codified in ethics simply be the product of politics? People do not want to believe this. It sounds false, even perhaps dangerously subversive of civilized standards. After all, our culture seeks to tell us that moral truths and the ethical code they fuel are by definition above and independent of the merely political. Politics as a necessary function may well be a permanent fixture in human social affairs, but it is a process and a source of dynamic outcomes that fits uneasily with what usually are believed to be enduring principles for the guidance of morally acceptable and therefore ethically compliant, behaviour.

There are excellent reasons why the human race has endorsed a thicket of laws, rules, principles, and norms in Walzer's 'war convention'.[46] Nearly everyone today believes that the ethical perspective on strategic affairs is a subject of high importance.[47] However, there are hindrances to understanding of the ethical dimension to strategy that are unique to this particular perspective. Morality and its desired ethics are held to express truths that are not merely the negotiated outcome of political argument and experience, but rather are epiphanies about eternal and universal values. There is much to be said in favour of this approach. After all, it is desirable that unwanted behaviour should be discouraged by whatever kinds of negative sanctions are judged likely to be effective.

For example, a code of military ethics that forbids the killing of prisoners of war should be strengthened usefully if it is regarded by soldiers not only as a matter of discipline, obedience to standing orders and the law, but also as rightful behaviour. Such killing should be discouraged when it is viewed by potential perpetrators not only as illegal, but also as morally wrong. But, no matter how insistent and rigorous one tries to be in employing an ethical perspective to strategic affairs, there is no evading the implication of the historical fact that the working presence of morality and its ethics, though indeed inescapable, offers no specific guarantees of substantive normative compliance. Everyone, everywhere and always, 'does' ethics and morality, but they do them as is generally accepted in the sense that they behave in ways that are morally acceptable; and therefore can be claimed to be ethically compliant, given the circumstances in which they find themselves. The pragmatic strategist and his military agents are apt to find themselves inclined to behave in ways that are ironic, given their sincere adherence to an ethical code, but which are not truly paradoxical. For a leading example, it is ironic to do great harm for the purpose of doing (greater) good, but it is not necessarily paradoxical. The two do not contradict each other, because it is in the nature of war, which is legitimate force or violence, to do harm. The strategist cannot fight the good fight without doing harm. This is rich linearity, not contradiction.

The discussion now must move on to consider whether there can be a meaningful ethics of strategic context, or rather whether consequentialist reasoning effectively jettisons moral compass as a concept not wanted on strategic voyages.

2.3.4 Situational Ethics (How Do We Know Right From Wrong?)

In the global and timeless domain that is the realm of strategy it is an enduring somewhat ironic truth that the law of war both licenses war as well as seeks to control it, and indeed licenses war by the effort to control it. Truly the ethical traditions of just war have fulfilled the vital function of providing moral justification for, thereby legitimating, violence. Historically viewed, law and ethics are very much the products of culture, while culture both shapes and is bullied into acquiescence by politics. There is an often underappreciated dynamic quality to the nature of war, politics, and culture that leads into the morally uncomfortable zone of situational ethics. Unless one is very careful one can blunder into a maze wherein the moral GPS does not function. If strategic behaviour is audited morally only by an ethic of strategic consequences, then whatever is judged necessary to do, *ipso facto* has to be morally right enough, simply because it is believed necessary. This circularity in moral justification is commonplace as well as superficially eminently reasonable. But, can it be moral in any meaningful sense? Judgements of perceived necessity typically are more than marginally subjective.

There is some inevitable tension in studies of the ethical perspective between, on the one hand, the need to speak truth to strategic history, while on the other hand there is a laudable if unscholarly desire to promote what the scholar regards as good behaviour. Understanding of the morality in the ethical perspective on strategy has long been harassed and hindered by scholars' unwillingness to accept facts that are morally discomforting and therefore unwelcome. The great French sociologist and occasional strategic theorist, Raymond Aron, spoke words of wisdom when he advised that 'prudence is the statesman's supreme virtue'.[48] Sad to admit, prudence as a value is compatible with much misbehaviour, as some moral compasses would indicate were they consulted. A problem with prudence is that it is intensely subjective. Political and strategic decisions are made by human beings, individually and collectively, who vary widely in their tolerance of risk. There is no escaping the need for judgement in all aspects of strategic affairs, a reality that obtains fully in the moral dimension. Wherever one looks for the intellectual security of certainty, one does not find it. This is not exactly an epiphany, but much public argument about strategic issues either pretends to a certainty of knowledge that its protagonists know they do not have or, more often, strategic claims are made in honest if still inexcusable ignorance of their fragility.

There is a 'war convention' in which just war doctrine long has figured as a major body of respected, if frequently ignored, standards. Unfortunately, the doctrine is as certain in its content as its application invites disputation. The ideas most closely associated with the concept of just war have so thoroughly penetrated the contemporary discourse in a form that has little if any detectable religious trace, that it is sensible to detach just war ideas for today from their theological provenance. Just war doctrine effectively is both secularized today and can be understood to tolerate so wide a discretion in application that the doctrine approximates a morality-light (or even absent) situationally empathetic consequentialist ethics.

Just war doctrine has at its core six criteria for *jus ad bellum*, all of which must be satisfied before a resort to war can be regarded as just, and two criteria for *jus in bello*.[49] For a war to be just, according to the doctrine, it has to be waged: for a *just cause*; for a *proportionate cause*; with a *right intention*; by a *right authority*; with a *reasonable prospect of success*; and only as a *last resort*. For a war to be waged justly, assuming it meets the just war criteria as cited, it has to be conducted with *discrimination* and *proportionality*. One does not have to be a pedantic logician in order to appreciate the potential for subjectivity in application of these eight large concepts that are required to function as standards. Given that international law in the form of the Charter of the United Nations recognizes unambiguously the inherent right of states to secure their self-defence, it is plain to see that one is very much in the realm of discretion over matters of war and peace. When one pursues the phenomenon of strategic discretion as it is implied in the UN Charter, one discovers unsurprisingly that what states and other collective political actors choose to do depends in no small measure upon the strategic situation in which they believe themselves located. An apparently unethical and illegal leap from peace to war thus arguably may well be morally, ethically, and legally justified as a prudent anticipatory response in aid of self-defence. International law does not oblige states to receive the first blow; pre-emptive military action taken in self-defence, or claimed not implausibly to be such, is ethical and legal. Preventive war is not ethically or legally licensed, but the distinction between pre-emption and prevention can be blurry or deliberately blurred.[50]

Whereas the plain meaning of the eight core concepts of just war doctrine are unambiguous, their meaning for almost any particular situation in strategic history is always more or less uncertain and contestable. When doctrine with intended ethical force lends itself so easily both to authentically as well as insincerely controversial interpretation, its moral authority cannot help but be diminished. So it is with the theory and doctrine of just war.

The basic problem with which this chapter in particular is wrestling is the fact that strategic behaviour is not 'lawfare' and neither is it applied morality (via an ethical code). Moral beliefs assuredly play a role in strategic behaviour, as also do legal constraints.[51] But, there is a fundamental disharmony between military violence and liberal values of morality in ethics, some of which find expression in law. Both politics and its sometimes servants, war and warfare, are indeed conducted ethically and often legally as well. Nonetheless, war and warfare have their own purposes and dynamics, and those do not naturally and inherently include law and morality. Security communities wage wars for political reasons, not immediately legal or moral ones. States do not fight proximately in order to obey the law (whose law and who says so?) or to affirm the right, though those purposes may be well served by the consequences of military success. The logic of warfare is the logic neither of law nor of morality. If one attempts to confine war within the bounds of law and morality, as we should and do, a measure of failure is either certain or at best is likely. So long as political communities are reserved the right to self-defence (in the absence of collective international action licensed by the UN Security Council) in a somewhat anarchic world, then for so long must state self-perception of its relevant strategic context be the final determinant of what is just and legally permissible behaviour. The challenge does not lie within the natures of politics, morality, or war. Rather is the problem the persisting fact that these distinctive categories are only uneasy partners at best. If this is appreciated, much inappropriate anger and unnecessary frustration should be avoidable. The uncomfortable historically enduring truth appears to be that it is not in the nature of war for it to be conducted morally or lawfully. By imperfect analogy, the warfare in war is akin to a wild animal that can be somewhat disciplined by reward and punishment, but it cannot reliably be tamed.

The situational ethics of anticipated consequences are all but mandatory for belligerents. But, consequentialism in strategic ethics is compatible with morally appalling outcomes, when one is willing to drag moral standards behind and subordinate to the chariot of a licensing strategic necessity. If ethically one is permitted to do what one believes is strategically necessary, then the only ethic with teeth is prudence: this would be a much bolder claim than Aron seems to intend.

2.3.5 Culture

Because culture is understood to embrace moral as well as other beliefs, it is close to a tautology to claim that culture is a potent source of moral authority. Whether or not culture is as powerful a shaper and driver of behaviour as it is of beliefs and other ideas, is a different matter requiring investigation that is not highly relevant to the discussion in this chapter. In much the same way that most apparent paradoxes are revealed after careful examination not to be true contradictions at all, but rather only ironies, so cultural phenomena tend to be too readily identifiable as a consequence of careless theorizing.[52] As the next chapter explains, currently there is a crisis in the cultural auditing of strategic phenomena because this concept can hardly help expanding its explanatory domain beyond meaningful bounds.

Any application of a moral lens and its derivative ethical perspective to strategic phenomena has to accord culture significant if not sovereign respect.[53] After all, if an ethical code, a legal framework, political attitudes, and a moral sense of the content of right and wrong behaviour are not to an important degree cultural, what are they? Since all people seemingly are biologically and psychologically programmed to think morally, and because their specific moral thoughts (with whatever content) are socially (and biologically?) transmitted, minds inexorably are culturally educated. Whether or not one can locate functional rationality behind particular beliefs, the moral authority of those beliefs is apt to be as robust as is their cultural nature. Public culture today is no more thoroughly global than are strategic and military cultures. That said, the 'so what' strategist's question now looms menacingly over this discussion. There is overwhelming evidence in support of the claim that culture is a potent source of moral authority. This claim is close to being a banal truth, though it does not point reliably to determining fuel for behaviour. Tautological traps lurk for the unwary. If thought and belief is key to action, if belief is accorded only to a moral authority, and if acceptance of that moral authority is socially learnt behaviour which means that it can be categorized as cultural, then thought, belief, and action, are all more or less cultural. This reasoning works well enough deductively, but approached empirically it is seriously fragile and it is so ambitious in claimed domain as to be notably short of meaning useful for understanding.

2.4 STRATEGIC ETHICS AND MORAL ADVANTAGE?

Does the application of a moral standard in an ethical code fit for effective strategic behaviour seize moral advantage in war?[54] Can strategic ethics be moral? The basic assumptions that undergird the just war traditions of ethical thought dismiss the possibility of any relevance to the second question. Among history's many ironies, it would seem indisputable that efforts to control and limited war, or armaments, both in theory and in practice have tended to have the reverse effect of that principally intended. It cannot be denied that rules for war-making and for arms retention, acquisition, and modernization yield restrictions upon political choice. But, the provision of rules of varying solemnity and specificity for war-making and competitive arming, functionally licenses the behaviour to be controlled, rather than comprises effective steps towards its eradication.[55] The repeated urge to regulate rather than eliminate has been realistic, but it continues to spark morally fuelled anger on the part of those who are not reconciled to the necessity for an ethics fit for strategic purposes that are resented. The core of the problem is that awful means need to be threatened or employed for the purpose of advancing desirable end-state policy goals. Much public political and moral debate is content to focus on the 'what' and the 'why' of policy, with scant attention paid to the 'how'. In other words, strategy tends to be alien to public debate.

2.5 NAVIGATING THE MORAL MAZE

This narrative has emerged from the moral maze with a few and clear enough conclusions that will serve as guideposts for the ethical perspective on strategy.

Moral thinking that distinguishes right from wrong conduct is inalienably human. Everyone needs a moral framework and everyone obtains one. Alas, moral frameworks are in some details plural rather than singular, and they differ both at one time between communities and over time as well. That said, moral thought is not optional, though it is not always determining of behaviour. Some thought and actions do not need to be fully compatible. It is a hallmark of properly strategic enquiry that it must ever be ready to pose the challenging question, 'so what?' No strategic commentary should be highly regarded if it advances the proposition that strategists can and ought to operate in a value-free bubble secure against harassment by moral considerations. It is human to think morally. When Clausewitz specifies 'violence, hatred, and enmity' (which he associates primarily with 'the people') as the first element in his trinitarian theory of war, he intends to emphasize the potency of moral force in all its pertinent forms.[56] People require some moral comfort if they are to perform effectively for strategy. This is not to deny that physical survival can serve as a good enough purpose that functionally meets the psychological necessity for confidence that behaviour is rightful. Identification of a minimally satisfactory goal capable of meeting a moral standard (bare physical survival?) is an exercise with subjective content.

In the marketplace for moral frameworks and ethical traditions the leading product is the Christian-founded doctrine of just war. The doctrine has been renewed periodically and not infrequently reinterpreted in its terms of application, but still it shines forth as the global exemplar of strategic ethics within a moral framework. Of course, Judaism and Islam also have morally fuelled ethical traditions that address the challenges of war and warfare. In addition, even the secular religions of communism and Nazism had distinguishable strategic ethics. This author has no quarrel with the estimable Guthrie and Quinlan when they say that

> The need for moral guidelines that will be clear, practicable and credible both to the armed forces and to the peoples they represent and serve therefore remains as cogent as ever it has been.

In our judgement the Just War tradition—which has lasted and evolved through centuries of change in the forms of warfare and of international affairs—still provides the best available foundation for meeting this need.[57]

A similar belief propels the argument in A. J. Coates' outstanding study of *The Ethics of War*. In his words:

Though the book examines alternative conceptions for war, its central focus is on the just war tradition of thought. This may seem an arbitrary narrowing of its subject-matter. The ethics of war is not after all exhausted by any single tradition. The just war tradition, however, is not simply one tradition among many— something that even its firmest critics acknowledge... The fact is that this tradition has monopolised the moral debate about war, at least in the Western world.[58]

Provided one is prepared to grant a moral licence for the resort to violence, the character of legitimate force applied for good enough purpose and in ethically acceptable ways, the strategic realm should be tolerably ethically tidy. The principles in just war doctrine can be used to guide politicians and soldiers along a straight enough path in the strategic ethics of applied morality. So far, so good, but closer examination reveals that just war doctrine with its relevant powerful principles is more of a stimulant for dispute than an effective arbiter. It is not probable that any government will be able to build, buy, or rent a just war testing kit that would spew forth authoritative reliable answers to the most vital questions of *jus ad bellum* and *jus in bello*. Moreover, even should such a testing kit be available, we can be sure that it would not be fit enough for all political and strategic purposes. While politicians and soldiers typically will seek to behave as justly as they believe prudent, they will not choose to fight for the purpose of behaving justly, and neither will they fight justly with justice as their primary and overriding concern. Commentaries that overprivilege moral concerns tend to underprivilege the natures of politics, war, and strategy.

Just war doctrine provides an invaluable educational guide to how to think morally about, and prospectively behave ethically in war, but it cannot yield answers to the scarcely less essential questions of what to think about, when to resort to, or how to conduct a particular war. It should be true to claim that a necessary key to knowing what to think about war and warfare has to be the grasping and exploitation of a framework of tests for moral compliance that offers moral education. The just war tradition serves that necessary end admirably, but alas to be necessary is not synonymous with being sufficient. Guthrie and Quinlan argue that '[a]ll this [all eight criteria as tests for *jus ad bellum* (6) and *jus in bello* (2)] continues to be a highly apt and robust framework of ethical reference. It is the best checklist there is of the aspects that ought to be weighed.'[59] Sad to say, their second sentence is all too true, while it serves somewhat to diminish the plausibility of the preceding sentence quoted. The just war tests for the moral acceptability of the resort to war and of ethical behaviour in its conduct are profoundly unsatisfactory in practice because they do not and cannot specify tests that are objectively answerable. Every one of the eight tests, when applied to particular cases, cannot be answered in ways that would merit ascription as being unquestionably ethically compliant and morally satisfactory. This is not the fault of just war doctrine and its theologian and secular theorists. Rather does the problem lie with the nature of morality, more specifically with moral authority. If the latter is weak, contestable and contested, widely ignored, or more often asserted on the basis of coercion, then there is not likely to be a context wherein ethical policing or moral order can reign and rule.

The last sentences in the main text of the book by Guthrie and Quinlan manage to be simultaneously correct and deeply troubling.

> But it is surely beyond argument that some framework for the moral analysis of war is necessary. Those who would reject the Just War approach have to face and answer the question of what other ethical road-map they would propose to put in its place.[60]

Those who seek certainties for the proper ordering of the moral universe and complete reliability in moral navigation aids would be well advised not to venture far into the domain of the strategist. There are few moral certainties to which the strategist can anchor his projects via an ethical code robust in its moral value as well as in its strategic practicability. Further research effort is not likely to reveal any startling epiphanies for the twenty-first century strategist that the thoughts and theories of millennia somehow have failed to discover. The ethical perspective and its foundation in moral belief about right and wrong is what it is because we humans are as we are. Morality and ethics are not usefully to be approached as a field for scholarly or other research in quest of new knowledge. But, both can be studied for deeper understanding of persisting human realities.

Morality and its strategic ethics have to rest upon authority, and authority is about influence generated by power. Of course, power is a contested relational concept, but whatever the character of its source, be it spiritual, secular, or both, its presence is indicated in the manifestation of its influence over thought and behaviour. With one caveat, the source of moral authority is relatively unimportant. It is the integrity and robustness of faith that matters, not its brand. However, although fully functional morality effected through a particular code of ethics can be founded with reference to any authority icon-figure, force, or object, some sources of moral authority are more likely to prove resilient in the esteem in which they are held in the minds of followers than are others. For a major example, secular religions whose moral authority is dependent upon the presumed and repeatedly asserted infallibility of a still living or only recently deceased human leader (and his creed), have proved fatally fragile in the face of adverse circumstances. Communism and Nazism provide exemplary illustration.

Morality, and even more certainly ethics, are really politics. This exciting thesis rests on the following logic: the standards of right and wrong of a particular moral order are laid down and enforced by those who have the influence, which is to say the power, to do so. This is politics. Even if one believes that the human agents of a moral order are divinely inspired, the process by which morality is applied as ethics is thoroughly political.[61] It is disappointing to appreciate even the possibility that ethics and morality are (merely?) politics, but as we struggle to deploy and employ them it is useful to see them for what they are. None of this discussion contradicts arguments that recognize the ubiquity of moral beliefs and reasoning or the necessity for them, and therefore their high relevance for the human project of strategy. History tells us that preferred standards are selected by winners, who then assert the moral authority that undergirds ethical codes. The readily evidenced fact of large-scale commonality between moral orders and ethical codes across time and space does not subvert the plausibility of this argument that privileges the potency of politics.

Morality and ethics are the products and expressions of culture. Ergo, it would seem to follow that different cultures, including strategic cultures as an admittedly porous sub-set, could have their own moral standards and ethical codes. To classify morality and ethics as cultural may demean their authority, but that need not be so. Culture changes and assuredly varies from community to community, but nonetheless some of its ideas will be held to be eternal truths and they, among other less central nostrums, will have determinative weight for judgements about ethical practice. Furthermore, to argue that an ethical code and its foundational morality are largely cultural, does not register as much of an advance in identified seniority of explanation. If culture is held to be the true moral authority that should govern strategic behaviour, it is necessary to enquire as to its sources. There is no escaping the prime-mover problem. Plainly, strategic ethics are cultural, but who or what is the authoritative parent of cultural values? Any search for moral authority is obliged by the nature of the issue either to assign that sovereign power arbitrarily and choose to regard it as conclusively rightful, or to live with moral and intellectual discomfort and tolerate an ultimate indeterminacy about the legitimacy of moral standards.

The contrasting natures of morality, law, and war have a malign consequence. Normative theory and doctrine tends to ignore, if it even recognizes, how different are the universes of morality, law, and war. Because warfare and its narrative of violence has a powerfully dynamic 'grammar' of its own, the categorical differences between itself and morality and law are always likely to dominate military behaviour.[62] Normatively expressed, war should serve political purposes and ought to be conducted for lawful reasons and in lawful ways with lawful means. But, often in historical strategic practice, moral beliefs, legal argument, and political goals serve the military goals of war and its warfare that effectively defines for itself—to risk some reification—in its own terms, what should be done. This is a moral, legal, and political nonsense; frequently nonetheless it is an accurate characterization of what happens. War is an untamed and in truth always in some measure an untameable beast that is let loose only at high risk. Clausewitz above all other interpreters of war understood this. His writing about an 'absolute' form of war was both strict logic and empirically founded theory.[63]

Pessimism and despair, ironically in tandem with optimism and hope, are not helpful in considering the practical meaning of the ethical perspective on strategy. People will wage war and they will seek to win strategic advantage. Alert though they are to the nature of competitive violence applied in war, morality and law have value in encouraging some control over the death and damage that might be inflicted. There is a place for a strategic ethics that knows it must accommodate some of the dreadful consequences of war's enduring nature and particular contemporary character. There is, however, a systemic difficulty about strategic ethics. Necessarily the ethics are consequentialist in their moral logic because they are situational. The ethical reasoning is that we do what we must do, given both the strategic context and the claimed moral and political worth of our purpose in war. While ethics will prescribe proportionality and discrimination in military effort, it is not usual for strategic performance to be notably troubled by ethical concerns. The historical reality typically has been that of political (for claimed moral) ends justifying military ways and means of violence. The moral, via ethical, and legal constraints may seem to have been accorded more directive force of recent years than in the past, though it transpires on close inspection that such constraints upon behaviour may not reflect a growing efficacy to the ever-burgeoning 'war convention'. This is probably a case of the context misleading. The character of strategic behaviour is shaped far more by its political propulsion, as Clausewitz argued, and also by its own categorical dynamics, than it is by ideational rules of the road set by law and moral norms. If a security community is seriously fearful, law and morality are enlisted to serve in the ranks of national security (or world order, and so forth). This may be regrettable, but empirically it is so and is likely so to remain. In the waging of war for high stakes, polities always are liable to break out from the fragile bondage of the ethics and laws that can have more constraining effect when survival and other vital interests are not believed to be at risk.

In the words quoted as the epigraph for this chapter, John Howard Yoder claimed that one can distinguish between morally warranted war and war waged amorally with a blank cheque. I have suggested here that as a practical matter, questions of moral authority rarely are permitted seriously to inhibit strategic choices. The reason is not because an amoral and probably immoral blank cheque is widely issued. Instead, strategic history reveals the persistence and ubiquity of a strategic ethics that, functionally at least, is worthy of the name. It is rare for soldiers to behave immorally, because typically their actions are licensed by a notably situational but functional ethics. If the situation is allowed to define what soldiers are permitted to do, which is to say that its needs are specified as they were perceived at the time and probably locally, then the actions taken will be judged ethical enough and *ipso facto* moral. The point is that strategic history does not show any absence of moral authority, any lack of concern for the moral warrant to do harm. What history does reveal, though, is that the idea of an amoral blank cheque to kill and cause damage is thoroughly erroneous. Without denying the persisting facts of some criminal military indiscipline, which is scarcely surprising given that the subject is human behaviour in the most stressful of contexts, nonetheless strategic ethics are all but infinitely forgiving and flexibly adaptable to circumstances. The moral problem is neither the absence of moral authority, nor is it the lack of a relevant ethical code (as strategic ethics), rather is it with the authority of the moral authority. As a practical matter, moral authorities are not subject to a fundamental test of inherent virtue. Moral authority is such because it is regarded as authoritative, not because it is in any sense verifiably right. This is not to dismiss as irrelevant or demean the endeavours of 'war convention' projects, with war-crimes trials and judicial punishment at their sharp end. But, it is to argue that the constructed nature of strategic ethics and its morality poses an unresolvable problem that the ethical perspective on strategy has to acknowledge. War is an instrument of politics and policy, as the great Prussian said, but it is not reliably tameable. War has its own grammar and that frequently can be something of a challenge if strategic ethics are to remain within morally defensible bounds. So long as Man insists upon waging war and its warfare, no matter for what blend of reasons, then for so long must he do strategic ethics. By so doing however, he is ever in danger of bringing claims for his moral warrant into disrepute.

Although the concept of moral advantage has little if any relevance to actual combat, it does have high significance for the statecraft that provides the political context for strategic behaviour. Legal scholars can have a field-day arguing over the intriguing issue of whether or not soldiers can wage an unjust war justly.[64] If initiation of a particular war is judged criminal (by whom?), then surely all behaviour in its prosecution must be criminal also. I choose to leave this legal conundrum to legal professionals. Suffice it to say that strategic history does not reveal beyond serious challenge a tendency to reward only those who occupy and keep hold of the moral high ground. No matter how one phrases the matter, it is obvious that because moral judgement is so quintessentially subjective, even the notion of testing strategic historical outcomes for the possible strategic advantage of some moral advantage is apparently absurd. However, absurd or not, yet again an apparent paradox is revealed to be only falsely identified as such.

There is some strategic advantage in plausible morally framed argument, even though moral virtue has no discernible combat value in fighting. Because all potential belligerents are prone to believe that their cause is just, moral advantage cannot fuel strategic benefit directly. Tests for the justice of rival political causes by expedient means of trial by combat are, perhaps regrettably, methodologically unsound by virtue of the circularity of moral logic in the exercise (i.e. I know I am in the right, because I won; I won because I was in the right). The strategic value of plausible moral argument is registered both in the quantity and quality of domestic political support for policy, including war, and also in the appeal that such argument has to other societies. The advertised purposes for war will be irrelevant to those locked in combat in the jungle or at altitude; for them their warfare is effectively morally neutral, warrior-to-warrior. But, people everywhere think morally, though with some local variation in definition of rightful and wrongful conduct. Given that all political leaders everywhere must put their strategic judgements in a moral framework, it follows that the political will of a domestic public and of some publics abroad is a variable asset or liability potentially of great value. For the pain and hardships of war to be bearable, societies need to believe that the costs incurred are for purposes that are morally worthy. The moral worthiness standard may not be high, but in most countries, popular democracies in particular though not uniquely, it does need to be met. Strategic failure is always likely to attract the charge that the lack of success are just deserts reflecting divine disfavour, or at least some measure of moral turpitude.

In conclusion, one must claim that although history is not a morality tale, strategists who elect to discount significance to the ethical perspective take foolish risks. Although people are capable of excusing almost any kind of behaviour on the grounds of its contextual necessity, they are not capable of excusing themselves or others from obedience to an ethical code. Even the issuing of a blank cheque for the government to fill in on one's behalf is not the denial of a moral authority, rather is it simply the conferring of such authority upon the government.

NOTES

1. John Howard Yoder, *Christian Attitudes to War, Peace, and Revolution* (Grand Rapids, MI: Brazos Press, 2009), 31.
2. The neologism of the compound, indeed hybrid, abstract noun 'lawfare', has been invented to describe the strategic phenomenon of the use of law to attempt to inhibit an enemy's military effectiveness (or constrain one's own country's

military style in warfare). Jeremy Rabkin, 'Can We Win a War If We Have to Fight By Cosmopolitan Rules? *Orbis*, 55 (Fall 2011), 701, is especially enlightening. Rabkin endorses the view that widespread notice, if not actual invention, of the hybrid concept of 'lawfare', can be traced persuasively to a lecture given at Harvard by USAF lawyer, Major General Charles A. Dunlap, on 29 November 2001. See also Adam Roberts, 'The Civilian in Modern War', in Hew Strachan and Sybille Scheipers, eds., *The Changing Character of War* (Oxford: Oxford University Press, 2011), 51. What is damaging to understanding, however, is not the strategically familiar phenomenon of legal and quasi-legal constraints deployed for advantage, but rather the confusions of war with law. The neologism 'lawfare' has misled some well meaning people into committing this error. This concept implies not merely that war should be conducted within the relevant law, which is scarcely a bold and innovative argument, but also that war miraculously has fused with law. The hybrid phenomenon of 'lawfare' thus is regarded as the law itself in arms and in action, not only as war waged according to authoritative laws and norms. This is a most important point. Warfare is defined in critical part by violence, this is its nature. It is not in its nature to be either lawful or unlawful. Given that warfare has altered radically in character but not in its nature over millennia, it would be absurdly unhistorical and illogical to agree that an unchanging legal framework is a part of war's eternal nature.

3. I have found three books in particular to be enlightening, though by no means always convincing, amidst a large library of offerings by scholars who typically reason more persuasively about philosophy than they do about strategy. A. J. Coates, *The Ethics of War* (Manchester: Manchester University Press, 1997); Christopher Coker, *Ethics and War in the 21st Century* (Abingdon: Routledge, 2008); and David Fisher, *Morality and War: Can War be Just in the Twenty-First Century?* (Oxford: Oxford University Press, 2011).

4. Frequently, the idea of moral compass, meaning simply an encompassed space of moral understanding or reach, defined by a circle within which moral behaviour is conducted, is confused with the metaphor of a moral compass as an imagined instrument that, like its real physical inspiration, points to magnetic north (presumably the morally acceptable direction) as a moral navigation aid. The metaphor of a moral compass, with the indefinite article, is attractive and useful, despite its categorical error. Perhaps it should be an acceptable metaphor, provided the user knows that the provenance of the idea is rather prosaic. I am indebted to Professor David Stevenson's excellent letter on the subject in 'Letters to the Editor', *The Times*, 14 July 2011, 27.

5. Michael Burleigh has come virtually to own the subject of the quasi-religious features of Nazism; see his books: *The Third Reich: A New History* (London: Pan Macmillan, 2001); *Sacred Causes: Politics and Religion from the European Dictators to Al Qaeda* (London: Harper Perennial, 2007); and *Moral Combat: A History of World War II* (London: Harper Press, 2010).

6. It would be agreeable to be able to label Cold War era writings on moral issues and nuclear weapons as period pieces and treat them simply as contributions to the intellectual history of the twentieth century. However, the nuclear age is very much alive and well today, even though it is in evidence as a second such age, post-

Cold War. The following works from the 1980s continue to have more relevance than one would wish: Russell Hardin et al., eds., *Nuclear Deterrence: Ethics and Strategy* (Chicago: University of Chicago Press, 1985); Joseph S. Nye, Jr., *Nuclear Ethics* (New York: Free Press, 1986); and Henry Shue, ed., *Nuclear Deterrence and Moral Restraint: Critical Choices for American Strategy* (Cambridge: Cambridge University Press, 1989). There is dust on the arguments in these books, but they address questions that continue to show life, at least half-life, today.

7. For one example, Michael Burleigh has done just this, and to good effect, with his *Moral Combat*.

8. Michael Howard, *War and the Liberal Conscience* (London: C. Hurst, 2008), is essential.

9. Thucydides, *The Landmark Thucydides: A Comprehensive Guide to the Peloponnesian War*, ed. Robert B. Strassler, rev. trans. Richard Crawley (c.400 BC New York: Free Press, 1996), 352–4. See the thoughtful comments in Peter R. Pouncey, *The Necessities of War: A Study of Thucydides' Pessimism* (New York: Columbia University Press, 1980), 37, 87–8.

10. See John A. Lynn, *Battle: A History of Combat and Culture* (Boulder, CO: Westview Press, 2003), 40–51. Sun Tzu claims that 'moral influence' is the first of his 'five fundamental factors' most essential to the understanding of war (the other four are: weather, terrain, command, and doctrine). He explains as follows: 'By moral influence I mean that which causes the people to be in harmony with their leaders, so that they will accompany them in life and unto death without fear of mortal peril.' *The Art of War*, trans. Samuel B. Griffith (c.490 BC: Oxford: Clarendon Press, 1963), 64. When Sun Tzu argues that '[a]ll warfare is based on deception' (66), he is talking about the fostering of disharmony and confusion in the minds of enemy military leaders and soldiers.

11. See Roger Chickering, 'Total War: The Use and Abuse of a Concept', in Manfred F. Boemke, Chickering, and Stig Forster, eds., *Anticipating Total War: The German and American Experiences* (Cambridge: Cambridge University Press, 1999), 13–28; and Talbot Imlay, 'Total War', *The Journal of Strategic Studies*, 30 (June 2007), 547–70.

12. Paul W. Schroeder, 'Napoleon's Foreign Policy: A Criminal Enterprise', *The Journal of Military History*, 54 (April 1990), 147–61.

13. A. J. P. Taylor, *The Origins of the Second World War* (London: Hamish Hamilton, 1961).

14. Michael Walzer, *Just and Unjust Wars: A Moral Argument with Historical Illustrations*, 3rd edn. (New York: Basic Books, 1977), 44–7. 'I propose to call the set of articulated norms, customs, professional codes, legal precepts, religions and philosophical principles, and reciprocal arrangements that shape our judgments of military conduct *the war convention*' (44; emphasis in the original).

15. Jeremy Black, *The Curse of History* (London: The Social Affairs Unit, 2008), is a powerfully argued and generally persuasive polemic that focuses on the politics of collective grief as history is used and abused to serve contemporary purposes.

16. See the classic memoir by ex-soldier and professional philosopher, J. Glenn Gray, *The Warriors: Reflections on Men in Battle* (New York: Harper Torchbooks, 1967).

A more recent powerful moral memoir is Karl Marlantes, *What It Is Like to Go to War* (London: Corvus, 2011).

17. Dave Grossman, *On Killing: The Psychological Cost of Learning to Kill in War and Society* (Boston: Little, Brown, 1995); and Rune Henriksen, 'Warriors in Combat—What Makes People Actively Fight in Combat?' *The Journal of Strategic Studies*, 30 (April 2007), 187–223, are instructive.

18. See two books by Daniel Jonah Goldhagen: *Hitler's Willing Executioners: Ordinary Germans and the Holocaust* (London: Abacus, 1996) and *Worse Than War: Genocide, Eliminationism, and the Ongoing Assault on Humanity* (Boston: Little, Brown, 2009). Also see Martin Shaw, *War and Genocide: Organized Killing in Modern Society* (Cambridge: Polity Press, 2003).

19. On the erroneous ascription of paradox, see Antulio J. Echevarria II, *Preparing for One War and Getting Another* (Carlisle, PA: Strategic Studies Institute, US Army War College, September 2010).

20. See especially Hardin et al., eds., *Nuclear Deterrence*, for a rich array of well-argued essays. Also, there is good value to be found in the writing of philosopher Gregory S. Kavka, *Moral Paradoxes of Nuclear Deterrence* (Cambridge: Cambridge University Press, 1987). Civil servant Michael Quinlan had much to say of considerable worth in his books: *Thinking About Nuclear Weapons: Principles, Problems, Prospects* (Oxford: Oxford University Press, 2009), esp. ch. 5; and *On Nuclear Deterrence: The Correspondence of Sir Michael Quinlan*, ed. Tanya Ogilvie-White (Abingdon: Routledge for the International Institute for Strategic Studies, 2011), 14–65. The moral challenges adhering to strategy for nuclear weapons have long faded from ill-tempered controversy since the peak of public and scholarly interest in the mid-1980s. However, they have not faded as a result of their being met and resolved. Technological change keyed to exploitation of the digital revolution is believed by many people to have reduced greatly the political and strategic relevance of nuclear weapons, but the assumptions behind this de facto demotion are disturbingly fragile.

21. I am grateful to my colleague Professor Alan Cromartie of the University of Reading for assisting my understanding of this historically important well attested point.

22. See Jeff McMahan, 'Deterrence and Deontology', in Hardin et al., eds., *Nuclear Deterrence*, 141–60.

23. The monitoring of an arms control regime is a technical function, whereas verification of compliance or non-compliance is a political judgement. Politicians would be distinctly uncomfortable with treaty verification rules that would leave no room for expedient discretion. If the discovery even of a single nuclear weapon could only mean that a treaty had been violated, it is a prudent if cynical expectation that it would not be discovered. States have a long history of not finding what it would be embarrassing to find. Many years ago Fred Charles Ikle identified a question that has never been answered satisfactorily, 'After Detection—What?' *Foreign Affairs*, 39 (January 1961), 208–20.

24. Colin S. Gray, *The Strategy Bridge: Theory for Practice* (Oxford: Oxford University Press, 2010), ch. 5.

25. This view drives the argument in Charles Guthrie and Michael Quinlan, *Just War: The Just War Tradition: Ethics in Modern Warfare* (London: Bloomsbury Publishing, 2007). Also see Gray, *The Strategy Bridge*, 57–9.

26. See Ken Booth, *Strategy and Ethnocentrism* (London: Croom Helm, 1979) and Robert B. Bathurst, *Intelligence and the Mirror: On Creating an Enemy* (London: Sage Publications, 1993).

27. Carl von Clausewitz, *On War*, trans. Michael Howard and Peter Paret (1832–4; Princeton, NJ: Princeton University Press, 1976), 75 (emphasis in the original), 89.

28. See Ian S. Markham, *Do Morals Matter? A Guide to Contemporary Religious Ethics* (Oxford: Blackwell Publishing, 2007).

29. See Burleigh, *Sacred Causes*.

30. See Yoder, *Christian Attitudes to War, Peace, and Revolution*; Coates, *The Ethics of War*; and Guthrie and Quinlan, *Just War*.

31. See Joseph Boyle, 'Natural Law and International Ethics', in Terry Nardin and David R. Mapel, eds., *Traditions of International Ethics* (Cambridge: Cambridge University Press, 1992), 112–34.

32. 'Objective criminality' is explained briefly and clearly in Coker, *Ethics and War in the 21st Century*, 11–12. In his words: 'This is the belief that a person (or fellow human being) can be seen as a criminal not because he/she has actually committed a crime—or is indeed subjectively responsible for one—but because they are members of a group deemed criminal by the state' (11). I prefer the wording of categorical guilt, which makes unmistakably clear the fact or claim that criminality is ascribed to individuals by virtue of their belonging to a particular category of people. The meaning of the alternative is the same, however.

33. Esperanto is a language created by a Polish doctor in 1887 in the hope and expectation that it would improve communication across political and cultural frontiers. Linguistically it did not work well for non-Europeans, while more fundamentally its invention rested upon the false premise that poor communication lies at the root of conflict. The idea is interesting and attractive, but alas it is wrong.

34. The English word control means close direction, including physical restraint if necessary. The French word *contrôle* has much looser connotations, implying only a distant supervision. However, such meanings do migrate transculturally over time as borrowings from other languages.

35. William F. Owen is the author of this unusual, not to say arresting, and certainly thought provoking dictum.

36. Harold D. Lasswell, *Politics: Who Gets What, When, How* (New York: Peter Smith, 1950).

37. Tony Blair, 'The Blair Doctrine', 22 April 1999 <http://www.pbs.org/newshour/bb/international/jan-june99/blair_doctrine4-23.html> accessed 12 July 2011.

38. Clausewitz, *On War*, 75.

39. Sun Tzu, *The Art of War*, 114.

40. See Lisa Randall, *Knocking on Heaven's Door: How Physics and Scientific Thinking Illuminate the Modern World* (London: Bodley Head, 2011). A Higgs boson particle now is discovered by good enough experimental evidence, but the question of the provenance of the so-called 'God particle' itself will be unanswered. As Julie

Andrews informed us in *The Sound of Music*, 'nothing comes from nothing, nothing ever could'. Even if one is minded to add a 'discuss' instruction to her dictum, plainly the quest for fundamentals inherently is unending.

41. Guthrie and Quinlan, *Just War*, 1.

42. See Burleigh, *Moral Combat*, which provides a fresh perspective on the Second World War, despite the familiarity of most of the individual topics in the book.

43. Fisher, *Morality and War*, is a better than average attempt to manage morally what at its core is beyond such management. Nonetheless, one applauds his worthy effort and, indeed, one is obliged by necessity to proceed along much of the same path.

44. '*War is thus an act of force to compel our enemy to do our will.*' Clausewitz, *On War*, 75 (emphasis in the original), also 87–90.

45. Clausewitz, *On War*, 605. Here, Clausewitz claims that '[i]ts [war's] grammar, indeed, may be its own, but not its logic'. This is normative rather than empirical. Warfare can and often does proceed beyond the influence, let alone the command, of political (or policy) logic. Instead it is driven by its own military dynamics to a military outcome, whatever that may mean in political terms. It is not in the nature of military force to be somehow political, but it is in its nature to have political consequences, intended or not. Clausewitz's often quoted short sentence on war's logic and grammar frequently is misunderstood.

46. Walzer, *Just and Unjust Wars*, 44–7.

47. In good part, one suspects, because of the discretionary character of most of the wars and quasi-wars waged by Western states of recent years, moral considerations have floated close to the surface of popular and scholarly debate. Fisher, *Morality and War*, is an impressive exemplar of this reality. But, it is important to remember that the reality that fuels moral debate on the ethical conduct of warfare is political and strategic. When the political and strategic contexts alter radically, so too will what one might call the moral climate and its ethics.

48. Raymond Aron, *Peace and War: A Theory of International Relations* (New York: Doubleday, 1966), 285.

49. For useful guidance on just war traditions and their ever arguable applicability to strategic practice, see particularly: Coates, *The Ethics of War*; Walzer, *Just and Unjust Wars*; Guthrie and Quinlan, *Just War*; and Fisher, *Morality and War*.

50. I pursue the closely connected topics of pre-emption and prevention in my *National Security Dilemmas: Challenges and Opportunities* (Washington, DC: Potomac Books, 2009), ch. 7, 'The Implications of Preemptive and Preventive War Doctrines: A Reconsideration'.

51. On the laws of war, see Adam Roberts and Richard Guelff, eds., *Documents on the Laws of War*, 3rd edn. (Oxford: Oxford University Press, 2000). Also useful are: Leslie C. Green, *The Contemporary Law of Armed Conflict*, 2nd edn. (Manchester: Manchester University Press, 2000); Michael Byers, *War Law: Understanding International Law and Armed Conflict* (New York: Grove Press, 2005); David Kennedy, *Of War and Law* (Princeton, NJ: Princeton University Press, 2006); Christine Gray, *International Law and the Use of Force*, 3rd edn. (Oxford: Oxford University Press, 2008); and Malcolm N. Shaw, *International Law*, 6th edn. (Cambridge: Cambridge University Press, 2008), ch. 20.

52. On paradox and irony, see Echevarria, *Preparing for One War and Getting Another*.

53. See John Keegan, *A History of Warfare* (London: Hutchinson, 1993); Lynn, *Battle*; Martin van Creveld, *The Culture of War* (New York: Ballantine Books, 2008); and Richard Ned Lebow, *A Cultural Theory of International Relations* (Cambridge: Cambridge University Press, 2008).

54. See Colin S. Gray, 'Moral Advantage, Strategic Advantage?' *The Journal of Strategic Studies*, 33 (June 2010), 333–65.

55. The empirical historical case against arms control as a useful approach to the control and moderation, let alone the eradication, of conflict is overwhelming and easily explained theoretically. See the effort to achieve this not unduly demanding goal in my *House of Cards: Why Arms Control Must Fail* (Ithaca, NY: Cornell University Press, 1992). Unsurprisingly, the book attracted, indeed probably invited, some unfriendly reviews. However, unfriendly commentary is not *ipso facto* proof of weakness in the argument attacked.

56. Clausewitz, *On War*, 89.

57. Guthrie and Quinlan, *Just War*, 4.

58. Coates, *The Ethics of War*, 1.

59. Guthrie and Quinlan, *Just War*, 14–15.

60. Guthrie and Quinlan, *Just War*, 46.

61. Historical examples of the political nature of religious doctrine are not in short supply. For a spectacularly grand example, see Philip Jenkins, *Jesus Wars: How Four Patriarchs, Three Queens, and Two Emperors Decided What Christians Would Believe for the Next 1,500 Years* (London: SPCK, 2010). Tom Holland, *In the Shadow of the Sword: The Battle for Global Empire and the End of the Ancient World* (London: Little, Brown, 2012), offers a challenging explanation of the rise of Islam, set in its historical, including ideational, context.

62. See Antulio J. Echevarria II, 'Reconsidering War's Logic and Grammar', *Infinity Journal*, 2 (Spring 2011), 4–7. The Clausewitzian conceptual contrast between war's 'logic' and 'grammar' (*On War*, 605), is sorely in need of more attention by strategic theorists. Echevarria's essay is a useful beginning, though more is required.

63. Clausewitz, *On War*, 78, 593, 606, *inter alia*.

64. See Jeff McMahan, *Killing in War* (Oxford: Clarendon Press, 2009).

3

Culture: Beliefs, Customs, and Strategic Behaviour

For if someone were to assign to every person in the world the task of selecting the best of all customs, each one, after thorough consideration, would choose those of his own people, so strongly do humans believe that their own customs are the best ones. Therefore only a madman would treat such things as a laughing matter.

Herodotus[1]

Different peoples can have dissimilar conceptions of war as it should be, and when they clash in battle, the fact that they are fighting by different rules creates a reality that neither adversary expected.

John A. Lynn[2]

On the surface, war tears people apart. But if we look closer, it drives them together. There may not be one universal soldier, uniform across time and space. But war has a culture of its own. Even as enemies stress their differences rhetorically, conflict with its reciprocity and strategic inter-action creates new syntheses.

Patrick Porter[3]

War will always be full of surprises. This point in itself has value. It can check one tendency within militaries, the quest for the 'magic bullet'. If the technology-driven revolution of the 1990s failed to deliver on all of its promises, we should also be cautious about the culture-driven revolution. A more careful reading of history demonstrates that East is not always East.

Patrick Porter[4]

3.1 SO WHAT?

If the ambitious concept of strategic culture was an aircraft, one would not issue it with a certificate of airworthiness. Nonetheless, it does fly for some useful understanding and it can transport its users to interesting places wherein knowledge might be sought. The concept has notable frailties of logic and evidence, but those weaknesses should not be judged fatally disabling for useful enquiry. The strategic scholar's skeleton key that is the 'so what' question should be employed even-handedly in debate over strategy and culture. On the one hand, the question is essential in its insistence upon an answer to challenge regarding conceptual utility. On the other hand, 'so what' is a relevant question, perhaps just exclamation, to pose as a response to critics of cultural analysis of strategic phenomena. The finding of actual or potential weaknesses in a concept or analytical approach need not be lethal to its value as a kind of intellectual nutcracker. This chapter argues that a cultural perspective on strategy is both seriously flawed, yet also is valuable and indeed essential. If one asks too much of the cultural view it must disappoint at best, or at worst it would be pressed to yield analytical results likely to be danger-ously oversimplified and misleading. Strategy is about life and death, often on a large scale. Ideas matter for their influence on behaviour. Strategy is a practical subject, which means that the concepts, other beliefs and attitudes, and habits that one can identify probably as having cultural content, cannot be judged for their logical elegance alone. Poor ideas about strategy will not merely be intellectually ugly, also they can result in destruction, death, and political failure.

Sun Tzu was correct when he claimed high significance for self-knowledge and for understanding of the enemy 'Other', but he was less reliable when he claimed such knowledge and understanding as a guarantee of victory.[5] Know-ledge and understanding can compound usefully as a great enabler of strategic effectiveness, but in and of themselves they neither sink ships nor bend foreign minds to one's political will. It is tempting to assert that knowledge of ourselves and of the enemy is a necessary condition for strategic success. But, this plausible sounding claim is not true. History shows that belligerents can win despite being culturally ignorant, and they are able to succeed strategically without an explicit and consistent strategy worthy of the name. Cultural ignorance or a disdain for strategy, perhaps both, can have lethal consequences, but it should be admitted that tactical and operational military excellence may deliver a quantity of net strategic effectiveness sufficient to meet political needs. The threat and the use of force generate strategic effectiveness, whether or not they are purposefully directed by a strategy.[6]

The epigraphs above highlight the vitally interactive nature of strategy in practice. It is my thesis that we have discovered and rediscovered both more and less than contending contemporary scholars have claimed in their debate about cultural influence on strategy. If it is agreed that strategies have to be in some measure, great or small, cultural (a matter to which I shall return), the 'so what' question remains.[7] Strategies also must be political, human, geographical, and technological, *inter alia*. It is not a notable scholarly achievement to recognize the logical chain that proceeds as follows: all strategies are designed and executed by particularly encultured people, therefore all strategies are influenced by culture. Since enculturation is unavoidable, strategic behaviour must bear a cultural stamp, be it ever so faint. Aside from its banality, this argument, to stretch terms, is likely to mislead seriously because it could encourage a side-lining of the competitive nature of strategic threat and action. Strategic history flows as the net effect of rival behaviours. And that effect is certain to be somewhat different from the intended, presumably preferred and optimistically anticipated strategic narrative of any single belligerent. But, given that our strategy requires engagement with 'Others', with their culturally influenced strategies, how useful is the claim that it is and has to be culturally shaped or influenced, and if so by how much? What happens when one belligerent's culture meets another's culture in war? Whose, if anyone's, strategic culture rules over the interaction?—and why? If both major belligerents have multiple cultures, as is common, the relevant cultural landscape may be too crowded to be mapped and analysed with confidence.

A minimal default claim on behalf of the role, if not relative influence, of culture simply is that which asserts the cultural identity, or identities, of all human actors and their organizations. Even if the US government needs to respond to strategic circumstances crafted by an alien strategic culture, the response will have some American characteristics. However, it is not entirely self-evident that those claimed characteristics are either decidedly singular to Americans, or have the significance ascribed to them as influences with consequences for behaviour. The concept of strategic culture is problematic both logically and empirically. This is the unpromising launch situation for this examination. One cannot assume that identity reliably drives norms, decisions, and behaviour. As often as not identity is swamped by the exigencies of circumstance. We think and behave not only because of who we are and what we believe we are, but also because of where we find ourselves, not necessarily by our own volition politically, morally, and strategically.

3.2 CONTESTED CONCEPTS AND THE RHYTHM OF DEBATE

The concepts of culture and strategy are individually contestable, while their intellectually exciting shotgun marriage provides a devil's playground for scholarly confusion. To talk of strategy and culture allows usefully for analytical discretion, while the familiar concept of strategic culture invites reversal to read seductively as cultural strategy. This minor example of conceptual magic achieved by syntactical sleight of hand is instructive because it prompts the thought that all strategy has to be cultural. Indeed, could there be strategy that was not to some degree cultural?

Definitions are arbitrary, but vary in quality of fitness for purpose and in the authority they acquire. Also, theory in the social sciences is understood as seeking and providing most-cases explanation. Some social science theory can have calculably predictive value, but the population size of relevant events for statistical treatment will need to be large and assuredly can deliver no reliably predictable outcome for a single near current possible happening. Those who seek correct answers to strategic questions through quantitative analysis are by analogy pursuing objective truth in astrology through better methodology. Such attractive terms as a calculus of deterrence, or strategic arithmetic, may flow glibly from our personal computers, but they offer fool's gold only. Strategies intended to deter certainly involve some calculation, but the most vital of currency conversions, those from military effect to strategic effect and from strategic effect to political effect, do not lend themselves to calculation and therefore to objectively checkable mathematical treatment.

Strategy and strategic are terms that are widely misused, but at least there is some authority worthy of the title behind the definition offered in this book (the direction and use made of force and the threat of force for the purposes of policy as decided by politics).[8] As for definitions of culture, the scholar is spoilt for choice. With culture and its contestable offspring, strategic culture, one enters an unregulated market. Given that strategy and strategic are terms typically deployed loosely, it follows that strategic culture and strategic cultural are unlikely to be precision conceptual instruments ready for use as keys to unlock doors for understanding that otherwise would remain closed. Exciting though some scholars, including this one, have believed to be the promise in strategic cultural enquiry, only the truest of true believers in its forensic qualities have entertained the hope that such investigation could be akin to scholarly keyhole surgery. In point of fact, culture, including its postulated strategic variety, is revealed to be ever more problematic a conceptual tool the more intensely it is scrutinized. However, the concept of strategic culture does survive more or less intact, albeit battered, as arguably important for the understanding of strategy.

There is and can be no correct definition of strategic culture, while it would be an exaggeration to claim that any one currently on offer in the marketplace of strategic ideas is more authoritative than others.[9] That said, I shall use the admittedly contestable concept of strategic culture as referring to the assumptions, beliefs, attitudes, habits of mind, and preferred modes of behaviour, customary behaviour even, bearing upon the use of force by a security community. The core meaning of culture is indicated incisively by the concept of 'a common stock of cultural reference' for a community, but just what is that? And what is it that renders this common stock cultural.[10]

Rigour rightly is demanded and expected of scholars, but the efforts to satisfy this requirement, indeed ethic, has a non-trivial ability to lead the earnest searcher after social scientific truth into substantial error instead. Quests in search of the El Dorado of a prediction-quality theory of the influence of culture on strategic affairs are certain to disappoint. To hunt an impossible quarry is a guarantee of failure. The academic literature on the subject of strategy and culture has been blighted by a determination to produce professional looking social science. This praiseworthy discipline has had the paradoxical and ironic consequence of hindering what could be done, in the interest of the quest for the impossible. Good practice in theory construction is challenged fundamentally by the very nature of the subject of strategic culture. Rigorous examination of anything is hard to do if one cannot distinguish it from its context. In the case here, the question is where does culture end and its influence begin, and how do you know? The obvious solution with respect to culture and strategy is to insist that culture is strictly ideational.[11] Concepts that appear to qualify for the cultural label for reasons of their persistent popularity might then be assayed for their presence in artefacts and behaviour that might give them some expression. Difficult though it can be to provide thoroughly persuasive evidence of this speculative cause and effect, nonetheless it has some merit on the scale of intended and attempted scholarly rigour. The subject, culture, is distinctive (as concepts) from its possible effects on material objects (e.g. tank design), and on style in grand and military strategic, operational, and tactical choices.

The trouble with the methodological tidiness of the approach just outlined is that it offends against reality and is contradicted by the general theory of strategy. The theory states that although strategy is cultural, it is so only to a variable degree because there is far more to strategy than culture (on any plausible definition).[12] The cultural analysis of strategic phenomena should not subscribe to the seductive belief that there is a theory of strategic culture with predictive value for policy, waiting out there for the sufficiently clever theorist to discover. Instead, the theory that can connect culture and strategy and is achievable is one satisfied to derive cultural insights to help cue recognition of plausible patterns in thought and behaviour. But, this cultural theory for insight can be valuable for strategic practice only when it is developed with the understanding provided by strategy's general theory. People educated by that theory should be immune to intellectual capture by a cultural theory of strategy, just as they ought to be deaf to claims for an ethical, geographical, or technological theory of strategy. People are culturally conditioned to a variable degree, but such conditioning should not be assumed to determine behavioural choices.

Definitions of culture abound and those of strategic culture now offer a range of choice near certain to enable scholars of most persuasions to find one they like. The major definitional matter still in dispute between scholars is the non-trivial one of identity of the subject. Does one look for the influence of culture only upon strategic phenomena, or can one find culture both upon and within those phenomena? Scholars agree that culture is ideational, but some—myself included—believe that culture can be identified both in material objects and also in behaviour. This latter belief is not an issue simply of intellectual taste. Rather is it a conviction that culture cannot sensibly be treated as a source of influence distinct from its usually debatable effect upon artefacts and action. Subject and object thus merge, indeed collapse into each other, which is rather challenging to methodology for analysis. No matter how appealing it is methodologically to postulate culture acting upon strategy, existential strategic reality commands a holistic approach that is inclusive of the intellect, the material, and the behavioural.

Definitions of strategic culture tend to be flawed in their giving offence to the minimalist rule of William of Occam. Encyclopaedism is a persisting sin among the coiners of definitions. In fear of damaging omissions, greater harm is done by needless qualifying specificity and inclusivity.[13] Prominent among the poisonous perils to strategic cultural analysis is the familiar methodological difficulty of distinguishing between variables that plausibly are sufficiently independent for meaningful analysis of their interaction. This challenge can be severe in methodological terms when one makes sensible allowance for the probable consequences of feedback. Since strategy is designed and executed everywhere and at all times by encultured people, how can one isolate the influence of culture both upon them and upon their decisions and behaviour?—and the latter question need not be answerable by the former. Even if one seeks to evade the methodological difficulty by insisting that the strategic culture to be tested is strictly conceptual, there is no reliable credible escape from the essential unity of strategic ideas and strategic practice.[14] Current strategic behaviour bears the imprint of a conceptual culture that itself was forged in part from past strategic behaviour. Understood in ideational terms, strategic culture cannot be regarded as a conceptual variable independent of strategic practice. Strategic ideas flow from what has been learnt from past practice and malpractice, while strategic practice is strategic theory in action in the field, no matter how imperfectly it is applied. When long preferred strategic ideas are refuted rather than validated by contemporary strategic experience, conceptual and other culture can and often does change.

Strategic culture can be understood as having a core meaning with intellectual integrity. Culture is important to the understanding of strategies because it directs attention to the customs, beliefs, and behaviours that persist and therefore presumably are relatively deep, rather than ephemeral and shallow.

To identify a decision as being notably strategic cultural, is to suggest that it reveals not merely a passing opinion, but rather an attitude expressing enduring assumptions and beliefs. A noteworthy contributor to the challenge in exploring strategy and culture is the fact that each lacks an analytically convenient boundary to its domain. Just about anything may contribute some strategic effect, while culture also is frontier-porous. Strategic culture provides context for strategic decisions and action, but Antulio J. Echevarria is correct when he claims that 'context itself has no objective end'.[15] Readers may recall that the previous chapter raised the disturbing thought that a source of moral authority itself requires moral authority. As Echevarria points out, the problem lies not with the integrity of the idea of context, but rather with the logical fact that all context itself has context without empirical limit. Where does one stop?

In order to attain a plausible understanding of the role of culture in strategy, debate has to move on from charge and countercharge. There is a normal rhythm to strategic debate, one that has manifested itself unsurprisingly over strategic culture. Debates typically follow a pattern of succession from thesis, through antithesis, to synthesis. These debates are triggered and for a while are sustained by perceived public policy need and also by the politics, economics, and sociology of defence professional career building. Radical change in the strategic environment fuels public anxiety that functions as intellectual and political licence and motivates financial gatekeepers to free up the resources necessary to enable strategic debaters to function.[16]

Generically the debate about strategy and culture is familiar to historians of strategic ideas. Recognition of this fact provides helpful historical perspective. When considered in the light of past defence, strategy, and security debates, the controversy over culture becomes easier both to understand and also resolve. Intellectual historians are addicted to finding schools of thought, which is to say rival camps. The greater strategic debates since 1945 have recorded attack, counterattack, and outcomes, if not quite conclusions worthy of the name, that were synthetical. For example, after brief initial epiphany in 1946, the great debate over nuclear weapons proceeded from imprudent enthusiasm, through no less imprudent demotion, to reluctant acceptance.[17] The latest pressing topic, cyber power and strategy for cyberspace, currently is still in its anxiety-rising phase with the thesis of maximum cyber potency generally ascending.[18] Inevitably, second thoughts as well as careerist opportunism will trigger antithetical claims to the effect that cyberspace is just another geographical domain for conflict, and that its distinctive menace has been much exaggerated.

Recent debate about counterinsurgency (COIN) and counterterrorism (CT) has given what amounts to a 'gravity assist' to arguments favouring a 'cultural turn' in strategic studies.[19] The historical cycle of debate was 'groundhog day', or *déjà vu* all over again in the immortal words of baseball legend Yogi Berra.

COIN all but vanished from the American strategic intellectual menu in the wake of Vietnam; the slaying of Soviet armoured dragons echeloned back from the inner-German border was the respectable subject area of the mid-1970s and the 1980s. Though initially hugely underprepared intellectually and materially for COIN, the incomplete victories in regular warfare in Afghanistan in 2001 and Iraq in 2003 presented COIN and CT challenges that, predictably and eventually quite impressively, the US defence community met with its customary enthusiasm. The conceptual wheels for COIN and CT were duly reinvented to the great self-satisfaction of many, and 'COIN-istas' briefly were in the political, but perhaps only arguably strategic cultural, ascendant.[20] To quote the French architect Le Corbusier, form follows function, but to expand on his thesis, functional priorities shift over time. Defence debate responded to the practical contemporary need for COIN doctrine in the 2000s. The form to satisfy that function had to be a COIN-educated, trained, and equipped military establishment. And it seemed to follow that for COIN, which is usually 'war amongst the people' and unarguably is always war about the people, a key to success in COIN has to be cultural understanding of the society in contention.[21] The cultural turn in much officially blessed strategic study was a response to undeniable failure in the field in Afghanistan and Iraq.

Thirty years ago one could not give strategic cultural studies to the US defence establishment, let alone aspire to sell them. In one meeting in the early 1980s with a US general and his loyal staff, I tried to make the case for some cultural analysis of America's foes, only to be met with blank incomprehension. The 'so what?' response to my cultural story was not the constructively sceptical reaction of the questioning strategic mind, but rather the 'so what!' of contemptuous dismissal. Against the odds, indeed strangely, strategic culture achieved a limited purchase in the realm of nuclear strategy in the 1970s, but in the 1980s and then in the 1990s it slipped beneath the radar of serious official attention.[22] After all, truly what need had the world's sole superpower of cultural understanding of its enemies?

Notwithstanding the experience of humiliation in Somalia in 1993, the strategic historical highway for the United States from Panama City in 1989 to Baghdad early in 2003 typically was the path of victory. A defence community overconfident about the lethality of its preferred way of war is not one that is going to seek to effect a major turn in its attitude towards cultural education and purposefully culturally adept practices. The cultural turn in US national security was the crisis-time response to unfolding strategic failure. The strategic history of the early and mid-2000s revealed beyond serious contention that although the American military machine could deliver swift regime change, it was unprepared for the conflicts that succeeded the easy initial victories. An obvious weakness in the American and allied war efforts was the cultural ignorance with which they were conducted. In short, the Western strategic endeavours in both Afghanistan and Iraq were plagued by a variant of the cardinal error flagged by Clausewitz when he insisted that '[t]he first, the supreme, the most far reaching act of judgment that the statesman and commander have to make is to establish by that test [of fit with policy and its context] the kind of war on which they are embarking; neither mistaking it for, nor trying to turn it into, something that is alien to its nature'.[23] Arguably, the American problem in Afghanistan and Iraq stemmed not so much from its policy, which plausibly was sound enough. That policy had as its minimum goal the neutralization of serious menace that could flow from Iraqi and Afghan national territory. Rather has the problem lain with strategy and its frequent misidentification as policy. US mission creep was the result of strategy failure. The impressively rapid military successes of 2001 and 2003 did not deliver the strategic effectiveness necessary to meet the policy goal. In both countries the United States needed to adjust and adapt its strategy to fit the local context. However, the rediscovery of cultural understanding as an enabler of strategic advantage predictably was over-celebrated in the later 2000s. It appeared to many, not least to some among its prophet-advocates, that the infusion of cultural understanding would make the vital difference between strategic success and strategic failure. If war is cultural behaviour, as John Keegan claimed robustly and as common sense affirms to be self-evidently partially true, then surely cultural competence must yield strategic rewards.[24]

The cultural turn in (American) strategic thinking and, albeit less so, in strategic practice, was over-advertised as a potential 'magic bullet'. Inevitably, the new cultural emphasis in American strategic thinking attracted intellectually counter-revolutionary theory. The counter-attack was both general and specific. The assumptions of culturalism as applied to strategy were challenged, as also were the more specific benefits claimed for it with respect to COIN and CT. Powerful critiques of strategic culturalism writ large, and of a major cultural tilt in the conduct of COIN, were written by Patrick Porter, Gian Gentile, and Rob Johnson.[25] Those scholars performed the function of raising the flag for argument plainly antithetical to that currently dominant. The market for strategic ideas needs bold would-be intellectual leaders, and if the strategic context lends plausibility to their arguments they fuel controversy sufficient to encourage the search for a resolving workable synthesis. The strategy and culture debate now has moved on from largely academic contention to and almost through major degrees of official adoption and popular acclaim, to the stage where it has encountered purposeful 'blowback', with culturalism seriously challenged.[26]

The dynamics of debate promote exaggeration, while the process of theorization necessarily requires reduction in the presentation if not the treatment of complexity. Both cultural and counter-cultural arguments have been advanced in oversimplified form. Given its prior relative neglect in strategic studies, it is tempting to excuse some over-enthusiasm for the cultural perspective.[27] Nonetheless, balance is needed for more reliable understanding of strategy. The pertinent challenge is to identify the elements in the cultural narrative that can withstand general and specific criticism.

3.3 ROOTS, FORMS, AND MANIFESTATIONS OF CULTURE IN STRATEGY

There are many reasons for scepticism over both the basic logical, as well as the evidential empirical, integrity of strategic cultural analysis. However, those objections need to be registered and weighed in the balance only against the more mature and moderate arguments that can be advanced in praise of cultural enquiry. The intention here is not to present the cases for and against culturalism in strategic analysis, rather is it to explain why some scholars persist in recommending such study despite problematic epistemological issues. It is my position that, 'warts and all', the eternal quest for strategic understanding mandates cultural enquiry.

The research hypotheses are that there are sources of influence on strategic behaviour that should be termed cultural and that they can be revealed to a useful extent by careful study. It is not hypothesized that strategic decision and action can be attributed either historically, or for the future predictably, to cultural influence. There are some historical cases of strategic behaviour for which cultural explanation appears overwhelmingly persuasive—Imperial Japan in the Second World War is a compelling example—but the purpose of this discussion is limited to explanation of the modest conviction that cultural argument is important for the understanding of strategic practice.[28]

A fundamental challenge to the methodological integrity of the study of culture is the porosity of the conceptual frontiers that theorization requires. Everything leaks into everything else. This is a classic example of a 'wicked' problem, one to which there is no fully satisfactory solution. On the one hand, it is tempting to identify candidate cultural evidence with an arbitrary but methodologically useful exclusivity (e.g. culture is defined wholly as ideational): this approach mandates that the scholar will neglect much that should be noted and considered. On the other hand, an attractive and apparently more sophisticated approach is one which accepts inclusively the near ubiquity of culture in its several forms: the trouble is that this tolerant view leads the scholar into a forest of evidential trees from which there is no escape, wherein everything is more, or less, cultural. If culture is everywhere it might as well be nowhere, because it cannot be distinguished from its contexts for examination. There is no authority to which one can appeal to resolve this dilemma of undue exclusivity versus undue inclusivity. The best one can do is flag the problem, decide on the flawed approach one will adopt, and then proceed with caution and loud caveats. The analysis here chooses to regard culture inclusively rather than exclusively, a view consistent with a holistic understanding of strategy (theory for practice, from conception, through execution, to desired strategic and political effect).[29] The fact that culture and its consequences are not reliably and unmistakably detectable by scholarly forensics is regrettable and methodologically unfortunate. But, what is possible to achieve by means of the cultural exploration of strategy is well worth the price paid in unsatisfactory research methods.

Several decades of culture-leaning, or at least recognizing, research by strategically minded scholars with a diversity of disciplinary and other professional backgrounds have yielded two candidate master conclusions. First, the cultural study of strategy provides a dimension to strategic education that is essential and unique. Second, because strategic decision and behaviour are the products of many influences in addition to those which should be regarded inclusively as cultural, even an excellent understanding of particular cultures cannot prudently be employed as the principal basis on which to act strategically. These claims are not mutually contradictory. What they assert, successively, is that: cultural knowledge is important in strategic affairs, and as a consequence of that appreciation it should be sought assiduously; but also that there is much more to strategy than sensibly is definable as cultural.

Where does culture come from? How can one organize the study of it? It is helpful to pursue the cultural perspective on strategy by means of a brutally reductionist rank-ordering discriminator among categories of cultural content of interest. I choose to identify roots, forms, and manifestations of culture on a descending order of relative importance of cultural phenomena of interest to strategists. These are sufficiently distinctive categories of subjects to be analytically useful as aids to the inclusive grasp needed of the cultural perspective on strategy. Table 3.1 provides a summary outline of the structure of the subject.

The first-order subjects of interest to pursuit of the cultural perspective on strategy have to be geography and history. Admittedly, these are perilously

Table 3.1 Culture and Strategy: Roots, Forms, and Manifestations

First Order: Roots

1. Geography	2. Historical experience

Second Order: Forms

1. Conceptual	3. Behavioural (customary)
2. Material	

Third Order: Manifestations

1. Social	4. Technological
2. Political	5. Military
3. Economic	

inclusive and porous candidate super-subjects, but that regrettable fact has to be acknowledged frankly and then set aside though not forgotten. Cultural enquiry cannot proceed productively if it neglects investigation of the spatial and temporal experiential contexts. It is somewhat true to argue that the meaning of geography is what particular human communities make of it. Similarly, it is necessary to register clearly that although there is an objectively existential sense in which 'geography just is', and 'history (i.e. the past) just was', and the objective realities certainly matter, there are assumed realities and narratives that people choose to believe. The all-inclusive items of geography and history encompass the whole subject of interest here. Unduly constructivist doubts about the objective facts of geography and the past are all but certain to lead to catastrophe, if one is sufficiently unwise as to take them at face value. What people believe to be true about geography and history matters for their behaviour, indeed is likely to matter decisively. But, if their beliefs are contradicted by a mix of physical geographical actuality that is contrary to their understanding, and by an interpretation of the shared past (history) substantially at odds with those of their enemies, the course of future political and strategic interaction is likely to reveal in events the ill consequences of constructed facts that owe too much to imagination.

There was physical geography before there were human societies with their cultures and their several histories. No matter exactly how one defines and understands culture, the geographical setting, both physical and perceptual, has to be recognized as the most pervasive and generically enduring of influences. This is not to endorse any variant of geographical determinism. Human imagination, skill, and effort embrace a range of possibilities with reference to what particularly spatially located societies and polities make of their geographical context.[30] Nonetheless, geography usually plays a significant role in shaping the menu of practicable policy and strategic choice, as well as of those options judged desirable to pursue.

This chapter is interested in the strategic influence of geography when mediated by the intervening variable of culture. The subject here is not geography, rather is it what the human strategic experience has been with geography. And that experience both was an objective reality at unique times and places, as well as a variably recoverable memory, individual and collective (in typically rival histories).[31] The physical geographies of particular security communities, including their spatial relations in all senses with other communities, always have had a large influence on strategic choice though not always as large as it should have been.[32] The perceived meaning of space, topography, climate, vegetation, wildlife, and their believed temporal implications often are in error, but they are no less important for that fact. Neither geography nor the human strategic experience dictates the course of history. Many pasts undoubtedly might have been, just as many interpretations of the single actual past joust for our endorsement. Contemporary strategic thought, decision, and behaviour in action is ever likely to be shaped by some understanding of physical geographical realities and by a somewhat accurate understanding of strategic historical experience. Scholars need to be both moderately sceptical, at the least untrusting, of nationally privileging historical narratives, while not denying their putative significance for future decision and action. Also, just because some strategic folklore is mythical, or at best legendary, it does not follow that cultural assumptions invested with specific strategic meaning have to be false in their essentials.[33]

Some discipline is imposed by the course of history on the cultural assumptions that may influence strategic choice and behaviour. Although polities and their societies are at liberty to adopt and adapt the culture(s) they prefer, the political and strategic realm beyond the national frontier will have a vote on the practical performance of the extant culture(s). Countries make their own history and interpret their own historical experience, but this making and interpreting is effected in the dynamic context of interaction in cooperation and conflict with other countries and their cultures. Objective history, which is to say the actual past, certainly must be interpreted subjectively by and for cultural comprehension. But, that cultural understanding generally cannot evade recognition and reflection of many of the facts along the way in the course of events, both welcome and unwelcome. Knowledge of the objective historical facts of a society's past cannot yield reliable understanding of the narrative of historical interpretation dominant in that society, but it should provide some helpful grasp of the menu of candidate evidence from which local interpreters make their selection. For example, even if a society prefers to tell itself lies about its past, nonetheless it can be enlightening to appreciate just what is being denied and to speculate why.

The first order of investigation of culture and strategy obliged us to endeavour to explain the relevance of geography and history. The centrepiece of this discussion has been the proposition that in every sense location is a key, possibly the key, to the diverse strategic historical experience of specific polities and their societies. From this overarching reasoning, alas, a host of reductionist and deterministic grand theories could flow. The ambition here is not to provide fuel for such conceptually imperial designs. Instead, it is only to indicate that the roots of culture relevant to strategy should be understood to lie inclusively in geography and history.

Moving on from the roots of culture, it is necessary to identify a second rank comprising the generic forms assumed by cultural influence. Three such forms command analytical attention: conceptual, material, and behavioural. Rephrased, when one seeks evidence of culture it is plausible to look at the realm of ideas, attitudes, and values (conceptual, including moral), artefacts (material), and actions (behavioural). One has to acknowledge the porosity of these three forms. For example, choice in aircraft acquisition will likely reflect in good part ideas on how air power should be employed and for what tactical,

operational, and strategic purposes. However, the aircraft acquired, for whatever blend of reasons (including cost-effectiveness and technical feasibility),
will themselves impose conceptual discipline on their owners, as their performance in effect polices what is and what is not tactically possible. There has
been a longstanding argument among scholars as to whether or not (military)
technology leads military ideas, ultimately for strategic ends. Fortunately, the
discussion in this chapter need only take note of the ongoing controversy, not
contribute to it (but see Chapter 5). Without registering a vote at this juncture
as to the relative importance of culture for the understanding strategy, one can
stake a minimal analytical claim with high confidence. Such evidence of
culture at work as there may be, grown from the variably sturdy roots
of geography and history, will be discoverable in the three inclusive forms of
concepts, material artefacts, and frequent, if not quite habitual customary
behaviours.

Much of the scholarly debate over strategy and culture has suffered from the
self-inflicted wound inflicted by the assumption of a binary choice in argument. Thus, there have tended to be culturalist and anti-culturalist 'camps'
and 'schools'. It should be clear enough today that both sides in the scholarly
debate essentially were correct. Summarized tersely: all of strategic history is to
a variable degree properly describable as cultural, but it is by no means only,
let alone always significantly, so. The particular value of the triadic organization of cultural forms suggested here is that it obliges a prudent inclusivity in
research and analysis that meets the reality test of common sense. As presented, three forms of cultural phenomena—concepts, artefactual material,
and behaviour—are recognized as plainly distinguishable, yet also are appreciated as mutually reinforcing. In addition, this argument recognizes both
porosity between the three categories and the unsoundness of monocausal
explanation. To argue that there is cultural influence upon a polity's preferred
strategic ideas, choice of material military systems, and persisting patterns of
favoured behaviour, is not to try and insist that culture rules the strategic
universe. It will rule when circumstances are permissive; it is always likely to
provide the familiar and therefore expedient default option. But, often culture
will only reign without executive authority; it may try in vain to command as
an intervening variable. Strategic history is too complex and uncertain for one
to make bold claims on behalf of an asserted general authority of culture. The
menu of competing explanations of cause and effect simply is too rich for one
to be able to vote for culture as the principal fuel for events.

Much that could be identified as being in part cultural lends itself more
readily to other labelling. A reason why evidence of culture can pass
undetected is because its roots are understood inadequately. Many of the
ideas, attitudes, values, and behavioural habits of action that typically and
plausibly are marked cultural, had material or other reality in historical
experience. As a result, a broader, deeper, and more accurate comprehension

of cultural phenomena becomes possible. Yesterday's material interests of a particular polity, if pursued with satisfactory results, are likely to acquire favour both in themselves and in the ways of the strategy that achieved them. What seemed to work well enough in past behaviour—as assumptions, ends, ways, and means—*ipso facto* will be candidates for future practice. The conceptual form in which a strategic tradition is expressed or evaluated assuredly will be ideational, albeit reflected to some degree in material means and customary ways, but it will be the reflection of a tradition anchored in, though not thoroughly faithful to, historical experience. That reflection will be of a selective communal memory of right enough strategic performance in times past, certainly in times historical and therefore assuredly somewhat legendary.

Those who demand reliable high predictive value as a reward for the cultural analysis of strategy are bound to be disappointed. As the better studies of strategy and culture have begun to argue, cultural analysis should help usefully to shorten the menu of an adversary's favoured alternatives that one can identify. All strategically rational choice is culturally informed; this has to be so because all strategic actions are human. The human actors are not only representatives of their strategic and other cultures, also they have individual biology and psychology, they have to perform in a more or less collective context, friction is ever probable, and then there is the semi-independent will of the enemy. And, simply, there are unique circumstances. Any study that portrays strategic decision and action as the product of people thinking and behaving like human cultural automata is bound to be nonsense. There are occasions when historical circumstance appears to compel all but strategic reflex reasoning that fairly could be termed cultural, but as a general rule the evidence will not be so apparently clear. For example, with reference to German war waging in the West in the spring and early summer of 1940 cultural analysis could lead one seriously astray. The escape of the British Expeditionary Force (BEF) from Dunkirk was feasible only because of Adolf Hitler's famous Halt Order, formally issued on 24 May (which ratified a close-up, effectively a halt order issued already by General Gerd von Rundstedt on 23 May) which halted the panzers, thereby preventing German encirclement of the lion's share of Britain's principal field army. This foolish decision, authoritative for a critical three days and eight hours, can be explained rationally with or without German cultural content. But, it is most plausible to believe that the decision was rational only in personal political terms, because the Führer was concerned lest his domestic authority be undermined by the rapidly ascending reputation of his generals. The issue of Hitler's Order will not now be resolved by further scholarship, but unsettled as it remains it illustrates the complicating richness of the diverse content of strategic history.[34] Motives are always mixed and even the key historical players themselves can rarely be certain which among the several reasons for a decision weighed decisively at the time. It is helpful to understanding to appreciate that although culture is always present in strategic history, it cannot with confidence often be crowned ruler of cause for unambiguously detected and verified effect.

The third category of potential evidence for investigation I choose to call manifestations of culture, which is to say of culture in action, generally as a conditioning influence providing spoken and unspoken assumptions. On a geographical stage that is mainly pre-set for a society and its polity at any one time, historical experience is endured and reflected in the sense of identity, the values, norms, and the perceptual lens that plausibly can be understood as cultural.[35] Culture(s) is usually plural rather than singular, but that complicating probability does not menace the integrity of my argument. The categorical forms for evidence of culture identified earlier—conceptual, material, and behavioural (customary)—encompass the entire field of strategy. All dimensions of strategy are subject to some cultural influence. In particular practice this expansive claim can be a weak one despite its ambitious domain. Some distinctive local characteristics of culture are offset by the commonality in the nature of our universal human species, as well as by the substantially common logic of Clausewitz's grammar of war.[36] In addition, the necessities of circumstance often are perceived as requiring cultural innovation or borrowing, adaptation, and adoption from abroad.

The cultural perspective on strategy has to be as deep, wide, and contextually appreciated as should be the study of strategy itself. Since there is always some cultural content to strategy, one ought not to struggle to achieve erection of an analytically impervious wall around that which is claimed as cultural. Strategy is cultural, period. This fact would be banal because it is a necessary truth, were it not for the additional fact that it attracts fierce arguments among scholars. Some of those heated arguments should dissolve when exposed to the reasoning that the necessary fact of strategy's cultural content is not synonymous with a claim for that content being dominant in any particular historical case.

Evidence of cultural influence can be sought in any and every aspect of strategy. To cite for illustration only a few of the principal dimensions of strategy, one can expect to find some cultural imprint in the political, social, economic, technological, and military realms. The imprint will be somewhat dynamic (it changes), it may be apparently confused and contradictory (because plural), and it will vary in weight, influence, and consequence from one historical context and situation to another. However, the moderating factors just cited as caveats should not be interpreted as good enough reason to discount or dismiss cultural manifestation in the ideas, material, and behaviour that we associate with strategy.

Most good ideas for and about strategy have the potential to be less meritorious when they are adopted, interpreted, and applied beyond their culminating point of common sense and evidential support. While it is always possible that a particular cultural perceptual lens will present a totally false view of objective reality, such ought not to be a standard assumption on the part of scholars. It is unusual, though not wholly unknown, for cultural assumptions about Other, more or less alien, polities and societies, to be so lethally erroneous as to be fatally disabling of strategic success. The historical reality is usually one of some cultural learning on the part of all rivals and belligerents, as the course of events in peace and war produces an actual objective narrative that no political participant (and his cultures) had anticipated even approximately.

Just as not all historically specific problems for strategy are solvable, so not all knowledge highly relevant to the practice of strategy is attainable. This is not a defeatist cry of despair, though some may choose to see it as such. Both those strongly favourable to a cultural turn in strategic study and practice, and those who remain robustly sceptical or even hostile, should appreciate that their rival assertions and arguments are apt to be overstated and misleading. On the one hand, the quest for cultural knowledge of potential use to the strategist is bound to fail if the pursuit identifies unreachable objectives of rigorously high standards in granular accuracy and strategically actionable relevance. Nonetheless, cultural knowledge is always potentially of some value. What it is not, save in truly exceptional circumstances, is a 'magic bullet' that guarantees strategic success. On the other hand, it would be foolish to dismiss out of hand the influence of explicit and implicit cultural assumptions and their consequences in culturally propelled inertia on strategic phenomena.[37] It may be a cultural pathology in the United States to approach conditions as problems, whether or not they are of a nature permissive of forensic analysis. As Clausewitz advises, in war friction happens.[38] Belligerents have to cope with its unpredictable manifestation in detail. It is an objective reality in relations between different communities that their cultures will differ. They will not differ entirely, and in the course of a protracted rivalry or armed conflict they are bound to find it necessary to learn, borrow, adopt, and even adapt some ideas, devices, and behaviours that are new to them. Unsatisfactory though it is to those who view the world in the neat binary terms of either/or—ignorance/knowledge, strategic success (victory?)/strategic failure (defeat?)—the cultural perspective on strategy is greatly in need of nuanced consideration and assessment.[39] If one is willing to grant that at any point in time over most issues of public policy there are extant relevant baskets of values, norms, attitudes, and preferred behaviours (customs), and that these may well shift as a consequence of their application in attempted effective practice, it is plain to see that the domain of cultural manifestation is broad indeed. Even when people strive honestly to behave politically, economically, or strategically on the merits of the case for the challenges of the day, they are unlikely to be able to preclude altogether the momentum of the inertia of culture. When knowledge obviously directly relevant to the perceived problem at hand is missing, it is unavoidable to rely on what for want of a better concept one can call intuition as well as habit or custom.[40] Scholars remind us that '[i]ntuition, a compass regularly employed by [intelligence: CSG] analysts, is culturally encoded and, by nature, ethnocentric'.[41] When strategists make judgements about different cultures, their own cultural lenses with their own assumptions are inescapable.[42] However, a willingness to recognize the Otherness of Others often leads not to a prudent recognition of some differences, but rather to cardinal error of the Orientalist kind wherein the strange and exotic is over-identified as different.

The making and execution of strategy is beset by a host of difficulties inherent in the subject's nature. Cultural diversity and its conceptual, material, and behavioural manifestation is just one, albeit pervasive, source of problems for the understanding that strategists seek.[43] Some cultural ignorance, even of one's own domestic situation and not only about Others, is normal and unavoidable. Cultural intelligence can be important and it should always be sought, though it is certain to be imperfect. But, even were it perfect one can predict with confidence that alone it would not point with total assurance to a strategic path that must lead to success. However, that caveat is no excuse for failure to achieve such cultural understanding as may be achievable. Culture, in its political, social, economic, technological, and military manifestations, is to be understood as dynamic and derivative from the geographically staged flow of historical experience that each security community has endured and evidently survived.

3.4 OF WEEDS AND FLOWERS: PRE-THEORY FOR STRATEGY AND CULTURE

Clausewitz tells us that '[t]heory should cast a steady light on all phenomena so that we can more easily recognize and eliminate the weeds that always spring from ignorance . . .'.[44] Over the course of the past four decades a shelf-full of studies have sought to penetrate the mysteries of the relationship between strategy and culture.[45] There has been much assertion and argument, some of it usefully foundational for scholarly enquiry. However, the time has come for conceptual contenders to strive harder than they have thus far to understand the concept in question by means of developing some relevant general theory. The remainder of this chapter offers thoughts intended to contribute to a pre-theory for the cultural perspective on strategy. What follows is a presentation of some of the more important persuasive claims and caveats from both culturalist and somewhat anti-culturalist camps (or perhaps tendencies), in order to try to identify the flowers in the field and save them from being choked by the weeds. It is necessary to review critically the intellectual landscape of the strategic culture, or strategy and culture debate, to see what remains standing on the field of recent conceptual battle that has value and merits being taken forward for further development.[46]

Culture is a high concept that invites the nominalist fallacy. If we simply discarded the concept of culture, let it pass out of intellectual fashion and therefore common usage, we would lose nothing of forensic value for strategic enquiry, so the argument proceeds. One need not endorse this proposition, but it is useful in that it obliges us to examine how we anticipate the concept of culture having value both for study and possibly, if probably indirectly as Echevarria suggests, for strategic practice.[47] There is some merit in most of the major criticisms of cultural argument and culturally flavoured analysis of strategic behaviour. Unsurprisingly, the relatively easy mission is the staking out of cultural claims and argument on the one hand, and finding those claims and arguments flawed on the other. Thus far, scholarly debate has identified positions, registered claims, and produced an intellectual meadow containing a riotous display of weeds and flowers. That granted, to date the literature on strategic culture (or culture and strategy) has yielded some candidate items for inclusion in a general theory designed to advance understanding of the subject.

Culture is only a conditioning influence upon behaviour and as such it cannot be operationalized as a reliable predictive analytical tool. This is not to claim that culture has little or no practical utility, but it is to say that that utility is constrained by the persisting nature but highly variable character of strategy. Monocausal explanation lurks as a temptation when a very big concept is released for undisciplined employment. In common with many of our grander concepts, culture and even strategic culture are revealed on close inspection to be misleadingly imperial. It is in the nature of scholarly enquiry for study to find claimed evidence for the need to make ever more granular classification. The concept of Revolution in Military Affairs (RMA) that so excited American and other scholars in the 1990s, plausibly was revealed by Williamson Murray as requiring augmentation by the yet grander concept of Military Revolution (MR) and, harking back to the Soviet conceptual roots of this theorization, of Military-Technical Revolution (MTR) also. Grammatical treatment of the RMA concept as a capitalized proper noun lent huge dignity and at least implied an empirical reality that inherently was alien to this intellectual construct. The RMA idea was theory.[48] In similar vein, some scholars in their innocence used to believe that the subject was strategic culture, but time and further scholarly forensic effort revealed that the relevant conceptual species had several close and highly relevant relatives; namely, public (and possibly civic) culture, and military culture that itself merited consideration as and with sub-species. It was convenient to simplify, reify, and expediently compound these subjects under the big tent of strategic culture, but in common with such useful concepts as a national way of war and national style in strategy, these great sweeping ideas are potentially flawed fundamentally by being under-evidenced and unduly reliant upon fragile assumptions.[49] They sweep away complexity in the interest of an elegant and potent economy and simplicity that usually pays too high a price for its virtues.

The relations between what should be sub-cultures within a supposedly simple national cultural domain, and between those sub-cultures and the much grander national level of culture (public and strategic), remains poorly governed intellectual space. How well does the impressive conceptual postulate of an American (*inter alia*) strategic culture, way of war, and national strategic style, hold up when interrogated by theories explaining both geographically and functionally focused military cultures? This is not to claim that the idea of military service and military sub-service (branch) cultures necessarily is seriously damaging to the singular concept of a unitary national strategic culture, or even military culture, but it is to suggest that it might be. The evidence and argument appear strong for what one might term sub-system strength. Such books as Carl H. Builder's *Masks of War*, J. C. Wylie's *Military Strategy*, Brian Linn's *Echo of Battle* (on the tribes persisting within the US Army), and Roger W. Barnett's recent study with the unambiguous title and sub-title, *Navy Strategic Culture: Why the Navy Thinks Differently*, point to the need for strategic and military cultures to be considered in a discriminating as well as a holistic way.[50] It would be challenging to theory development were scholars to discover inductively that soldiers, sailors, airpersons, space persons, and cybernauts had more culturally in common with their fellow geographical and functional domainers abroad, than they did with those in their sister armed services at home. To continue this theoretically subversive line of thought, it could be troubling to some cultural theory were one to discover that the special warfare warriors' tribe was (political) frontier-free in terms of culture. To illustrate with a question, do Chinese cyber warriors wage cyber warfare in a distinctively Chinese way? Is that possible? Tactical choices certainly are influenced and sometimes determined by the geographical and historical contexts for particular militaries. It is not difficult to detect the stamp of particular cultures on weapons and their tactical employment. However, to what degree do fighter pilots, submariners, or gunners, share a common worldview because of their branch specialisms? Can one pilot an aircraft Chinese-style? An appropriate answer would be that although equipment for military use that is common across frontiers mandates some common technical skills, the tactics chosen for those skills to serve may differ markedly. It can be that even if military cultures and sub-cultures bear unmistakably particular national or other community hallmarks, the attitudes, beliefs, and preferred behaviours of their human agents owe more to the nature of their specific military instrument than to a national cultural authority.[51] This thought is expressed neatly by Dominick Graham in his memoir of the performance of the British Army in the two world wars, when he writes, simply, '[e]ach arm of the army had a distinct view of the battlefield'.[52] This claim is so obviously true that its implications tend not to attract the notice they should.

When one begins to take seriously the proposition that soldiers, sailors, and air persons (*inter alia*) may have worldviews sufficiently distinctive as to merit description as cultural, insight should be gained on some of the endemic problems in combined arms and joint warfare. Much intra- and inter-service disharmony is rooted in notably different military cultures. Each military geographical focus fosters a small basket of strategic attitudes that can prove severely dysfunctional for military efforts that need to be adequately combined and tolerably joint for a single strategic purpose. Understandably, armies incline to believe that warfare is really all about the control of land and people via persisting physical presence; navies necessarily approach warfare as a struggle to secure (maritime) lines of communication; while air forces are prone to regard warfare as an exercise in targeting for kinetic effect from altitude, viewing the strategically relevant world as akin to a dartboard. These cultural leanings are complementary and can mesh constructively for a whole military effort much greater than the sum of its parts. But, often this is not the case. Instead of recognizably combined and joint military effort, reality frequently is the conduct of several styles in warfare, loosely stapled together and sponsored rather than commanded and controlled by an only nominally unified command structure. The concept of culture has value for understanding diversity and its challenges with respect to what needs to be combined and joint.

The complexity and dynamism of statecraft and strategy in peace and war mean that cultural information, and one hopes knowledge for understanding, primarily should be valued for its educational worth. For an imperfect analogy, the general theory of strategy is all about education; as Clausewitz insisted, it is not a 'sort of *manual* for action'.[53] Cultural understanding of an enemy is not adequate as a basis for strategic decision. What such understanding achieves, assuming it is superior understanding, is comprehension of an enemy's values and probably inferable preferences. But this understanding, though important, does not itself include in its domain the full measure of considerations, enduring and ephemeral, that will work to produce the enemy's particular decisions at unique times, in specific places and circumstances.

Culture, to be such rather than mere opinion, must have an enduring quality. However, much as historical research on the evidence for the RMA postulate tends to locate revolutions in abundance, so the cultural postulate can hardly help but bias the scholar in favour of persistence over change, custom over innovation.[54] This can be unfortunate, because it is in the nature of culture to change, occasionally radically and suddenly, though sometimes slowly by evolution. Culture and custom take time to bed-in, they cannot shift with agility in an instant. It is close to being a matter of definition. This caveat can be overstated. Plainly, if the cultural thesis has substantial merit it should be able to cope with the fact of change by arguing fairly plausibly that, to cite one recent specific example, there is a 'Revolution in Military Affairs with Chinese Characteristics'.[55] A friendliness toward innovation, especially of a technological kind, is thoroughly compatible with a cultural leaning in one's analysis.[56] Nonetheless, scholars do need to be alert to the historical reality of extensive and sometimes rapid cultural change through a process of learning and borrowing, when pressure of circumstances provides the motivation.

The heavily contingent nature of politics and war works by rewarding expedient adaptation to under-anticipated events. Cultural borrowing (and theft), learning, and perhaps recovery and discovery (of extant but underprivileged sub-cultural traditions), is an important theme in strategic history. Belligerents and their several military (*inter alia*) tribes and branches may well bring stable bodies of cultural lore, expressed in customary behaviour, to the struggle. But, armed struggle, the violent duel itself, with its many calories of chance and surprising epiphanies will encourage attitudes and preferred modes of military behaviour that constitute a marked alteration from those that were traditional, effectively meaning cultural, before battle was joined.

It is an error to dismiss culture as merely ideational froth that rapidly can be blown away from the top of the material realities of competing power by the pressing strategic and tactical needs of the moment. The reason is because strategic culture cannot simply be a matter of current intellectual discretion, which is to say of choice, rational or otherwise. Culture is organically existential and is not discretionary at any one moment. Only the passage of time reveals whether an opinion or decision today merits classification as cultural. We are what we are, culturally and even multiculturally, in ways and to results that largely are inalienable in the short term. By analogy, an American may leave America, but he is not likely to cease being detectably culturally American, most especially by himself (e.g. you can take the boy out of Arkansas, but you cannot take Arkansas entirely out of the boy). The cultures that people acquire are not selected from a catalogue of alternative culture options. The reason why particular attitudes, beliefs and behaviours are preferred is because they have the moral authority of being perceived to be right rather than wrong according to the local ethical code. And the moral authority of the pertinent ethical code rests upon a particular understanding of the security community's grand strategic historical narrative. No matter if the culturally authoritative narrative is entirely mythical, notably legendary, or substantially well evidenced culture is about belief, which is to say subjective, not objective, truth. Self-styled practical, problem-solving people are mistaken if they neglect the influence of culture. Mind usually rules muscle, to risk undue simplification.[57] There is some essential circularity in cultural influence. Cultural themes in strategic matters are themes believed locally to bear directly upon strategic success, though remembrance of heroic failure also can have high cultural significance. Consider Serbia's heroic defeat in Kosovo in 1389, the romance of the Lost Cause that was the brief Confederate States of America, or Britain's 'miracle' in the defeat (or successful retreat by sea) that was Dunkirk 1940. Strategic culture indicates theories of and for community strategic benefit. This quality of perceived advantage helps explain why particular attitudes and beliefs warrant the label cultural. They endure because those so encultured understandably find them attractive, and not infrequently there is moral victory in military defeat. It is a short step from a desire to believe, to belief itself. Strategic cultural belief is not likely to be unconditional, but the immediate consequence of an apparently undeniable objective disproving of cultural tenets by events is as likely to be confusion, demoralization, and despair, as rapid cultural re-education and reprogramming.

3.5 HOW CAN CULTURE INFLUENCE STRATEGY?

It may appear strange to observe that culture, which by definition is socially acquired, nonetheless should be thought of as an organic and even quasi-biological phenomenon. Cultures need to be, and therefore even feel, a seemingly natural fit for the people and organizations that acquire, adopt, and adapt them. The apparent paradox in the claim just made is important, because appreciation of the significance of culture for strategy often is weakened by critical judgements that are accorded more weight than they merit. First, culture is believed to be too insubstantial and relatively slight in comparison with objective material realities and historical context.[58] Second, culture is predicted to be too vague to be analytically helpful, even were one blessed with a methodology roughly fit for purpose. The concept of culture suffers generically from the same limitation as does that of strategy. Both are very high concepts, but that elevation contributes nothing of note to their permissiveness of disciplined treatment for analytical endeavour, indeed quite the contrary. In order to avoid giving unintended religious offence, I will refrain from extending this argument into the realm of theology, where it appears to fit with discomforting ease. Both strategy and culture are contested concepts, at least in the unarguable sense that they are contested by people who use them in different ways and for distinctive purposes. The core of culture, as also of strategy, cannot be directly represented physically. One can identify the strategy that directs behaviour, or that directed choices in military procurement. But, strategy itself cannot be photographed (except as physical plans), because it is inherently conceptual. Similarly, iconic representations of culture, including the artefacts of custom, are easy to find and make, perhaps unduly so, but the culture itself that takes conceptual, material, and behavioural forms is both everywhere to some degree and yet nowhere unquestionably concrete and representable. When scholars impose an intellectual marriage for the attempted fusion of strategy and culture, the theoretical and analytical result is more than marginally unsatisfactory.

A right enough way to approach culture, including strategic culture, is within an organic biological framework, perhaps an ecological one. One must concede the phenomena of accidents, other sources of friction, and occasional apparently non-linear unanticipated change. But still it is fruitful to think of culture in all respects, including the strategic and military, and its plural and overlapping manifestations, as the natural product of historical experience as a community has come to perceive it. This is not a deterministic story, and neither does it offer a simple single track. A country's sub-communities will prefer their own exceptional or perhaps even deviant, dominant historical narratives from which they draw their sense of identity(ies), values, norms, and overall perceptual lenses. The closest that one can and ought to proceed in the direction of determinism, is with respect to the relatively dominant role of an inclusively understood geography in the making and refinement of culture. Not all apparent opportunities are recognized, grasped and then gripped, but there is little doubt that geographical location on the planet is a greater conditioning source for strategic historical experience than is anything else that one might choose. This is not to prefer geography as the golden key that can be exploited by ingenious theorists to explain both the *longue durée* of strategic history as well as the crisis of the moment. But, it is to argue that of the many sources of influence on culture, and on culture for strategy, both objective physical geography and the geography of the imagination have to be assigned pole position. For example, if American culture should be understood as the ever dynamic outcome(s) of the unique history of North America, so that unique history is no less uniquely, primarily though of course not exclusively, the product of America's geography.

A seven-fold response answers directly the question posed in the title of this section—'How Can Culture Influence Strategy'.

First, culture influences strategy because mind moves muscle, and muscle moves material. Not all ideas for strategy and tactics warrant the label cultural, but culture, usually cultures plural, is always in play as a factor in the preferences expressed in decisions and actions. We humans do not reconstruct our mental universe, reorder our norms and values, and shift our identities, according either to objective need or to passing whim. Even radical change in some ideational or material features of a country's defence posture will coexist with features that are traditional and plainly have become cultural and customary. For diverse examples, it was not entirely self-evident how machine guns should be employed, or for that matter tanks, aircraft carriers, or submarines. Machine guns could be regarded and employed as light field artillery, as a close support weapon for the infantry, and in sub-machine gun form as personal weapons for individual soldiers.[59] Tanks could be viewed as mobile artillery to support the infantry or as mechanized cavalry. The choice of meaning attached to new military tools is subordinate to a community's dominant concept of the character of contemporary and near-future warfare. This concept inevitably is disciplined, and as a result adapted, to fit events, but it can be termed in some measure cultural. Ideas persist about the character of war and warfare, and how military forces should be used in war. There is change and continuity and the concept of culture accommodates both.

Second, it is necessary to highlight the phenomenon identified earlier as the momentum of cultural inertia. In his grand narrative of world history, Roberts wishes to privilege

> ... the weight of the historical past and the importance, even today [March 2002: CSG], of historical inertia in a world we are often encouraged to think we can control and manage. Historical forces moulding the thinking and behaviour of modern Americans, Russians, Chinese, Indians and Arabs were laid down centuries before ideas like capitalism or communism were invented. Distant history still clutters our lives, and perhaps even some of what happened in prehistory is still at work in them, too.[60]

Roberts sails perilously close to mystical historicism, with his reference to vague, but by implication irresistible, 'historical forces'. But, that caveat duly noted, his major proposition that historical inertia has a lot to answer for is powerfully persuasive. Furthermore, his insistence that due recognition be accorded to the influence of the weight of the past on the present and the future is more than faintly reminiscent of Karl Marx's judgement in *The Eighteenth Brumaire of Louis Napoleon*, when he observes pejoratively that '[t]he tradition of all the dead generations weighs like a nightmare on the brain of the living'.[61] Whether one's view of the weight and inertial momentum of history and its implacable 'forces' is somewhat negative, as was that of Marx, or broadly neutral, as is that expressed by Roberts, all such argument speaks in favour of culture as an influence with historical significance. Roberts' 'historical forces moulding ... thinking and behaviour ...' can reasonably be termed cultural in their claimed effect. When assumptions, attitudes, values, ideas, and behaviour are sufficiently enduring as to warrant being called traditional, usually they will merit the descriptors habitual and customary as well. Persisting notions and patterns of behaviour acquire historical momentum by inertia. Familiar ideas and traditional behaviour influence ideas and behaviour in the future, often simply for existential reasons. They are what they are, and in the absence of considerable effort and a possible willingness to accept high or unknown risks, they will continue as the culturally extant default setting.

Culture usually is dynamic, while also there is a contest for dominance among rival sub-cultures because typically there is a cultural market-place which is a site for cultural competition. But, scholars can be hyperactive in their forward leaning analysis at the expense of continuities. In seeking and inevitably finding change and complexity, it is not hard to miss the cultural assumptions, values, ideas, and habitual behaviour that endure. Even in the presence and aftermath of undoubted revolution, societies and their ethical codes, political practices, and strategic preferences are apt to continue bearing what can be characterized as a cultural stamp on their historical DNA. Generic continuities in historical experience stemming most essentially from geographical circumstances, do seem to be propelled onwards in time by an inertia that, *ipso facto*, becomes more than modestly cultural.

Third, one needs to be alert to the danger of neglecting the obvious simply because it is so obvious. Many assumptions, values, norms, ideas, and behaviours of relevance to strategy that merit the label cultural, enjoy that assignable quality because they are perceived to be advantageous to the society and its polity in question. Strategic ideas and practices that reflect cultural assumptions, and that have the inertial force of the perceived past, cannot be assumed to be foolish just because they represent the default setting for their political and social bearers. Some strategic assumptions and practices endure for the excellent reason that they are superior to canvassed alternatives, rather than because of culturally inertial force. Great powers habitually, which in a key respect is to say culturally, are strategically sensitive to any potentially hostile intrusions into their 'near abroad'. Empire tries to insist upon imperium beyond the formal frontiers of continuous physical control. The United States has long tried to insist in practice upon the imperium that it believes is due its hegemony throughout the Americas, north and south. Russia has been slimmed down in its colonial and imperial holdings, but the post–1991 polities in its near abroad in the Baltics, Ukraine, Central Asia, and Caucasia are not confused about their geopolitical and geostrategic status in Moscow's culturally stable strategic world-view. Continuity of geographical context finds important expression in much generic continuity in strategic historical experience, at least in the menu of choice. Strategic ideas bid to become cultural preferences when they yield perceived community advantage. And strategic success, accurately attributed or not, feeds upon itself; its presumed and therefore attributed ideational, behavioural, and material causes are replicated as societies strive hopefully to repeat past success and glories.

Fourth, the values, norms, ideas and behavioural patterns that warrant description as cultural tend to acquire some moral force as an influence over a community's strategic affairs. Cultural assumptions include moral judgements that find prescriptive reflection in an ethical code (see Chapter 2). It is in the nature of cultural beliefs to have moral force. This is both because those beliefs typically are well rooted in local soil for good enough local reasons, and also because the passage of time required for a belief to be worthy of the cultural tag itself confers at least some moral authority. Traditional beliefs and behaviours frequently are more than merely habitual; their persistence is likely to be recorded in, and possibly policed by, an ethical code that expresses cultural attitudes towards right and wrong that reflect assumptions long unchallenged and therefore unexamined. Customary behaviours are anticipated, expected, to a degree policed and can have a quasi-sacred authority. But, the influence of culture is the issue here, not its objective merit. This is not to argue uncritically for an ethically relativistic view of culture. I am not suggesting that the possible moral sincerity of a German on the rightfulness of his conduct as an active participant in the Holocaust is a sufficient excuse for atrocity. But, I am claiming that a person's belief is an influential psychological enabler of killing/murder. Culture can hardly help but be an influence over behaviour. It may be ignored and contradicted under duress, but it must always lurk ready to seize control of thought and action, because everyone's culture has educated and trained their moral and other ideational taste buds.

Fifth, there is an important and functionally necessary sense in which culture enjoys influence over strategy because it works by what amounts to a complex process of indoctrination. Homo sapiens is universal. Our individual and collective culture, more accurately our cultures, work universally to produce encultured people. But, the universality of encultured people does not mean that people share a universal culture. While people universally share cultural features, also they differ markedly in some respects. Humans are globalized both physically and also in many of the situations with which they have to try and cope. But, even when personal circumstances are roughly identical across cultures, in deadly combat for example, cultural passports usually provide the meaning to a situation and for behaviour in it. An undoubtedly universal physical and psychological humanity, a single species, is thoroughly compatible with an eternal history of episodic warfare. One can attempt to argue that war is the objectively explicable result of human competition for scarce living space and resources.[62] In historical experience, cultural pulls privileging inter- and also intra-communal cooperation usually have contended with rival theories of security that favoured episodic struggles for advantage. Humans are assailed from the cradle to the grave by tolerably coherent narratives that make sense, or profess to do so, of their political, social, economic, and strategic situation. These narratives are socially constructed; they have some objective basis but they are nonetheless subjective. Such narratives are unavoidable because our species lives and functions in societies with polities that have grand and military strategies. Societies transmit to us fairly distinctive sets of tolerably coherent cultural assumptions. The process of enculturation is purposefully directed as well as simply existential. We are what we are, in terms of values, beliefs, and preferred behaviour, in good part because of the bequest to us of a unique culturally mediated historical experience—'our nation's story' and so forth—anchored in a particular geographical location, a homeland. The stories we tell ourselves about ourselves, especially those that function doctrinally through formal schooling, change over time as our national context alters and we reappraise the past. The past is done and cannot change, but we can and do change the meaning we assign to it. Nonetheless, dynamic though they will be, community-wide values and beliefs on all subjects, which are cultural by any definition, do have an indoctrinating effect that has meaning for, and influence upon, strategic ideas and behaviour.

Sixth, potent values and beliefs worthy of description as cultural are apt to be socially and legally policed and when necessary enforced. Most people will be culturally orthodox and compliant for reason of personal conviction, no matter how that conviction was secured, or even if it were better described as acquiescence. But, cultural orthodoxy is promoted and reinforced by rewards and enforced by punishments; there is a coercive dimension to cultural compliance. Security communities, especially their military organizations, insist upon loyalty and tend not to take a nuanced permissive view of values, ideas, and behaviour that express a complex reality of multiple cross-cutting, and sometimes mutually contradictory cultural identities, beliefs, and habits. Culture functions to advance and sustain social conformity as an aid to social and political harmony (for survival), to borrow a favourite Chinese value. Recognition of the importance of culture as a supporting enabler of social, political, and military cohesion, helps protect one against discounting its influence as a factor in strategic decision making and behaviour.

Seventh, culture needs to be considered holistically, which means inclusively rather than exclusively. Scholarly specialists are prone to deconstruct and analytically disassemble ambitious concepts in order better to appreciate their several possible parts and, sometimes, for the purpose of investigating how the concept works. Such academic dissection is always feasible. Indeed, its progress usually is limited more by the imagination of the scholar, the potential reward for the effort, and the time available for the exercise, than by the inherent intractability of the conceptual material. It is necessary to consider each of a historical strategy's three most essential parts—ends, ways, and means—and possibly its pertinent assumptions also. However, it is important never to forget that although each link in the strategic triad needs to be connected purposefully to the others, the sense in each link is provided only by the whole concept of strategy.

The big idea of strategic culture is subordinate to the yet bigger and still higher concept of culture, unqualified by any modifying adjectives. This is why it is preferable to consider the cultural perspective on strategy in terms of strategy and culture, rather than strategic culture. The enculturation of the people who think, write about, decide upon, and strive to do strategy is never a process confined to the transmission and absorption strictly of strategic content. Intellectual biographers of Clausewitz emphasize that the great man and his strategic professional work can only be understood with the necessary empathy if his historical cultural context is appreciated in the round, holistically.[63] This is not to say that a theorist cannot transcend his historical circumstances and speak wisely to and for times other than his own. But, it is to say that the products of every strategic thinker must bear the stamp of their time, place, and professional situation of authorship, as well as the imprint of individual genius and personality. This concluding point registers the claim that strategic performance of an intellectual or of a practical executive kind is effected by a whole encultured person. Values, norms, attitudes, ideas, and even practices from areas of life experience that are distinctly non-strategic (e.g. sport and other forms of popular entertainment, literature and other arts), share emotional and intellectual space. These cultural influences spill over into considerations that are unquestionably strategic in the meaning preferred here. When seeking to identify and consider possible cultural influence on a security community's strategy, it is prudent to cast the net of enquiry inclusively. The values, some concepts, and customary practices, of a society and polity's life in general, carry over to its strategic thought and behaviour. At the least, this claim should be treated as a working hypothesis sufficiently robust as to merit consideration.[64]

3.6 CULTURE, ESSENTIAL BUT PROBLEMATIC

What is one to make of all this? Scholarly combat has been waged, episodically but vigorously, and some initially attractive beliefs and arguments can be classified today as damaged though still breathing, while one or two are dead if not yet buried. The discussion concludes with general observations on the state of play in the understanding of the relationship between strategy and culture. Culture reigns universally over strategy, as it must because all strategy is devised and executed by encultured people. But, although culture must reign, it does not always rule. Unless one is careless with one's preferred definition and in effect places no defensible boundary around culture's domain, plainly it is the case that only rarely is cultural preference allowed sole sovereign command authority over a community's strategy.

It is ironic and it may be paradoxical to note that although it is easier to demolish than to defend cultural interpretation of strategic behaviour, such interpretation usually is plausible as a contributor claimed to be needed for explanation. Methodologically regarded, one might well grant cultural argument a passing grade of the kind that translates as a condoned fail. But, cultural analysis delivers insight, despite weaknesses in the methodology on which it rests uneasily.

For the strategic scholar and operator, the half-full glass of culture is of high, though immeasurable and certainly unreliable value. It is a serious error to discount some cultural explanation of strategic history on the grounds that it does not, and one suspects cannot, pass an examination as rigorous social science. Culture speaks potent volumes to the moral and political vision that lies behind the politics that generate the policy that in its turn guides particular strategic thought and behaviour. Cultural influence always is potentially important, though it is not always, let alone determinatively, relevant to specific strategic decisions.

In preference to the familiar grand notion of strategic culture, a combination of large ideas compounded by brutal reductionism as an over-simple unified concept, the subject is strategy and culture. Endless granularity is a feature of scholarship. The more rigorously academics examine phenomena, the more strategic and military cultures and sub-cultures they discover. Security communities typically contain multiple cultures, though the ill potential of such multiplicity to promote confusion tends to be ameliorated in practice by rank-ordering hierarchy (e.g. Queen, country, regiment, comrades, personal honour, in whichever rank order is preferred). Nonetheless, the concept of an overarching national community-wide strategic culture has sufficient possible merit to warrant retention by scholars as a useful source of insight. This is not to deny that a source of insight is not necessarily a safely usable tool of analysis, so *caveat emptor*! The culminating point of victory for the value in cultural analysis to the strategist probably is reached relatively swiftly and over the less challenging of empirical terrain. The inherent reductionism of strategic culturalism is likely to mislead because it may prejudice the observer against noticing the inconvenient reality of competing cultures, while obviously it can encourage an oversimplified assessment of adversary thought and likely behaviour. However this is only a danger, not necessarily a lethal pathogen.

The constructivist push of cultural explanation is apt to undervalue the importance of the distinctive natures of the levels of conflict with their dependent grammars. There is a logic and a tactical and operational grammar for each level that is an awesome challenge to what needs to be a purposeful process of command and control for cohesive and tolerably harmonious strategic performance.[65] Even if one can detect what seem to be cultural phenomena in operational artistry and also in tactical behaviour, those phenomena may well be superficial when compared with the influences that are trans-cultural. Ideas on best military practice, which is to say doctrine, certainly vary between security communities, particularly in peacetime when they are bereft of the discipline of first-hand contemporary experience. But, actual combat experience is a great educator and trainer, as cultural preference is field-tested and typically revised, sometimes radically.

British Minister Tony Blair's problematic claim on 22 April 1999 (in the context of Kosovo) that our values and our interests merge, was a statement that, in its fallaciousness ironically serves a useful purpose.[66] Since American values, for example, canonically can be summarized in the triptych of liberty, democracy, and the free market, and given that these high notions are quintessentially cultural, it is unarguable that culture frequently does not rule over American statecraft and strategy. Considerations that belong in the category of *Realpolitik* are not usually overruled by policy desiderata that are obviously cultural in the narrow sense of being dominated by values. Interests vary in weight and intensity, as they do in feasibility and prudence of effective promotion in particular cases. Cultural push helps explain the terms and heat of public debate, but it cannot be relied upon as the determinative fuel for political decision and consequent strategic action.

The ideas of national style and culture (as an influence on strategic behaviour), and of a national way of war (and peace), need to be retained in the scholar's conceptual toolkit as having some value for understanding and explanation.[67] One must add hastily the conceptual health warning that these expansive concepts should be handled only with caution, because when misapplied beyond their analytical reach and grip they rapidly become perilously unsound ideas. Unhappily for elegant scholarship, notwithstanding its broad endorsement by John Keegan, the exciting proposition that there have been and remain extant contrasting and eternally distinctive Eastern and Western Ways of War has been shown by careful historians to be an implausible oversimplification in its overbold presentation of sharp alternatives (the Orientalist fallacy traceable to Herodotus, if not Homer).[68] Alas, some conceptual formulae are too imperial to withstand brutal challenge by empirical audit. When the exceptions exceed the claimed norm, it is usually time to discard the rule. Intellectual boldness and claimed utility do not suffice as tests for the merit in a theory.

The perceived value in the cultural perspective on strategy has been damaged by overstatement and uncritical adoption, but the quality of insight it can offer should be beyond serious challenge. The cultural glass is only half-full and it does have cracks, but nonetheless it can yield a depth and quality of understanding and explanation that is essential and unique. Nonetheless, cultural insight cannot be trusted as a predictor of strategic behaviour. Strategy is too complex a subject to yield reliably to monocausal analytical assault.

NOTES

1. Herodotus, *The Landmark Herodotus: The Histories*, ed. Robert B. Strassler, tr. Andrea L. Purvis (*c*.450–20 BC; New York: Parthenon Books, 2007), 224.
2. John A. Lynn, *Battle: A History of Combat and Culture* (Boulder, CO: Westview Press, 2003), 335.
3. Patrick Porter, *Military Orientalism: Eastern War Through Western Eyes* (London: C. Hurst, 2009), 191.

4. Porter, *Military Orientalism*, 197.
5. Sun Tzu, *The Art of War*, tr. Samuel B. Griffith (Oxford: Clarendon Press, 1963), 84.
6. The concept of strategic effect and effectiveness is explained and examined in Colin S. Gray, *The Strategy Bridge: Theory for Practice* (Oxford: Oxford University Press, 2010), ch. 5.
7. Gray, *The Strategy Bridge,* 16
8. My definitions of military and grand strategy are strongly Clausewitzian. See Carl von Clausewitz, *On War*, tr. Michael Howard and Peter Paret (1832–4; Princeton, NJ: Princeton University Press, 1976), 177.
9. Lawrence Sondhaus, *Strategic Culture and Ways of War* (Abingdon: Routledge, 2006), 124–5, examines a range of definitions instructively.
10. Editorial, *The Times*, 22 April 2011, 2. The editorial writer was explaining the cultural significance of the King James Bible of 1611.
11. Alastair Iain Johnston is admirably clear when he states in the Preface to his path-breaking book that '[t]his book, then, is about ideas and their relationship to behavior'. *Cultural Realism: Strategic Culture and Grand Strategy in Chinese History* (Princeton, NJ: Princeton University Press, 1995), ix. It is interesting that he did not declare his subject to be ideas in or as behaviour. Also, Johnston has explained that to him strategic culture is '[a]n integrated system of symbols (e.g. argumentation structures, languages, analogies, metaphors) which acts to establish pervasive and long-lasting strategic preferences by formulating concepts of the role and efficacy of military force in interstate political affairs, and by clothing these conceptions in such an aura of factuality that the strategic preferences seem uniquely realistic'. 'Thinking About Strategic Culture', *International Security*, 19 (spring 1995), 46. My own definition of strategic culture has oscillated only to a small degree around the following example from 1999: strategic culture comprises '[t]he persisting socially transmitted ideas, attitudes, traditions, habits of mind, and preferred methods that are more or less specific to a particular security community that has had a unique historical experience'. *Modern Strategy* (Oxford: Oxford University Press, 1999), 131. Both the Johnston and Gray definitions are ones favoured for illustration of contrasting approaches in Sondhaus, *Strategic Culture and Ways of War*, 124. Other useful discussions of definitional issues are provided in David G. Hagland, 'What Good is Strategic Culture?', and Thomas G. Mahnken, 'U.S. Strategic and Organizational Subcultures', in Jeannie L. Johnson, Kerry M. Kartchner, and Jeffrey A. Larsen, eds., *Strategic Culture and Weapons of Mass Destruction: Culturally Based Insights into Comparative National Security Policymaking* (New York: Palgrave Macmillan, 2009), respectively 16–19, and 70. See also Thomas G. Mahnken, *Understanding Dominant Features of Chinese Strategic Culture*, IDA Paper P–4614 (Washington, DC: Institute for Defense Analyses, August 2010), esp. 5–10.
12. See Gray, *The Strategy Bridge*, 59–60.
13. Clausewitz provides a concept that the coiners of definitions should take as a guide to sufficiency: 'the culminating point of victory', which can be expressed pithily as more is often less, *On War*, 566. This point typically is attainable with fewer words than official definers find adequate. Examples abound, especially in official

publications. A well intentioned work especially rich in the number of targets on offer to a critic of unwise encyclopaedism, or definitional detail creep, is the US Joint Chiefs of Staff, *The U.S. Department of Defense Dictionary of Military Terms*, rev. edn. (London: Greenhill Books, 1990). Successive editions of this worthy publication would appear to have found the encyclopaedism virus to be ineradicable. Definitional bloat is the result.

14. Lynn, *Battle*, focuses heavily on the conceptual dimension to cultural influence on strategy.

15. Gray, *Modern Strategy*, ch. 5, 'Strategic Culture as Context'; Antulio J. Echevarria II, 'American Strategic Culture: Problems and Prospects', in Hew Strachan and Sibylle Scheipers, eds., *The Changing Character of War* (Oxford: Oxford University Press, 2011), 432.

16. See Raymond Aron, *Peace and War: A Theory of International Relations* (New York: Doubleday, 1966), 1.

17. See Bernard Brodie, ed., *The Absolute Weapon: Atomic Power and World Order* (New York: Harcourt, Brace, 1946); Colin S. Gray, *Strategic Studies and Public Policy: The American Experience* (Lexington, KY: University Press of Kentucky, 1982); Lawrence Freedman, *The Evolution of Nuclear Strategy*, 3rd edn. (Basingstoke: Palgrave Macmillan, 2003); Keith B. Payne, *The Great American Gamble: The Theory and Practice of Deterrence from Cold War to the Twenty-First Century* (Fairfax, VA: National Institute Press, 2008); and Beatrice Heuser, *The Evolution of Nuclear Strategy: Thinking War from Antiquity to the Present* (Cambridge: Cambridge University Press, 2010), ch. 14. The open-ended character of contemporary debate over nuclear weapons and strategy is a source of some fragile satisfaction. The kind of empirical evidence needed to provide a healthy base in experience for strategic theory would be hugely unhealthy in all other respects.

18. Franklin D. Kramer, Stuart H. Starr, and Larry K. Wentz, eds., *Cyberpower and National Security* (Washington, DC: 2009); Richard A. Clarke and Robert K. Knake, *Cyber War: The Next Threat to National Security and What to Do About It* (New York: HarperCollins, 2010); and David J. Betz and Tim Stevens, *Cyberspace and the State: Toward a Strategy for Cyber-Power* (Abingdon: Routledge for the International Institute for Strategic Studies, 2011). For two vigorously worded contrasting arguments that 'book-end' the debate thus far, see John Arquilla and David Ronfeldt, 'Cyberwar is Coming!', in Arquilla and Ronfeldt, eds., *In Athena's Camp: Preparing for Conflict in the Information Age* (Santa Monica, CA: RAND, 1997), 23–60, and David Beitz, 'Cyberwar is not coming', *Infinity Journal*, 3 (summer 2011), 21–4.

19. Patrick Porter, 'Good Anthropology, Bad History: The Cultural Turn in Studying War', *Parameters* 37, (summer 2007), 45–58, and Montgomery McFate, 'Culture', in Thomas Rid and Thomas Keaney, eds., *Understanding Insurgency: Doctrine, operations, and challenges*, (Abingdon: Routledge, 2010), 189–204.

20. See US Army and Marine Corps, *Counterinsurgency Field Manual* (Chicago: University of Chicago Press, 2007); David Kilcullen, *The Accidental Guerrilla: Fighting Small Wars in the Midst of a Big One* (London: C. Hurst, 2009). Daniel Marston and Carter Malkesian, eds., *Counterinsurgency in Modern Warfare* (Botley: Osprey Publishing, 2008) offers useful historical perspective.

Undue culturalism is assaulted credibly in Rob Johnson, *The Afghan Way of War: Culture and Pragmatism: A Critical History* (London: C. Hurst, 2011).

21. Rupert Smith, *The Utility of Force: The Art of War in the Modern World* (London: Allen Lane, 2005), xiii.

22. For period pieces, see Jack L. Snyder, *The Soviet Strategic Culture: Implications for Limited Nuclear Operations*, R–2154–AF (Santa Monica, CA: RAND, September 1977) and Colin S. Gray, *Nuclear Strategy and National Style* (Lanham, MD: Hamilton Press, 1986).

23. Clausewitz, *On War*, 88.

24. John Keegan, *A History of Warfare* (London: Hutchinson, 1993).

25. Porter, *Military Orientalism*; Gian P. Gentile, 'A Strategy of Tactics: Population-centric COIN and the Army', *Parameters*, XXXIX (autumn 2009), 5–17; and Johnson, *The Afghan Way of War*. An earlier assault was mounted in Michael C. Desch, 'Culture Clash: Assessing the Importance of Ideas in Security Studies', *International Security*, 23 (summer 1998), 141–70.

26. Johnston, *Cultural Realism*, esp. 4–22, was an important sophisticated study that commented critically on previous works with cultural leanings, including my own. I replied in my *Modern Strategy*, ch. 5.

27. A book that has stood the test of time is Ken Booth, *Strategy and Ethnocentrism* (London: Croom Helm, 1979). Booth's argument for cultural awareness in strategic studies reads as well today as it did when he wrote it, possibly even better.

28. Imperial Japan is an irresistible subject for strategic cultural scrutiny. Particularly helpful studies include Forrest E. Morgan, *Compellence and the Strategic Culture of Imperial Japan: Implications for Coercive Diplomacy in the Twenty–First Century* (Westport, CT: Praeger Publishers, 2003), esp. ch. 2, which primarily tackles the more challenging issues of methodology, and does so with some success; Porter, *Military Orientalism*, ch. 3; and Sally C. M. Paine, 'The Japanese Way of War', paper delivered to the Conference on Asian Strategic Studies, US Naval War College, Newport, RI., August 2011. For a strongly positive appreciation of Western Orientalism, see Robert Irwin, *For Lust of Knowing: The Orientalists and their Enemies* (London: Penguin Books 2007).

29. As I explain at length in *Modern Strategy* and especially in *The Strategy Bridge*.

30. A classic statement of this ecologically 'possibilist' view is Harold Sprout and Margaret Sprout, *The Ecological Perspective on Human Affairs with Special Reference to International Politics* (Princeton, NJ: Princeton University Press, 1965).

31. See Colin S. Gray, 'Inescapable Geography', in Gray and Geoffrey Sloan, eds., *Geopolitics, Geography and Strategy* (London: Frank Cass, 1999), 161–77.

32. For example, in 1942 General Douglas MacArthur was apparently massively ignorant of the objective geographical fact that he was directing American and Australian soldiers in battle in Papua New Guinea in what has to be a leading candidate for the title of most hostile geography for warfare on the planet. The proud general, smarting from his humiliating defeat in the Philippines and over-eager to restore his reputation, demonstrated little interest in understanding the physical challenges posed by the extremely hostile physical geography of New Guinea. MacArthur's operational level commander in the Buna campaign, Lt. General Robert L. Eichelberger, observed in December 1942 that his American

forces 'were prisoners of geography'. Eichelberger is quoted in James Campbell, *The Ghost Mountain Boys* (New York: Crown Publishers, 2007), 223.

33. Jeremy Black writes intriguingly about the 'cultural perceptions of the past'. *Geopolitics* (London: The Social Affairs Unit, 2009), 21. Also, see his excellent *Rethinking Military History* (Abingdon: Routledge, 2004), chs. 2–3.

34. The most convincing explanation of the Halt order imbroglio, with its plausibly fatal consequences for German hopes to prevent the evacuation from Dunkirk, is Karl-Heinz Frieser, *The Blitzkrieg Legend: The 1940 Campaign in the West* (Annapolis, MD: Naval Institute Press, 2005), ch. 8.

35. I am pleased to record a methodological debt to Jeannie Johnson and Matthew T. Berrett, 'Cultural Topography: A New Research Tool for Intelligence Analysis', *Studies in Intelligence*, 55 (Extracts, June 2011), 1–22.

36. Clausewitz, *On War*, 605.

37. I am grateful to Johnson and Berrett for the concept of 'cultural inertia' in their 'Cultural Topography', 1. For their part, they are indebted to J. M. Roberts for the root idea of 'historical inertia' in his book, *The New Penguin History of the World*, 5th edn. (London: Penguin Books, 2007), xii.

38. Clausewitz, *On War*, 119–21.

39. This is an important argument in Porter, *Military Orientalism*.

40. Clausewitz makes a closely related point when he claims that '[s]o long as no acceptable theory, no intelligent analysis of the conduct of war exists, routine methods will tend to take over even at the highest levels', *On War*, 154. Routine methods can fairly be described as customary.

41. Johnson and Berrett, 'Cultural Topography', 2.

42. See Booth, *Strategy and Ethnocentrism* and Robert B. Bathurst, *Intelligence and the Mirror: On Creating an Enemy* (London: SAGE Publications, 1993).

43. See Gray, *The Strategy Bridge*, ch. 4, for a detailed treatment of the strategist's woes.

44. Clausewitz, *On War*, 578.

45. Notable works include Johnston, *Cultural Realism*; Peter J. Katzenstein, ed., *The Culture of National Security: Norms and Identity in World Politics* (New York: Columbia University Press, 1996); Lynn, *Battle*; Sondhaus, *Strategic Culture*; Johnson, Kartchner, and Larsen, eds., *Strategic Culture and Weapons of Mass Destruction*; Porter, *Military Orientalism*; and Johnson, *The Afghan Way of War*.

46. Echevarria's 'American Strategic Culture' is a leading example of analysis inclining strongly towards scepticism, yet which manages to see heuristic value in cultural argument. His conclusions include the following pair of plausible claims: 'In the realm of policymaking, where some degree of uncertainty is unavoidable, studies of strategic culture do not appear to reduce it in any appreciable way. Studies of strategic culture can, however, help indirectly by offering conclusions that can be challenged and critically examined' (442). His argument is reminiscent of a major rationale for the Anglo–American Combined Bomber Offensive, which was that it would oblige the Luftwaffe's fighter force to offer battle at altitude, where it could be destroyed attritionally. Echevarria may be correct in both of his claims, but I incline to take a more positive view of the cultural perspective, provided it is taken with caveats as well as a healthy pinch of salt.

47. Echevarria, 'American Strategic Culture'.

48. See MacGregor Knox and Williamson Murray, eds., *The Dynamics of Military Revolution, 1300–2050* (Cambridge: Cambridge University Press, 2001); Dima Adamsky, *The Culture of Military Innovation: The Impact of Cultural Factors on the Revolution in Military Affairs in Russia, the US, and Israel* (Stanford, CA: Stanford University Press, 2010); and, for a well-informed updating analysis, Barry D. Watts, *The Maturing Revolution in Military Affairs* (Washington, DC: Center for Strategic and Budgetary Assessments, 2011).

49. Gray, *Nuclear Strategy and National Style*, was an early under-nuanced venture by this theorist.

50. J. C. Wylie, *Military Power: A General Theory of Power Control* (Annapolis, MD: Naval Institute Press, 1989); Carl H. Builder, *The Masks of War: American Military Styles in Strategy and Analyses* (Baltimore, MD: Johns Hopkins University Press, 1989); Brian McAllister Linn, *The Echo of Battle: The Army's Way of War* (Cambridge, MA: Harvard University Press, 2007); and Roger W. Barnett, *Navy Culture: Why the Navy Thinks Differently* (Annapolis, MD: Naval Institute Press, 2009).

51. One should not be overimpressed by the potential for common technical choices that resides in a fairly common technical capability. Alan R. Millett has provided convincing evidence in support of the proposition that '[s]ome weapons even showed national characteristics' because different countries' militaries prioritized performance characteristics differently. For example, America's highly motorized and mechanized army in World War II was seriously lacking in tanks with hitting power fully competitive in battle. Millett, 'Patterns of innovation in the interwar period', in Williamson Murray and Millett, eds., *Military Innovation in the Interwar Period* (Cambridge: Cambridge University Press, 1996), 345.

52. Dominick Graham, *Against Odds: Reflections on the Experiences of the British Army, 1914–45* (Basingstoke: Macmillan, 1999), 5.

53. Clausewitz, *On War*, 141.

54. More research reveals yet more RMAs, when the quest is founded on the assumption that there are as yet undiscovered RMAs hiding out there in a past undergoverned by the historian as theorist.

55. Jacqueline Newmyer, 'The Revolution in Military Affairs with Chinese Characteristics', *The Journal of Strategic Studies*, 33 (August 2010), 483–504.

56. As Thomas G. Mahnken shows in his *Technology and the American Way of War Since 1945* (New York: Columbia University Press, 2008).

57. Lynn, *Battle*, xvii–xix.

58. Historian John France makes a strong statement to this effect when he writes that '[w]ar may exercise the intellect, as Sun Tzu asserted, but the material conditions of society imposed remarkably similar methods of fighting upon peoples, no matter how diverse their cultures'. France did concede, perhaps grudgingly, that '[o]f course cultural experience has some influence upon war, and particularly on why we fight.' He sets out his stall of argument by claiming that 'this book is primarily about how we fight. It will argue that down to the nineteenth century the major world civilisations, including the western, fought in distinctly similar ways'. *Perilous Glory: The Rise of Western Military Power* (New Haven, CT: Yale

University Press, 2011). France's thesis concerning the limited scope of cultural influence in the global history of warfare is overstated and apt to mislead.

59. See John Ellis, *The Social History of the Machine Gun* (Baltimore: Johns Hopkins University Press, 1986); and C. J. Chivers, *The Gun: The AK–47 and the Evolution of War* (London: Allen Lane, 2010).

60. Roberts, *The New Penguin History of the World*, xiii.

61. Karl Marx, *The Eighteenth Brumaire of Louis Napoleon* [1852] in Marx and Friedrich Engels, *Selected Works in Two Volumes*, Vol. 1 (Moscow: Foreign Languages Publishing House, 1962), 247.

62. The 'why war' literature is exceedingly large and hugely inconclusive. It is open season for exciting theories that might explain the phenomenon of war satisfactorily, but the season has been open for a very long time and seems unlikely to be closed anytime soon. The following stand out among the more thoughtful basic studies of war produced by scholars of recent years: Stephen Peter Rosen, *War and Human Nature* (Princeton, NJ: Princeton University Press, 2005); Azar Gat, *War in Human Civilization* (Oxford: Oxford University Press, 2006); and Martin van Creveld, *The Culture of War* (New York: Ballantine Books, 2008). Or, for an alternative superior to modern scholarship, see Thucydides, *The Landmark Thucydides: A Comprehensive Guide to The Peloponnesian War*, ed. Robert B. Strassler, rev. tr. Richard Crawley (*c*.400 BC; New York: Free Press, 1996).

63. See especially, Peter Paret, *Clausewitz and the State* (Oxford: Oxford University Press, 1976) and Hew Strachan, *Clausewitz's On War: A Biography* (New York: Atlantic Monthly Press, 2007).

64. The study of strategy is predominantly a male profession, and strategists in the countries with which this strategist has some first-hand familiarity typically are deeply encultured by and with the concepts, rules, norms, and behaviours fairly specific to their favourite sport(s). My tri-national experience as a strategist, in Britain, the United States, and Canada, has bequeathed me a tri-national enculturation deriving from the 'grammars' of cricket, American football, and (ice) hockey.

65. See Edward N. Luttwak, *Strategy: The Logic of War and Peace*, rev. edn. (1987: Cambridge, MA: Harvard University Press, 2001), xii and, following Luttwak, Gray, *The Strategy Bridge*, 65.

66. 'The Blair Doctrine' <http://www.pbs.org/newshow/bb/international/jan-june99/blair_doctrine4-23.html>.

67. See van Creveld, *The Culture of War* and Richard Ned Lebow, *A Cultural Theory of International Relations* (Cambridge: Cambridge University Press, 2008).

68. Victor Davis Hanson, *The Western Way of War: Infantry Battle in Classical Greece* (London: Hodder and Stoughton, 1989); Victor David Hanson, *Why the West Has Won: Carnage and Culture from Salamis to Vietnam* (London: Faber and Faber, 2001); and Lynn, *Battle*. Hanson's concept broadly is endorsed in John Keegan, *A History of Warfare* (London: Hutchinson 1993), but is flatly rejected in France, *Perilous Glory*, 5, and Johnson, *The Afghan Way of War*, 5–6.

4

Geography: Geopolitics and Deterrence

Both the real and the arm-chair strategists lacked a global view. How could they acquire such a view in a generation without the intellectual tools or imaginative feeling for analyzing and reconstituting the world in global terms? Global geography was simply not in our blood. The conception of geography in its profound relation to man's destiny remained superficial. Geography had been taught for too long a time by men who failed to grasp that politics is destiny, and politics had been directed and also taught for too long a time by men who failed to grasp that land and sea spaces, too, are destiny.

Hans W. Weigert[1]

Mackinder had a point [in 1904: CSG]: whereas Russia, that other Eurasian giant, basically was, and is still, a land power with an oceanic front blocked by ice, China, owing to a 9,000-mile temperate coastline with many good natural harbors, is both a land power and a sea power.

Robert D. Kaplan[2]

The Italians knew what they wanted [in 1919: CSG]. Geography forced them to think seriously about the Balkans.

Margaret MacMillan[3]

4.1 GEOGRAPHY AND DESTINY

Geography, meaning the physical features of the world, would seem to be qualitatively different from the perspectives on strategy examined in this book thus far: the conceptual, the ethical, and the cultural. Strategic concepts, morality and its strategic ethics, and strategic culture are all in their rich variations constructions of the human mind. They are invented and applied or ignored by human discretion. By way of sharp contrast physical geography is materially existential. Mankind discovers what it is and makes of it what he can, but nonetheless geography is massively 'given', substantially beyond near-term (at least) alteration by human effort. That said, strategic history shows that human security communities attach political and strategic meaning to physical geography that can have profound consequences for the course of events. The physical features that constitute world geography comprise the material stage upon which humans contrive their several grand narratives. Because of the ubiquity and pervasive relevance of the geographical context to all strategic phenomena, I am sharpening this discussion by providing it with a focus on the theory and practice of deterrence. How is the geographical perspective on strategy manifested in deterrence phenomena?

One can hypothesize that the prospects for success with a strategy of deterrence may be improved by a better understanding of its geopolitical dimension. It is necessary to conceive of strategies in the plural. Although there is only one general theory of strategy and one general theory of deterrence, in application a strategy of deterrence needs to be unique in detail for a good enough fit with its historical context.[4] The general theories of strategy and deterrence are valid eternally and universally, but particular strategies of deterrence are neither. What deters one polity may well be inappropriate for another. General theory covers the deterrence projects of all polities, but the details of each case will be distinctive. The United States would like to deter unfriendly, let alone actually damaging, behaviour by a potentially nuclear-armed Iran, just as it sought to deter, and may have deterred, the Soviet Union during the Cold War. However, it would be a gross and avoidable error on the US part were it to assume that the deterrence lore that it discovered and sought to practise from 1946 to 1989, must fit well enough the circumstances for attempts to deter in the twenty-first century. In common with the strategy function to which it is subordinate, the deterrence function is identical in the two periods, but much of the vital detail is situationally distinctive.

A neglect of geographical perspective is lamented in the words quoted from Hans Weigert as the first epigraph to this chapter. Weigert's book can be read as a period piece, reflecting a moment in modern history when the political dimension to geography and the geographical dimension to politics briefly seized the popular imagination. Global maps decorated with exciting and sometimes menacing arrows were daily fare in the popular press in the early 1940s.[5] It was fashionable at the time to believe that an evil Professor Karl Haushofer, who held the rank of major general in the German army, and his Institut für Geopolitik in Munich, had crafted a Nazi grand design for world conquest.[6] The popularity of a geographical view of world politics was both well and ill founded. In the latter regard, although Adolf Hitler's designs for foreign adventure certainly had a large geographical dimension with reference to Slav-tilled soil to Germany's east, no less assuredly those designs owed little to the particular theories advanced by the sometimes scholarly general.[7] Hitler's policies indeed owed much to his understanding of Germany's geographical context, both actual and another subjective one that in his view was far more desirable. But, they owed even more to a non-scientific ethnographic view of Germany's destiny. Race was more important to the Führer than was geography.

Due to its somewhat unmerited guilt by association with Nazi Germany,[8] geopolitics departed from the scholars' shop window of fashionable concepts and respectable valued fields of study, almost as swiftly as it had appeared in the late 1930s and early 1940s. There has been a modest revival of scholarly and official interest in recent years, but the subject continues to be regarded with suspicion.[9] There are both sound and unsound reasons to be sceptical of the value of geopolitical analysis. This examination argues that it is possible to avoid the genuine perils among the claimed hazards of geopolitical enquiry. So imperial is the global domain of geopolitical theory—its area of responsibility theoretically is limitless—that in careless hands it can pretend to the unwary to be the master theory of everything.[10] Geopolitics may strive to explain too much, and as a consequence it fails to contribute that of which it is capable when ambitions for understanding and explanation are more modest. I am not exploring the hypothesis that 'geography is destiny'. Geopolitics offers an important and frequently neglected or misunderstood perspective upon national and international security, including issues of deterrence: it is neither offered nor examined here as a serious candidate itself to provide a complete theory of statecraft and strategy. Ironically, to claim less is to enhance the prospects for the delivery of more.

4.1.1 Concepts and Definitions

I define geopolitics deliberately in a neutral fashion simply as the political implications of geography.[11] This definition is crystal clear about its subject in general in an inclusive way, yet does not prejudice particular discussion. It does not seek to specify what is meant by political, and neither does it suggest any particular meaning to geography. The content of 'political' has varied widely, while 'geography' covers a range of subjects when adjectival modifiers are added (economic geography, cultural geography, military geography, and the like). For the purpose of this discussion 'political implications' are understood as referring to those that bear upon the distribution of power among and within polities; while 'geography' refers both to physical reality and to mental images of that reality. Although there is a brute force existentiality to physical geography, as a generalization it is geography in the mind, of the imagination, that matters most.[12] Physical geography imposes discipline upon manifestations of the human will in behaviour, but it is the will that is in the driving seat, to coin a somewhat perilous metaphor. Given that the focus of this analysis is upon deterrence, and that for deterrence to work well enough the deterree has to choose to be deterred, it is obvious why mental geography counts for more than physical geography. The latter may cause the human will to crash in failure, so, plainly, physical geography triumphs. But, the human will that crashed was brought to its fatal collision with material reality by what it believed would be possible.

Just because the subject here is deterrence regarded in geopolitical perspective, it would be a serious error to take a holistic view of geography that collapsed physical and mental geography into a gestalt. Rational strategic analysis has a bad habit of failing to register and make allowance for the variability of rational behaviour. The rational and a culturally shaded understanding of the reasonable tend to be confused. Functional rationality on the part of a strategist requires only that he or she seeks to connect political ends purposefully by employing means in ways believed suitable and effective. The actual content preferred in this decidedly rational process should not be assumed to be common across polities, cultures, communities, civilizations, institutions, or even individuals. The political implications of geography can never be assumed to be objectively so obvious as to be self-evident and therefore incontestable, at least not across frontiers, legal and tacit. To illustrate: the political implications of the geographical setting of Gibraltar and of the Falkland Islands differ as between London and, respectively, Madrid and Buenos Aires. The geography is as unarguable as its perceived political meaning is contestable.

Geography can impact the prospects for success with a strategy of deterrence in both the objective physical and the subjective mental realms. Physical reality matters: for example, it can and frequently does impose itself to preclude flying in bad weather, an intervention that constrains necessary logistical support operations.

Geopolitics is as important a dimension to the feasibility of deterrence as it is difficult to control conceptually and employ operationally in a disciplined way. It may appear unduly academic, in the pejorative meaning of the adjective, to insist upon clarity in definition and rigid consistency in the use of key terms, but there is acute need for such apparent pedantry. Carl von Clausewitz advises persuasively that

> The primary purpose of any theory is to clarify concepts and ideas that have become, as it were, confused and entangled. Not until terms and concepts have been defined can one hope to make any progress in examining the question clearly and simply and expect the reader to share one's views.[13]

The core meaning of the definition of geopolitics provided here is as plain as its boundary is contestable. In common with culture and economics, for parallel examples, geography potentially has a limitless domain. This is why strategic analysts are reluctant to yield undue intellectual space to those who allow their demand for the concept of security to be privileged over strategy.

The logical precedence of the former over the latter is beyond challenge. However, in practice this rank ordering achieves so pervasive a securitization of strategic subjects that the latter lose their necessary focus. It is a considerable analytical challenge to distinguish between subject, in this case deterrence, and context(s). Undue diligence in contextualization encourages an inadvertent demotion in significance of matters that are somewhat autonomous with much of their own 'grammar', vis-à-vis their context.[14] By analogy, it is possible as a teacher so to contextualize a great war politically, socially and culturally, and so forth, that little space is left in the explanation for the course and consequences of the actual fighting. Although a grasp of context usually is essential for understanding, it does not follow that just because some contextual knowledge is valuable, a great deal more must be proportionately so much more valuable. The social scientific law of diminishing returns to effort applies to contextual analysis. Geographical context always must have yet more geographical context, literally ad infinitum. The strategist can be saved from having his battlespace devoured by context only by applying that quizzical saviour of common sense, the question 'so what?'

It is necessary to recognize the historical authority of the specific over the general. In the immortal words of US Supreme Court Justice Oliver Wendell Holmes, Jr, '[g]eneral propositions do not decide concrete cases'.[15] Deterrence theory educates, but it can do no more. It explains the nature of deterrence and how and why it works in general. But, the strategist well educated in theory must apply his education in translation for fit with the circumstances of the challenge of the day. One may be a master of the theory of deterrence, but such intellectual achievement is worse than useless if it does not include recognition of the likely sovereignty of context. Whether or not context proves sovereign over the would-be imperial force of a menace uttered for the purpose of deterrence can only be decided by the specific details of time, place, strategic occasion, and people.

It is easy to err in making either too much or too little of geopolitics. It is useful to indicate two responses to the perils, on the one hand, of conceptual imperialism, and on the other, of undue modesty. The besetting temptation of the big idea is that of the panacea. When one stumbles upon and into recognition of the salience of a potent seeming factor, there is the danger that the epiphany of the moment will be overvalued. Similarly, people with a variety of professional foci are apt to discover that their particular tool can be applied to provide the answer to almost every question. This all too understandable human proclivity is especially noticeable among strategists. Thus we find theories of warfare that privilege, even exclusively privilege, land power, sea power, air power, space power, and now cyber power. Scholars of International Relations are scarcely less prone than are strategists to overvalue their most favoured tools. Hence, one finds theories of world politics that overemphasize the leverage claimed for economic, psychological, cultural, legal, or geographical factors, to cite but some among the more popular tools in the academic's tool-box.[16]

A phenomenon common among competent and indeed honest theorists and analysts, is for them to permit definition creep to serve as the vital ingredient that permits expansive employment of their favoured idea. For a case in point, once one has grasped the inescapable pervasiveness of culture, it is extremely challenging to rein in its seemingly irresistible ability to explain everything.[17] There is a sense in which everything about statecraft and warfare as an instrument of that statecraft might merit definition as cultural.[18] The result is that a potentially valuable conceptual tool, culture, is misused by the unwary so that its deployment—with apologies to Clausewitz—far exceeds its 'culminating point of victory' in analytical utility.[19] Because culture appears to explain so much, typically it explains nothing quite satisfactorily. If everything is and has to be cultural, then everything might as well not be regarded as cultural. The adjective has lost meaning because it adds no value. Theory must distinguish what is from what is not. Ironically, perhaps, the only way in which geopolitics can be deployed and employed as a potent analytical tool is by insisting upon meaningful restrictions to its domain. As with the case for the allegedly cultural, if everything is in one or more sense geographical, the adjective cannot serve the purpose of improving understanding.

This book is content to define geography in unproblematic and minimalist style simply as 'the main physical features of an area'.[20] This elementary dictionary definition is entirely innocent of political, strategic, or any other non-physical content. But geography per se is of no interest. What matters is the political and strategic meaning ascribed to geography, and how that meaning may influence the willingness and ability to deter or resist being deterred. The austerity of the definition just offered enables an analytically helpful inclusivity. The stability of physical geography, even the relatively high stability of its elements of instability (seasonal weather patterns that reflect climate, for a leading example, tidal ebb and flow for a lesser case), contrasts significantly with the variability of content to geography's 'political implications'. If physical geography is stable, politics assuredly is not. Moreover, even if both politics and geography betray far more continuity than change, the same cannot be said of strategy. The dominant strategic narrative is one of instability, notwithstanding the unchanging character of physical geography. The English Channel can be a barrier or a highway; indeed, it can be both in a single conflict. In the Second World War it functioned strategically as a defensive moat for Britain, because it was more than adequately defended by the Royal Navy and the RAF. But, less than four years on from the eponymous battle for national survival in summer 1940, that same Channel was a highway to continental Europe inadequately defended by German forces. The geography was identical in the two cases, but the politics and the strategy could hardly have been more different.

On the Eastern Front in that same conflict, winter was the period in both 1941 and 1942 wherein the Soviet Red Army exploited its relative advantage in cold weather fighting to launch major ground offensives. Winter had some different strategic meaning for the Red Army as contrasted with that for Germany's *Östheer*. To the former it was the prime season of opportunity; to the latter it was the season to be endured in preparation for the resumption of decisive operational effort when the weather predictably would be more permissive of German effort.[21]

The historical examples given emphasize that geography 'just is': it is what people make of it that signifies politically and strategically. This may seem to approach perilously close to an unduly constructivist view. Of course there is a sense in which geography is thoroughly neutral as a (non-)purposeful player in human affairs. What matters is the need to steer a prudent course between the hazard of determinism ('geography is destiny'), and the scarcely less misleading siren call of constructivism ('destiny is what we choose to make of the geography that is "given"'). Physical geography can be either enabler or disabler, depending upon how wisely it is exploited. Geography is a stage set by forces beyond much human control. The ability to work with it varies hugely with context, but geography is always present as a source of greater or lesser discipline that charges a price for the rewards sought through its exploitation. For example, to move across space of almost any geographical nature comes with some transaction costs in time and attenuation of strength.[22] Even in a contemporary strategic context characterized in part by the widespread exploitation of orbital space and of cyberspace, physical geography—perhaps geographies—cannot be taken as a given factor of no significance. Cyberspace does not really bypass, let alone conquer geography, at least not without material assistance, and it may not be destiny, at least not sufficiently so as to be strategically decisive.[23]

This enquiry into the geographical perspective needs a way to be found to operationalize geopolitics as a variable that may influence the feasibility of deterrence. One must insist that deterrence cannot be regarded as capable of delivering a general effect upon whom it may concern, with occasions and addressees left unspecified. Historical and other contextual granularity is important for the prospects for deterrence success. Whereas reference to 'the nuclear deterrent' unquestionably is a categorical confusion of means with ends, even discussion of a 'strategy of deterrence' risks mistaking ways for ends. When commentators are careless in their lack of adequate distinctions among ends, ways, and means, misuse of the concept of deterrence hinders the ability to grasp the nature of the strategic challenge. Such confusion promotes a spurious authority of the general over the particular. The problem is that deterrence is not general; overwhelmingly it functions with reference to particular time, place, players, stakes, and occasion.

It can be argued that the messy details of geopolitics matter far less than does the global distribution of power and influence. In this view, geographical particulars in their political implications typically are swamped for significance by, say, the general deterrence that flows as an all but ubiquitous leverage from America's relative power position considered globally.[24] Rephrased, states and others should be discouraged from serious misbehaviour because there is a hegemonic and self-appointed American global community policeman. This is not a thoroughly foolish idea, but nonetheless it cannot withstand close scrutiny for authoritativeness. It is tempting to argue that good enough order on the global maritime common is maintained in part by the existence of a dominant US Navy. There is a general deterrent effect discouraging of maritime misbehaviour that flows from military maritime power appreciated existentially. This argument is not wholly unpersuasive, but its virtue is more than offset by its limitations. For example, Somali pirates seem underimpressed by this logic of dissuasion.

There are political benefits to a strategy intended to achieve a general deterrence. Belief in such a benign condition excuses the would-be general deterrer from making specific geopolitical/geostrategic commitments that could prove embarrassing to meet with action. But, the attractions of ambiguity necessarily carry a burden of risk of loss of deterrent weight. Politicians eager to believe that fortune is with them and who are not risk-averse, will be more than ready to read or misread America's lack of specificity of threats as a modesty of interest and determination. This is not to deny that risk-averse policymakers will probably choose to be deterred by general and distinctly latent menaces when they should not be. However, to make that point is to register nothing more insightful than the observation that some politicians are far easier to deter than are others. Moreover, the seriously risk-averse among them are unlikely to need deterring anyway.

It is necessary to admit of exceptions. If ever there was a topic concerning which it is necessary to be open to some unreasonable argument, it is deterrence. This is a subject that seems easier to master in practice than in theory. The core of the explanation for why this should be so lies in its pervasively human nature. When one seeks to unwrap and reveal the connections between geography and politics for strategic choice, one is venturing into a human terrain that far transcends what the unwary policy observer might anticipate to be the meaning of geography.

4.1.2 Geopolitics and Geostrategy: Why and How Does Geography Matter?

Geography is context for human thought and behaviour. It is not an active, intelligent, and self-willed player in the drama of history, though there are occasions when it can seem to warrant identification, duly anthropomorph-ized, as an independent player obedient to some usually malign purpose of its own. Human beings can feel an affinity for a particular geography such that their very identity somehow is dependent upon the integrity of the link between their blood and the soil. While geography needs to be regarded dispassionately as an often contested physical context for human behaviour, in historical experience all too frequently it is valued by people far from dispassionately, or even rationally, let alone reasonably. Because the subject here is the relevance of geography in the form of geopolitical factors bearing on the feasibility of deterrence, the human core to the politics in geopolitics must temper what might seem to be an otherwise sound geographical analysis, were it mistakenly to privilege physical reality. Because people must decide about the political implications of their physical environment, it has to be their beliefs that require emphasis. When one voyages into would-be deterrence country, the mind is more relevant than is physical geography.

It is principally through the mind that geopolitics provides fuel for, as well as resistance to, intended deterrence. The feeling that 'this land' is/has been/ should be/will be 'my land' is exceedingly strong, even in a globalized and variably de-nationalized world. When one considers the logically descending hierarchy from vision of the desirable as to what is believed to be 'right', down through politics, to policy, and then into execution by strategy directing operations and tactics, it is important to note that geography provides political and strategic contextuality to the whole cascade of descending levels of belief and behaviour. Human beings are territorial animals whose affinity for par-ticular terrain is a matter of prudence for security. This geographical associ-ation is expressed politically, and since politics primarily is about power the affinity requires a military dimension. Human self-interest in connection with particular territory finds expression in what have to be termed sentimental and even mystical claims. Many societies have cultures that venerate their physical geography. 'Blood and soil' is a primitive, but nonetheless potent pairing.[25] Early in the twentieth century, Frenchmen were not alone in regarding their soil as sacred in a way that was not accidentally quasi-religious. The road to Verdun that sustained the French Army defending Verdun in 1916 was called *la voie sacrée*. The Mother Russia assaulted by a Teutonic horde in June 1941 was portrayed and regarded in notably sentimental territorial terms. America's Manifest Destiny was a big idea that contained much high ideational content. But, also it carried a clear geographical and geopolitical (indeed *Realpolitik*) message, and that message necessarily had geostrategic implications. Manifest Destiny took Americans from the Alleghenies to California, and thence via Hawaii to the Philippines: it provided a master narrative to explain why it was right and proper that the American empire should expand. Even if geography per se is not destiny, ideas about it can be.[26] The principal challenge to this analysis is not any difficulty in locating the ways in which geography can have political implications. Rather is the problem the difficulty in constraining the search for answers within bounds that allow for meaningful conclusions.

The relationship between geography and politics is more intimate than one might be misled into believing, were one to be unduly isolated ahistorically on the mobile small island that is today. The aphorism to the effect that 'geography is what we make of it' implies a well ordered and stable relationship between people, their society with its polity, and the territory they occupy. Historical perspective, however, brings into focus a sometimes fluid, even oscillating, relationship between soil and polity: frontiers can ebb and flow, and polities fracture, fuse, and divide again. The contestable maxim quoted already which claims that geography is destiny, has been known to suggest to some people that the territory over which they hold sway can and should be augmented, almost certainly at the expense of those currently in residence. Appreciated historically and strategically, geography is not always a given of which people must make what they are able, but rather is an expandable, or shrinkable, quantity. Physical geography is stable, but political geography is not, while even the former has a shifting meaning as technology alters space–time relations.

Geopolitics is regarded here as a house with five rooms: geophysical resources; location; human resources—skills and culture; experience—the past, history, legends, myths; and mental cartography. These categories capture the sources of the political implications of geography. When geopolitics plays to facilitate or hinder deterrence, it functions with fuel from these overlapping categories.

4.2 GEOPHYSICAL RESOURCES

Several generations ago, the authors of textbooks on international politics favoured the presentation of what could be pedestrian details about what used to be known as the 'foundations of national power', or some like rubric. Such necessary, though rarely sparkling, discussion had an influential precedent in Alfred Thayer Mahan's brief treatment in 1890 of the 'general conditions affecting Sea Power'.[27] The first three of his general conditions were geographical position, physical conformation, and extent of territory. Quality can trump quantity, but when quantity is with you there is less need for a quality that may be hard to achieve. Physical geography matters. All aspects of terrain are significant. Indeed, even when the terrain under discussion is bereft of features strongly contributory to natural wealth, that fact of barrenness can have political implications. The wealth necessary for advanced civilization must have geophysical referents. The extent, conformation, and material content of terrain by no means tell the whole geopolitical story, but they are important. It is true to claim that the political meaning of physical geography is what people make of it. But, it is scarcely less true to argue also that some physical geographical settings have been more stimulating than have others of human behaviour geared to the expansion of that ever contestable asset, power. Physical geography provides much of the power base, the fount of wealth fundamentally enabling of politics and strategy. Size is not everything. Very large, but very cold territories, even if amply endowed with mineral resources, do not provide a setting permissive of wealth and hence political power creation and sustainment comparable to that likely to be achievable from territories of comparable extent that are favoured with a more benign climate. 'It is no accident' that Canada has not become a great power. And a similar comment would apply to Argentina, albeit with some caveats pertaining to culture inclusively understood. There can be high strategic value in sheer space, brute terrain one might say. But, as a general rule extensive terrain per se is not a strategic asset. It matters critically where the terrain in question is located and what culture recommends and enables.

4.3 LOCATION

The cartographic coordinates of territory are most literally vital to any and all political and strategic narratives. Whereabouts on the map is the land in question? Location is not a neutral stage for politics and strategy. Latitude and longitude determine climate and weather, and that unavoidable physical reality has near conclusive implications for probabilities in power relations. However, not only does geographical location load the dice heavily in a way favourable or unfavourable for wealth creation, also it determines the political and strategic character of the neighbourhood. Given that virtually all human security communities are territorial, and that territory is an essential multidimensional enabler of a community power that is relative, obviously the geographical coordinates of immediate neighbours and near neighbours are a matter of high significance. Where one is on the map is crucially important. Position, as well as size, territorial shape and conformation of terrain, places one in relation to Others. And that position will have had political and strategic implications throughout the past of one's society and polity. Recall the real estate valuation mantra—'location, location, location'.

Logistically regarded, it is bad news for the United States of America to be located an ocean away in every relevant direction from the main engine of human history on the great 'World Island' of Eurasia–Africa.[28] But, the attenuation of strength imposed by the strategic need to project power at a great distance overseas, has been more than offset by the geopolitical and geostrategic reality that America's nearest continental neighbours pose no menace worthy of note to the homeland. A neighbourhood crowded with worthy rival polities is apt to motivate for high competitive performance, but as the great European civil wars of the short twentieth century demonstrated, also it has a way of encouraging exhausting conflicts.

Physical geography does not determine political and strategic history, but latitude and longitude combine to provide a unique historical stage for every polity there has ever been. It matters greatly that Russia is located as it were between China and peninsular Europe (NATO, EU), just as it does that the United States lies between both Canada and Mexico and Europe and Asia. The location of Belgium and Poland between rival great powers in modern Europe has been a primary source of national misfortune.

4.4 HUMAN RESOURCES, ECONOMY, SKILLS, AND CULTURE

The contest of wills that is a deterrence relationship is conducted by people in organizations on behalf of the legal abstractions with definite physical territories that are states. Even when either deterrer or deterree is not a state, the human dimension to the project often is obscured by scholars who refer to notional dehumanized 'actors', or to political collectivities reified as actors, such as America or Russia. There is sense in biasing analysis to favour arguments that recognize the leverage of considerations of *raison d'état*. Individuals performing official roles on behalf of their polities and conducting the affairs of state from within a governmental structure are not likely to behave as they would were the stakes entirely personal. That said, policy and strategy are decided upon and executed by individual human beings born and bred in particular social and other contexts. A very few politicians rise to perform well at the level of statecraft, but even the most effective statesmen cannot help but be shaped by the influences derivative from a more or less unique geographical setting. In a far less than wholly globalized world, the rich variety of social, economic, and cultural influences upon individuals have consequences for outlook and habits, including habits of mind, that can have significance for deterrence relationships. There is a need for analysts to beware of the 'Orientalist' fallacy, but still there is a powerful case for alertness to Other's values.[29] Strategic rationality, the ability to function purposefully and coherently in relating ends, ways, and means, is a universal and eternal facility.[30] It is as much a mistake to assume patronizingly an irrationality, or even just bizarre exoticism in alien values, as it is to commit the cardinal ethnocentric error of assuming that all foreigners really think like us.[31] In the latter case, the intended deterree of the moment is viewed, for example, as an aspirant American in the most key of respects.

It is necessary not to overcomplicate and overclaim for the meaning of the point registered here. One can make the obvious claim that, geographically regarded, everywhere is somewhat distinctive, and that each human security group (state, tribe, clan, class, extended family, even contestably civilization) has an individual stamp on its thought and behaviour. Obvious or not, this claim can matter greatly. But, what scholars and policymakers need to understand is that just because every individual charged with official performance has been conditioned by culturally acquired, as well as inherited biological, DNA, people, polities, and their challenges also have much in common across space as well as time. Strategic logic, though potentially subject to the conditioning influence of culture, is still strategic and logical. And, *Homo sapiens* is exactly that, a single species, regardless of cultural variations. To seek influence over an adversary via deterrence, coercion, and if necessary by brute force, requires an effort to understand what both parties bring to the trial. The local detail of the adversary's values must be important, because that will shape his relative weighing of perceived interests. However, the distinctive geographical setting that is vital for the shaping and performance of society, economy, and culture, is in no way challenging to the authority of the strategic function of ends, ways, and means. The aspiring deterrer should benefit from cultural intelligence, but he ought not to be looking too hard for 'Otherness'. Most good ideas in the complex realm of strategy cease to be such if they are allowed a hegemonic sway that encourages or requires heroically monocausal reductionism.

4.5 EXPERIENCE: THE PAST, HISTORY, LEGENDS, AND MYTHS

'Nothing comes from nothing, nothing ever could', as *The Sound of Music* affirms. Experience is pervasively geographical. We live in geography and the physical environment impresses itself upon us in so many ways that its influence literally is untrackable. But when a factor is ubiquitous it loses forensic value as a tool for analysis. Although physical geography is stable, political geography often is not. The human past was experienced in a geographical setting that was both a physical 'given' that provided opportunities to be exploited, but also was a source of constraint. Regarded over the *longue durée*, security communities have been able to make and remake some of their own physical geography competitively by choice and determination, with the leverage yielded by the power at their command. In practice, however, collective human experience, the real past, shows how frequently political will fails to triumph. And a potent reason for the frustration even of a strong political will to enforce a favourable redistribution of power has been the vote cast indifferently by physical conditions. It is a cliché about the nature of strategy to claim that 'the enemy too has a vote'. It is scarcely less true to claim that the physical geographical context also commands a vote, even if it is bereft of preference for one human political party or another.[32] Climate as weather has had an eternal and ubiquitous conditioning influence on the practicable possibilities for human behaviour of all kinds, as well as a specific impact on the prospects for political success at particular times and places.[33] It would be an exaggeration to assert that climate is human destiny, but such a claim does have merit. The human experience has been one of survival and even prosperity in the face of geographical adversity. Indeed, physical adversity often has been the trigger that set whole communities in motion in search of literally greener pastures. But, it is necessary to be alert to the pathetic fallacy. Strictly viewed, geography, climate, and weather did not trigger anything in the human past. Geographically adverse conditions provided a challenge that some communities found ways to meet well enough, but others did not. Climate change can provide the principal reason for, say, the westward movement of tribes from Central Asia and beyond towards the Roman (East and) West. But, that geographical trigger, if it be so regarded, has to be pulled effectively by human political action which carries a strategic narrative.

To maintain merit in the proposition that geography is destiny, it is essential that 'Destiny' is not implicitly capitalized and promoted to play a purposefully deterministic role as a strategic agent. For example, while there can be no question that the Russian climate played a, but only a, major role in the Wehrmacht's failure in 1941, there is no less question that the real problem was not so much the climate itself, but rather the inadequacy of German preparation to cope with it. The Russian climate was always going to pose a huge challenge, but the strategic and hence the political intensity of that challenge was within Germany's ability to influence.[34]

I am registering a claim for the importance of physical geography as a factor in history, all the while laying emphasis upon the ability of human beings to overcome geographical difficulties. Whether geography is regarded as a forbidding problem or an opportunity, as a constraint or a stimulating challenge, is a matter that finds answer in factors that transcend the geographical. Somewhat crude anthropology can lead one to claim that whereas some geographies favour, and some all but inhibit, agriculture, those that do not have tended to produce economies and life-styles conducive to the development of predatory warrior skills, habits, and preferences. Nomadic hunters and herdsmen were likely to view settled farming communities as victims for exploitation by domination achieved coercively. Hunting and even food gathering skills had more carry-over value for competence in combat than did those well-honed for farming.

It is ironic that the implications of geography for politics are hard to specify precisely because they are so many and so pervasive. By analogy, today it is impossible to distinguish clearly among land power, sea power, air power, space power, and cyber power, so intimately are they interwoven, interdependent, and sometimes integrated. The human past necessarily is inherently geographical. Plainly, for geography to be accorded the weight that often it should merit as a factor in analysis for policymaking and strategy making there is a need to render it operationally more useful. There is no small danger that geographical content simply collapses into everything else, rendering it frontier-free and hence effectively unusable as an analytical key.

Experience is not always quite as it may appear to the unwary. It is not merely scholastic to insist upon recognition of the distinction between the past and history. The latter should be plural, as histories, because commonplace reference to history, meaning the past, is unintentionally ambiguous. On the one hand there is the true unique past that did happen. Our ability to recover understanding of that past is variably always imperfect and unreliable; even simply to be certain of what occurred, let alone to be able to explain with no room for doubt just what happened and, of most value, why it happened, frequently is a requirement too far. In practice we are obliged to recover the past through the interpretations, which is to say the theories, offered by historians who research and write history(ies). The geographical dimension to the past as incorporated in the history of historians, features both as adequately verified or verifiable narrative and explanation, as well as categories of material attested as such less satisfactorily. In sharply descending order of reliability: there is the objective (actual) past; then there is the history written by historians that honours an obligation to seek and provide supportive evidence; the next step down the factual reliability ladder is the category of stories about the past termed legends, which are believed, at least expected, to be based on some facts; while myths 'are ideas that exempt themselves from any systematic authentication process'.[35] The relevance of this typological pedantry is revealed in the next few paragraphs, which explain that the geography that counts most in a relationship of deterrence may well be more in the mind than the physical environment.

4.6 MENTAL CARTOGRAPHY

Although physical geography has a way of disciplining those who misunderstand it, a particular course in political behaviour will be chosen on the basis of what is believed, not necessarily what verifiably is so. Some potent political beliefs that credibly can have a clear audit trail to would-be deterrent behaviour, literally are neither true nor false in geographical terms. For an important categorical example from all accessible periods of history, consider the mental maps that the statesmen of great powers bring to their duties of statecraft. For example, historian Jeremy Black claims persuasively that '[p]owerful states expect to dominate their neighbours and do not appreciate opposition to this aspiration, as Russia has demonstrated in the Caucasus in the 1990s and 2000s—for example, in its aggressive policy towards Georgia'.[36] Usually there will be some strategically rational, if not always reasonable, grounds for a great power to wish to dominate its neighbourhood geopolitically and geostrategically. However, the logic of statecraft that advises statesmen to seek a friendly near-abroad, readily creeps over the line from recommending a relationship of cooperation to a measure of strategically coercive co-option. Moreover, great powers incline to slide from reason into belief, even moral belief. For example, a reviving Russian Federation judges it prudent for its national security that its geopolitical belt of near-abroad polities comprising erstwhile Soviet peripheral republics, should be more or less obedient to Moscow. This understandable judgement is not only strategically rational, in addition it has some normative authority. A great power may not be globally or continentally hegemonic, but it is near certain to believe that the very fact of its relative greatness entitles it to dominate its neighbours.

Both Russia and the United States believe they are entitled to be hegemonic in their geographical regions. What else did the Monroe Doctrine suggest as it was proclaimed, practised, and occasionally malpractised? It said 'hands off, this [the Americas] is ours. And to the degree that it is not quite ours, politically and strategically, it certainly is not going to belong to any other great power.' Although such *démarches* of a hegemonic geopolitical and geostrategic nature have specific historical contextual meaning, it is not inappropriate to see them as addressed generally 'to whom it may concern'. It is commonplace to contrast a dominant Russian political culture that pre-eminently frames its security narrative in a territorial way, with its American cultural counterpart that is quintessentially ideational and legalistic-institutional.[37] Such a contrast is fairly persuasive, but it is apt to mislead if it is understood to imply that Americans do not frame their security thinking in territorial terms. Americans are not confused about the geography that enables the hegemony they believe is their due as the super-persons owning superpower. Soviet missiles in Cuba constituted not only a material geostrategic move in the central Cold War chess game. Also, those missiles were a normative insult to American understanding of geopolitical propriety. Americans have always known that their state's greatness in the several dimensions of power entitled them to extraordinary influence in Havana. This belief, or conceit, has not been much dented by the political and strategic negation of it by the local Cuban politics enabled by the former Cold War context.

Of course, there are reasonable grounds for the United States to be displeased by Cuba's international course since 1959. However, it is well to recognize that the American mental map of American superpower does not allow any legitimate space to a notably unfriendly and uncooperative offshore island. One can cite in addition to the US example vis-à-vis Cuba, the cases of Russia's perspective upon its 'near abroad', China's view of its status in East Asia, and England's fundamental attitude towards Wales, Scotland, and Ireland. The *Great* Britain that was created legally in 1707 by the Act of Union with Scotland, gave explicit official expression to a great-power attitude, including a matching mental map that already had been fairly authoritative politically and even normatively for nearly 600 years. When projected mechanistically into a global arena, some democratic theory may honour the principle of 'one state—one vote', but that is not the reality of geopolitics and its derivative geostrategies.

Physical geographical realities matter deeply for statecraft, including strategy. Objective truths about space and terrain discipline the flights of human imagination. Most especially do those truths function by impressing their contemporary implications upon the several ways in which statecraft is made manifest. People act on their beliefs, but when those beliefs are thwarted in practice by underanticipated realities, including the geographical, the experience should trigger learning that argues for a course correction to behaviour. The reasons for a shift in policy and strategy may not be strictly geographical. Over Kosovo in 1999, Slobodan Milosevic was obliged to cease to exploit the mental map of most Serbians concerning the rightful territorial possessions of Serbia, because it became dangerously imprudent for him to do otherwise. Cynically exploitative though Milosevic was in his successful effort to excite his fellow Serbs over Kosovo, and even though that province unquestionably was legally Serbian, the political geography at issue was far more psychological than material in its value to Serbs. When a people feel deeply attached to a particular space, the conventional arguments that pertain most obviously to Thucydidean 'fear' and 'interest' can be augmented by his other specified motivation, 'honor'.[38] The Greek general-historian's triptych provides a potently explosive brew; which is the principal reason why war and its warfare have been so characteristic a feature of human history.

The geography of the imagination is revealed and functions in mental maps that contribute to emotions as attitudes and opinions relevant to the feasibility of deterrence. Why is this so? Because, deterrence is human behaviour, and the balance in rival strength of motivation, as well as the balance in rival material strength, is apt to be decisive in the contests of the will that are intended to be episodes of deterrence.

4.6.1 Geopolitics

For the purpose of this enquiry into the geographical perspective on strategy, with its illustrative focus upon deterrence, a minimalist approach has been adopted towards geopolitical theory. The literature on geopolitics that might be of relevance to questions of deterrence is large and varied. If theory is understood inclusively to refer to systematic effort at explanation, geopolitical theory should be capable of functioning to help policymaking and strategy-making at several levels. These levels may not be quite as distinctive as is claimed here, perhaps being better regarded as way-stations on a continuum. Nonetheless, it is important for policymakers and strategists to register these distinctions if they are to make suitable use of geographically charged arguments that often are labelled geopolitical.

4.7 GEOPOLITICS AS EDUCATION, JOURNALISM, AND COMMENTARY

Scholar-educators endeavour to explain in some detail why there is a geographical dimension to politics and to the policies and strategies that politics produces. This literature seeks only to ensure that policy and strategy is appropriately alert to geography and is equipped with geographical concepts; it is not prescriptive. The educators beat the drum for geographical alertness, not (necessarily) for the acceptance of political implications that might be drawn from appreciation of geography.

Between the scholar and the policymaker and strategist lies the zone of journalistic commentary. In terms of theoretical rigour this literature is noticeably light, which is, of course, a necessary condition for its ease of public accessibility. Also, the application of general theory to specific cases nearly always must be controversial. After all, the journalist-commentator needs a story to tell in an engaging manner, and he or she typically personally will add value to the tale with a point of view that has to be presented persuasively.[39] Given that a week, let alone a month or a year, can be a long time in politics regarding policy and strategy debate, it is unavoidable that there is apt to be some tension between the 'presentist' bias of journalism, and the relatively long-term or structural perspective inherent in a subject anchored to the fundamental stability (at least, slow to change) of physical geography. Instant geopolitics come so close to being oxymoronic that essays by journalists that seek to borrow the believed authority of a geopolitical label should carry intellectual health warning notices. There is no discipline of geopolitics to which one can turn for policy guidance. Rather should geopolitics refer to the education in geography for politics that scholars can provide. The geopolitical implications of events are simple, indeed they are all too easy, to explain, though not necessarily understand correctly, if one is forearmed with geopolitical theory fit enough for predictive purpose.

4.8 GEOPOLITICAL GRAND THEORY

To this point no mention has been made of the greatest among Anglo-American grand theorists of geopolitics, Sir Halford Mackinder (1861–1947) and the Dutch-American Nicholas J. Spykman (1893–1943).[40] The third member of the Anglo-(Dutch) American trio of leading, now often elevated to the approving category of 'classical', theorists of geopolitics, Alfred Thayer Mahan (1840–1914), was cited earlier, but with reference to his theory of sea power as education, not his geopolitical theory for application in policy and strategy.[41] As grand theory, geopolitics endeavours not merely to explain why geography matters for politics; in addition it specifies how and where it matters. The step from education to advice is short. Moreover, the step is a proper one. After all, geography does feature significantly in the general theory of strategy, and that is theory for education for practical purposes.[42] There is nothing inappropriate about geopolitical theory with what one might term attitude. It is difficult to see how defence professionals could employ an education in the general potential relevance of geography other than with respect to its particular meaning for them in the present and the near future. That said, politicians, officials, and soldiers need to be alert to the vital distinction between a geopolitical worldview which, at one extreme, simply argues that geography provides vital context to political behaviour and sometimes has an influence beyond what contextual modestly implies, and grand theory at the other extreme with its explicit implications for policy and strategy stated boldly if not imperatively. The theoretical minimalist is content to educate as to the potential relevance of geographical elements. But, the grand theoretical maximalist will organize the physical world conceptually in political and strategic terms for ready intellectual digestion by policymakers in need of guidance, or at least public explanation. The grand theorist may well offer theory fairly ready for use. Moreover, given the global domain of geopolitical grand theory, there will be little about the Earth's physical geography that will not yield to grand theory's grasp and grip for orderly explanation of its political meaning. One need hardly stress the appropriateness of the advice, *caveat emptor*. A typical trouble with grander theory is that it is evidence-proof. A theory that can explain everything is certainly capable of explaining away apparently contradictory data. Cognitive dissonance does not long trouble those thoroughly persuaded by a truly inclusive theory.

The relevance of geopolitical grand theory, as opposed to merely a geographical alertness, to deterrence issues, is not hard to identify. Such theory can provide the understanding that appears to yield the explanation for events framed in geographical terms. Geopolitics all but encourages the creation of grand theory that 'joins up the dots' on a vast canvas. Geopolitical grand theory is neither policy nor strategy neutral, because it specifies relationships that carry implicit, or more, political and strategic recommendations for action. For example, by far the most perceptive and persuasive of geopolitical grand theories, that devised and revised by the British geographer Halford Mackinder, initially was created in 1904 to explain a rapidly evolving menace to the security of his primary concern, the globally dispersed British Empire.[43] Mackinder's intellectual successor, even though he briefly predeceased the Briton, Nicholas Spykman, theorized geopolitically essentially from the perspective of an American concerned most to protect and advance US national security.[44] The details of their theories are not strongly pertinent to this discussion, but what is relevant is the fact that their somewhat rival explanations of the political and strategic meaning of spatial relationships carried explicit implications for policy and strategy. The theories of Mackinder and Spykman explained what should be deterred in territorial geographical terms with political and strategic content. It would be hard to exaggerate the importance of this potential contribution to policy and strategy. This was geopolitical theory for use in practical statecraft and strategy. Mackinder authored a grand historical narrative that was geographical. His narrative identified a Eurasian 'Heartland' power as posing an ever possible, though periodically seriously menacing, threat effectively to unify the 'World Island' of Eurasia–Africa. This unification would translate as a polity so well resourced that it should be able to rule the whole world. The theory was well understood in the United States in the 1940s, and it played some role in explaining the need for, as well as intellectually legitimizing, what was adopted by the United States as its policy and grand strategy of containment.[45] And, need one point out, the central pillar in the US-led containment of the Soviet Union for nearly half a century was a strategy keyed to nuclear threat designed to deter, rather than deny by active defence.

4.8.1 Geopolitics at Work

It is useful to distinguish between modest and ambitious claims for the salience of geopolitics to the relevance and feasibility of deterrence. The former strives to confine its argument to what it suggests is, or can be, geographical fuel for politics. The latter is not content merely to fuel journeys of geopolitical reasoning, but rather provides explanation of whither the geographical fuel will, or at least could, transport politics. By rough analogy, if geopolitics as raw geography is content to supply the ingredients from which a wide range of meals might be concocted, ambitious geopolitics as high theory specifies the 'specials' on the menu. Mackinder and Spykman, notwithstanding their differences over the respective strengths of the Eurasian Heartland and Rimland,[46] explained to Britons and then to Americans why the age-old struggle for bi- (even tri-, with Africa) continental domination was of the utmost consequence to them. Untidy though it may appear, it is appropriate to be inclusive rather than exclusive in explanation of the political implications of geography, which is, after all, the most basic definition of geopolitics. The discussion that follows is organized in the form of four claims that are raids planned to interrogate plausible claims for geopolitics.

First, physical geography as resources provides potent stakes for political conflict. It may be true to claim that 'geography does not argue, it simply is',[47] but it is also true to argue that political ownership of tracts of terrain, stretches of water, and airspace, have been a steady motive for political behaviour. Access to the resources of the Earth and the right to exploit them always has been a fundamental requirement as a basis for the power that is central to politics. Although politics is about values and ideas as well as the distribution of power (understood as influence and the right to command, albeit legitimately as authority), the condition of the latter decides whose values and ideas enjoy a privileged position. Geography impinges upon politics because it is the source for the material referents necessary for political behaviour. Whatever the political narrative, in whatever period, and regardless of the stage of technological and social development, there has to be a physical geographical story unique and essential to the historical case in question. Much as the strategy function expressed in the triptych of ends, ways, and means is authoritative eternally and universally, notwithstanding the open-ended variability of its details in application, so physical geography always plays politically and strategically.

Apparently plausible challenges to the claim just recorded do not survive close scrutiny. For example, one might try to argue that security communities engage in political conflict for many reasons, including some that are not obviously geographical in reasonable assessment. The most suitable reply to this argument takes several forms, but it has to begin by asserting that regardless of the character of polities' motives in conflict, their antagonism must have physical, political, and strategic geographical referents. Human politics and strategy necessarily are conducted in physical geography: we cannot function outside such. One or more of land, sea, air, orbital space, and cyberspace must be the context within which our political quarrels are pursued. In human conflict the plot will be political, but the stage must be physical. Moreover, political struggles that are fuelled heavily by ideas, the appalling recurrent record of religious and other substantially ideological wars, for example, invariably have consequences for territorial influence which, in its turn, enables a firmer, if contested grip upon human minds.

For another example of the ubiquitous and perennial relevance of geography, consider claims for the meaning of competition in the virtual reality of cyberspace. Does the placelessness of cyberspace trump old fashioned physical geography?[48] Certainly cyber warfare collapses time and space at close to the speed of light, but so what? The immateriality of cyberspace only appears to be supra-geographical. In reality, cyber behaviour and misbehaviour is only strategically significant because of its ultimately material consequences. Cyberspace is an artificial creation by material agencies with a physical infrastructure that has geographical coordinates; it may be everywhere and therefore nowhere in particular, but such cannot be said for cyber warriors, their computers, or the behaviours influenced by the uses made of cyberspace.[49]

Second, territorial association lends credibility to efforts both to achieve and resist deterrence. Aside from political commitment to territory judged reasonably to allow for more or less discretion, there is a particular quality of human political territorial association that is in a class of its own for shaping the prospects for success with a strategy of deterrence. Herman Kahn explained this point half a century ago. He distinguished among three types of deterrence. He wrote: '*Type I Deterrence* is the deterrence of a direct attack. It is widely believed that if the United States were directly attacked, its response would be automatic and unthinking.'[50] He proceeded to define his '*Type II Deterrence . . .* as using strategic threats to deter an enemy from engaging in very provocative acts, other than a direct attack on the United States itself.'[51] Finally, '*Type III Deterrence . . .* refers to acts that are deterred because the potential aggressor is afraid that the defender or others will take limited actions, military or non-military, that will make the aggression unprofitable.'[52]

Kahn argued persuasively that although his 'Type I Deterrence' can fail, it does not lack for credibility. He reasoned that it should not be a problem to persuade a putative deterree that he would trigger an all but automatic US (nuclear) military response were he to attack US home territory. While it might be a challenge to convince enemies that one really cares deeply about foreign soil, it is not difficult to assert credibly an open ended commitment to the protection of native sod.

There are strategically rational reasons for deep commitment to homeland security. In addition, often there is a quality of commitment to a particular space in physical geography that is politically owned which transcends strategically rational cost-benefit analysis. Kahn applied his logic of nuclear deterrence to the hardest of hypothetical cases—hardest because of the catastrophic character of nuclear risks. On the one hand, he favoured a determined US effort to be able to wage and survive a nuclear war. But, on the other hand, he was discussing the extreme category of historical cases wherein national annihilation might be the confidently predictable consequence of a failure of deterrence. Whereas his logic for 'Type I Deterrence' is incontestably sound for scenarios not involving WMD, it is at least tolerably compelling even for nuclear contexts. The commitment to one's homeland generally is held to override the prudence that otherwise might dominate strategy with self-deterrent effect.

Soil is not just land. For we humans it can be what the French emotively mean by the earthy word *terroir*—it can be our own sacred native national soil. When the emotions behind the politics propelling strategy are of this visceral kind, a rigorously rational education in the 'grammar' of deterrence will not be fit enough for purpose.[53] The feasibility of deterrence can depend critically upon the very human emotions that tie particular people to specific tracts of physical geography. Strategic analysis that strives rigorously and even metrically to match menaces to anticipated estimates of intended deterree interest, are more likely than not to miss their mark if they neglect the associative element in the human relationship to the geographical environment. Threats to take action against a foreign land 'unless . . .' may well fail because they rest upon assessment of enemy interests that undervalues the quality of emotion in the geographical nexus between intended deterree and the relevant geographical stage. In this case the 'logic' of policy to which Clausewitz refers will be heavily indebted to the first of the three elements in his trinitarian theory of war, the passion of the people.[54] The categories in his trinity are porous.

There should be maximum deterrent reward from the posing of threats to the highest values of the enemy. But, in action as spurs to behaviour those values can vitiate expectations for the early limitation of hostilities. Almost any tract of land is likely to be regarded as more than mere geography by the people who own it, and sometimes by those who believe they should own it. Householders as homeowners have been known to behave imprudently when their domestic sanctuaries (homes) are violated by uninvited intruders, so security communities are apt to believe that any and all measures are justified in defence of their (currently) native land. This argument exemplifies why it is that would-be deterrers and intended deterrees have to consider the whole of the equation that specifies that 'threat = capability × motivation'. The will to act and the will to resist are not reliably computable from material grand strategic, let alone narrowly military, metrics.

Third, credibility in geographical association for effective deterrence is not reliably discretionary. It may not be essential for territory to be owned politically and legally for one to be able to deter attacks upon it with high confidence, but such qualities of possession should help. Because deterrence is a human enterprise, as well as a political and strategic one, there is no way in which a polity can be absolutely certain that a prospective bid to deter either will or will not succeed. However, since the would-be deterrer may succeed or fail depending upon foreign perceptions of the quality of his concern for the stakes at issue, the more plausible the deterrer's attachment to those stakes, the more likely he is to be successful. Americans do not need to persuade anyone that they care deeply about potential damage to their American homeland, with all its resources, human and material. Moreover, America's human assets, and at least some of its non-human ones, are valued for their own sakes, not only instrumentally for their assessable strategic worth. Hence, the generally convincing logic of Kahn's 'Type I Deterrence'. Ironically, it is that very depth, indeed that inalienable, care about Americans by Americans, that renders a strategy of deterrence especially problematic. It is exactly because America's geography in all meanings is so beloved by Americans, that American state-craft can have difficulty trying to deter attacks upon distant foreign lands that might lead to a process of violent escalation that would place the American homeland in the most deadly peril. 'Ours' and 'not (really) ours' is a distinction crucial in the construction of deterrence theory and the conduct of attempted deterrence practice.

It is by no means a simple matter to persuade people that implausible promises would be honoured in the dire event. It may be undemanding of American competence in policy and strategy to convince those who might need convincing that awesomely bad consequences for them would flow from any assault upon America itself. But, to threaten or even attack an American ally, friend, or candidate friend is likely to be judged a challenge of smaller magnitude. Georgia was not a US ally in 2008, but it had been declared to be an American friend. Indeed, so much was this widely advertised to be so that Georgia appeared set on the road to NATO membership. The Bush Administration made it known that it favoured such a development, and notably warm words of mutual admiration passed back and forth between Washington and Tbilisi. Far from this unmistakable political romance failing to deter Russian aggression in 2008, rather did it fuel Moscow's determination to reassert some of its hegemonic and erstwhile ownership rights over Georgia. The United States was angry, more than a little humiliated, but ultimately impotent. Had Georgia been admitted to NATO membership, as had the Baltic states, it is unlikely, though not impossible that Russia would have dared risk the political and strategic ambush that it set and executed for an imprudent Georgia (and America) in 2008.

The Georgian case in 2008 is especially illuminating for the theory and practice of deterrence. Georgia is regarded by Russia as rightfully 'theirs', albeit temporarily politically estranged. Russia defines its security mainly in geographical terms, unsurprisingly given the location of its territory in, and as, the 'Heartland' of Eurasia. In Moscow's eyes, Georgia: is strategically 'theirs' because it is in the very 'near abroad', and they are, or aspire to be again, the regional hegemon; is 'theirs' by historic right of conquest and rule, and only recent loss; and its strategic significance is high both because of its location and because its political fate tells a story that has profound political meaning to and for all whom it may concern. The Georgian government appeared to believe that it was becoming a member of America's 'gang', which is to say NATO. However, the 'becoming' proved a critical qualifier. In the event of challenge, as in 2008, Russia demonstrated that it cared more about Georgia than did the United States. Despite the mutual US–Georgian dalliance, for Americans Georgia was a far off and exotic country about which they did not care enough to confront Russians militarily. *De facto*, there had been a road-test of dissuasion, if not quite of deterrence. The United States seemed not to have understood that it would need to deter Russian aggression, and in the event Washington decided to pretend not to define Russian misbehaviour as a challenge.[55] This may have been prudent on the US's part.

The Georgian illustration emphasizes the significance of geography—physical, political, economic (energy in, through, and from the Caucasus region), and strategic. Georgia's geography, with the history it has staged, manifestly has a profound relevance to the feasibility of American authored deterrence on its behalf. It is interesting to deploy some more words of the ever-quotable Herman Kahn. In 1960 he wrote that

> If we wish to have our strategic air force contribute to the deterrence of provocation, it must be credible that we are willing to take one or more of the above actions [military measures on an escalating scale: CSG]. Usually the most convincing way to look willing is to be willing.[56]

Kahn ought to be correct. His assertion sounds plausible. Alas, his reasoning is flawed, or at least is likely to mislead. Even though it should be easier to look willing if one actually is willing, there is no evading the sovereignty of the intended deterree's right to decide not to be impressed. No matter how willing one really is, deterrence can only work if the deterree believes you, and even then he may decide to trust to luck and not desist from his political and strategic course.

Deterrence is complex, uncertain, and perilously all too human. Some Cold War era theorizing suggested to the unwary that the prospects for successful pre-war, and if need be intra-war, deterrence (i.e. coercion or compellence), could be enhanced by skill in the art of political commitment.[57] Because deterrence is highly situational to time, place, and circumstance it is perilous to venture generalities about feasibility. But, for my purpose here it suffices to register the salience of a geographical dimension to deterrence. The clearest way to explain the core meaning of this claim is to affirm the significance of the homeland/foreign distinction. As Thomas C. Schelling wrote in 1966: 'As a tentative approximation—a very tentative one—the difference between homeland and everything "abroad" is the difference between threats that are inherently credible, even if unspoken, and the threats that have to be made credible.'[58] In the 1960s and early 1970s, the United States failed either to deter or to coerce and compel North Vietnam to cease its violently active commitment to conquer the South. A major problem with deterrence is that it cannot be guaranteed to succeed by a sufficiency of skill. There are some possible commitments to action which no measure of skill will render sufficiently credible in the estimation of concerned foreigners; these are 'wicked problems'. Contrary to the implication of Kahn's logic, it will not matter that one is determined to act, at the least to behave dangerously, if the adversary either declines to believe you or believes you but is insufficiently impressed by the damage he anticipates suffering.

It should be true to claim that deterrence can be facilitated and enabled by cunning statecraft effected by artistry in political commitment. However, it is an error to believe that a polity has discretionary authority over the geographical writ of its sufficiently credible deterrence efforts. Success with deterrence cannot be achieved strictly as a triumph of the will, directed artistically or otherwise. Deterrence is a game that more than one must play. If your adversaries are not impressed by a contingent promise intended to have deterring effect because they choose not to believe that you care as much as do they about a geographically referenced issue, no artistry will compensate adequately for their 'cartographic psychology'.[59] Improbable and hence implausible commitments typically require physical demonstration of resolve if they are to overcome a substantially geographically shaped expectation of acquiescence. Examples include the American commitment to sustain blockaded Berlin in 1948–9 and to defend South Korea in 1950, and the British determination to eject Argentinian invaders of the Falklands in 1982. In each case purposefully focused pre-crisis deterrence had been weak or absent, but even had it been attempted it might well have been discounted. Cartographic psychology would seem to assign all of Berlin to Soviet hegemony, all of Korea to the strongest local force, and the Falklands to their giant, if overseas, regional neighbour.

Fourth, the mental maps and metaphors drawn and drawn upon by geopolitical theory shape assessments bearing on the need for, and feasibility of, deterrence. Armed with Big Concepts from geopolitical theory, the policymaker and strategist is equipped with grand designs that make sense enough to minds predisposed to find them agreeable. The geopolitical theories that claim to explain at least the broad structure and essential dynamics of world history have some potential to inspire and encourage political and strategic choices.

It is plausible to argue that geopolitical theory can be deployed as an expedient legitimizer for power politics. Particularly if one is able to suggest a strong element of geographical pre-determination about events, then geopolitical theory may provide an intellectually semi-respectable cover story for one's behaviour. However, it would be a mistake to dismiss all geopolitical high theory as vacuous nonsense, pretentious nonsense, cynically self-serving nonsense, or as all three combined. There is insight and sometimes persuasive understanding of the *longue durée* of world history in geopolitical theory. One should not condemn what appear to be honest theories just because they are misused. Clausewitz's *On War* offers education to all, for the unprincipled dictator as much as for the well intentioned defender of civilized values, much as nuclear physics can serve any political intent. For good or for ill, geopolitical ideas organize what otherwise can appear as a chaotic reality that eludes comprehension. A peril in such service by geopolitical theories is that they seek to explain too much. 'Magic geography' can suggest seductively that geographical relationships are more, or less, geopolitically and geostrategically threatening, depending upon the motives behind, and skill in the artwork.[60] Grand geopolitical theory is more than capable of joining up that which truly is scarcely connected at all, and certainly is not connected in the suggested way. For example, persuasive cartography can appear to illustrate, even demonstrate to the credulous, the danger of falling state 'dominoes'. And yet, geopolitical theory can imply political and strategic relationships that need to be suggested. For a leading case in point, the only somewhat contrasting Heartland–Rimland theories of Mackinder and Spykman do help, though only help rather than make definitive sense of the course of world history.

Geopolitical theory has proffered useful advice for American and British statecraft in particular. It is not wise to dismiss grand geopolitical theory as does Jeremy Black when he complains that '[i]f it is seen along the line of Mackinder's "he who controls the Eurasian Heartland controls the world" or similar adages, then geopolitics is too vague and of use largely for rhetorical purposes'.[61] Big ideas, even would-be hegemonic concepts, are valuable, though there is need to be wary of them. Policy and strategy are devised pragmatically and expediently, but their context usually includes some normative vision of how things ought to be, as well as a typically vague general notion of desirable goals and strategies that should advance progress towards realization of such vision. Behaving pragmatically, the statesman and the strategist are likely to be somewhat educated, possibly miseducated, by a distinctively geographical (evolving) revelation as to whither he or she would prefer to move. Statesmen and strategists need a comprehensive grasp of the context for their decisions, and geopolitical theory provides just that. There is always the danger that such theory will offer more advice more seductively than the evidence can support. Ideas can be hazardous as well as helpful to public security. But, by analogy, the fact that motor cars kill is not reason enough to ban motoring.

4.8.2 Deterrence is Geopolitical and Therefore Geographical *(Inter Alia)*

Deterrence needs to be understood as many things, one among which is that it is the product of a geopolitical relationship. The political implications of physical geography frequently have meaning for the feasibility or otherwise of deterrence. Not only must all human behaviour have a geographical context, in addition identifiably geographical influences can shape the decisions of security communities.

Geography is a conditioning factor for political and strategic behaviour. Physical geography is not an autonomous agent intruding upon human security affairs. Nonetheless, geography in all its physical variations does enable and disable particular human political and strategic projects. The local geography of terrain and climate act via economic necessity and opportunity upon political will and strategic choice. Horse-riding armies of nomads were all but propelled by climate change from East-Central Asia upon a collision course that drove them piledriver-like upon the settled civilizations of the Middle East and Europe. The Vikings were not just violent tourists bent upon loot, fun, and glory. They were motivated to shift by brutal geography, and their raids, expeditions, and migratory movement had great political significance for what eventually became Russia and the entire western and southern fringe of peninsular Europe. The political importance of geography varies from historical case to case, but to claim that it is always a factor of some significance, and often is a matter of high relevance, is beyond serious challenge. Jeremy Black is persuasive when he argues as follows:

> However, if what is meant by geopolitics is that geography is an essential factor in understanding a country's foreign policy, then geopolitics is very important. For example, it is near impossible to understand the history of British and Russian foreign policies without taking into consideration their geographic circumstances.[62]

Beyond serving as a conditioning factor for human thought and behaviour, physical geography comprises assets of variable worth to societies that are more, or less, well equipped to exploit them. Geography is an asset and therefore is a stake with value that attracts competitive human behaviour. People fight not only in geography, but also for geography. Assuredly, not all of human conflict is about territory, literally and directly. However, to claim that political and strategic history must have geographical referents risks understating the political salience of physical geography. People can be motivated by ideas, but whatever their mixture of motives, when ideas are translated into action geography as potential net enabler or disabler plays a role. America's continental size, indeed effective near insularity—to risk giving offence to Mexicans and Canadians—is on balance a robust source of national security. Unfortunately, most assets inherited and acquired have some downside. America's geographical isolation has posed an enduring challenge to its ability to extend US-generated deterrent effect over distant polities. Wherever and whenever one looks historically, the spore of geographical content unmistakably was present. To cite but a single, albeit almost grotesquely obvious, example, how could one begin to understand the contemporary Middle East were one to ignore the geographical elements of the grand narrative? The land of modern Israel that is the national homeland for the Jewish people is viewed very much as a value, virtually regardless of its intrinsic physical resources. By way of sharp contrast, how could one aspire to make sense of the Arab world today were one to pay scant attention to the mineral facts of the oil industry and its multidimensional consequences?

Human psychological attachment to particular local terrain, and sometimes to the notional geography of mental maps as imagined geography, can be even more important for political and strategic decision-making than is physical geography itself. The latter assuredly has the last word as a limitation upon what the imagination can achieve when translated into action, but the former is what drives decisions on behaviour. In historical times, the British Isles remained off-shore to continental Europe. That stability of physical geography has been permissive of radical shifts in 'British' attitudes towards their political identity. Are Britons European or something else, apart—and are they 'Britons'? Moreover, Great Britain, the United Kingdom, is a modern invention that rested upon the political hegemony that reflected the military superiority of England. Most of the Irish deny any political legitimacy to the concept of the 'British Isles', while many Scots similarly do not accept the thesis that geographical unity must mean geopolitical unity also. Attitudes towards identity have potent influence upon state policy and strategy. For another case in point, does the US location in North America imply the correctness of an identity keyed to a secure sanctuary, by and large effectively isolated by oceanic distances from most of the troubles of less happy lands? Or, is North America to be regarded as an impregnable base—a kind of modern variant of Byzantine Constantinople with its triple Theodosian land walls—from which Americans can venture forth to impose order and do good in the world, secure in the knowledge that their homeland is all but untouchable by malefactors? The idea of sacred native soil can have profound meaning for the feasibility of deterrence.

Consider the episode of conflict over the Serbian province of Kosovo in 1999. That land, though populated in the 1990s largely by Muslim Albanians and not by Serbian Orthodox Christians, nonetheless was regarded by most Serbs as especially sacred to them, indeed to their historically stamped identity. This widespread Serbian sentiment was hugely exploitable by then President Slobodan Milosevic. He could and did appeal to Serbian legends from the fifteenth century, 'Balkan ghosts' indeed, in order to excite support at home, to justify brutality against the Albanian majority in Kosovo—a brutality that was matched in quality if not quantity by the victim population.[63] Also, the close historical and somewhat legendary Serbian national association with Kosovo was exploited by Milosevic as a source of credibility for counterdeterrence. He hoped that the historical narrative of geographical association reasserted as an inseparable stapling of Serbians to Kosovo, would enable him to avoid being a designated deterree, let alone the object of a campaign of coercion by NATO. Since the relational variable that is deterrence depends upon human will, Milosevic sought to boost NATO's estimate of his will by exploitation of Serbs' known sentimental attachment to Kosovo. History abounds with examples of assertion, sometimes competing assertions, of national geographical association.

Although the assertion of historical association is manipulable for political theatre, it is not necessarily *ipso facto* only a constructed reality. Most security communities have some variant of the sacred soil legend, not merely myth, as a component of their identity. And such legends, usually somewhat rooted in an actual past, have consequence for the feasibility of deterrence. Understood inclusively, not solely in a religious sense, the somewhat geographical concept of Holy Places has eternal and universal relevance.

The geography in geopolitical theory can have profound influence upon the need for, and prospects of success with, deterrence. States may need to be deterred over geographical stakes that can be presented as geopolitical anomalies and anachronisms. For some examples: Britain periodically has to discourage Spain from exerting pressure over Gibraltar (acquired by the Treaty of Utrecht in 1713); Argentina has needed to be deterred, coerced, and defeated over the Falkland Islands, seemingly an anachronistic colony; while episodically in the Cold War the erstwhile American, British, and French sectors of Berlin, collectively in the character of West Berlin, were the focus of a relationship of deterrence at its most dangerous. Moving from the small, if dangerous, to the very large picture, geopolitical theory provides grand narratives that claim to help explain the course of millennia of history. A Truman Administration armed intellectually with Halford Mackinder's Heartland theory of geopolitics, with the value added by George F. Kennan's essentialist theory of Russian/Soviet (mis)behaviour, was provided with a global geographical context pre-sorted and ready for policy and strategic treatment. The policy and the strategy were packaged and explained as containment, though many people were confused over whether containment was a political 'end' or a strategy.[64] Similarly, though less persuasively, it was easier for the Kennedy and Johnson administrations to make sense for US national security of events in South-East Asia, when geopolitical theory provided an explanation of the structure and dynamics of what was perceived as a challenge. For all its crudity, perhaps because of its crude simplicity, the theory of (falling) dominoes served as the master rationale for an escalating American commitment to the region.[65] Geopolitical theory could explain why, and how much, it mattered to America that South Vietnam should be helped to resist coerced communization.

Even when it is possibilistic rather than deterministic, geopolitics as theory can be fit enough to be enlisted in the service of guidance for policy and strategy.[66] Whether or not the United States would choose to intervene in the Second World War in Europe could not be predicted by geopolitical theory, but that theory could explain why it should do so, and therefore why logically one could anticipate that it would.[67] Had Adolf Hitler sought actively to deter American intervention, instead of declaring war gratuitously on 11 December 1941, part of the difficulty of his task would have been to counter the influence of a particular geopolitical theory over American minds. Americans had been told why the domination of Eurasia by a single state or coalition would be incompatible with US national security in the Americas in the medium-to-long term. When America went to war in 1941, admittedly as a consequence of compelling events, it seemed to be well armed with a geopolitical theory that made sense of the conflict. Furthermore, that theory applied no less well to US relations with the Soviet Union after 1945. Big organizing ideas matter as providers of a framework of assumptions within which the details of policy, grand and military strategy, and military force posture can be determined and executed as cohesively as human frailty, contingency, and a somewhat adaptive enemy permit.

The relevance and feasibility of deterrence is highly situational. It is always conducted in a particular geographical context, but this does not mean that geography rules, not even as geopolitics. The influence of physical and psychological geography can be swamped by other pressures. Often there is an apparent logic to brute physical geography, or to a favoured mental cartography. But, there is always likely to be a logic of cost and benefit estimation, of strategic reasoning attentive to the coherence of ends, by suitable ways, with necessary means, that is the 'last man standing' in a policy debate. There is an unequal dialogue, to borrow Eliot A. Cohen's loaded concept, metaphorically between geography and politics with its servant strategy.[68] Geography translated into geopolitics usually is more discretionary than directive, while even in geopolitical form it is interpreted as offering possibilities as well as imposing costs as limitations, rather than commanding certainty of outcomes. In common with such other large ideas as culture or air power, geography as geopolitics is potent indeed, provided one does not expect too much of it. The culminating point of the value in theory is hard to divine in practice, but, hard or not, that point is there. Deterrence is geographical. Geopolitics is important for the relevance and feasibility of deterrence. But, deterrence is by no means only geopolitical.

Deterrence as a relational variable is both human, with all that that implies, as well as strategically rational, though not always strategically reasonable in the views of all interested parties. Both the human and the rational, if not necessarily reasonable, dimensions of deterrence performance—by would-be deterrers as well as intended deterrees—can be influenced by the perceived political implications of geography. And those implications flow from objective physical as well as psychological realities. The general theory of deterrence can only educate, it cannot provide doctrine specifically applicable to particular historical cases. Geography matters, but exactly how much it matters is decided by the narrative of the situation at issue.

NOTES

1. Hans W. Weigert, *Generals and Geographers: The Twilight of Geopolitics* (New York: Oxford University Press, 1942), 4.
2. Robert D. Kaplan, 'The Geography of Chinese Power', *Foreign Affairs*, 89 (May/June 2010), 22.
3. Margaret MacMillan, *Peacemakers: The Paris Conference of 1919 and its Attempt to End War* (London: John Murray, 2001), 132.
4. This argument is foundational in Colin S. Gray, *The Strategy Bridge: Theory for Practice* (Oxford: Oxford University Press, 2010).
5. See Halford J. Mackinder, *Democratic Ideals and Reality* (1919, 1942; New Brunswick, NJ: Transaction Publishers, 2007). A recent biographer of Mackinder has written that '[i]n 1941 and 1942 Mackinder's ideas became well known in the US as publications like *Newsweek, Life,* and *Reader's Digest* carried articles on geopolitics, the Heartland, and Mackinder himself. In 1942 Mackinder's *Democratic Ideals and Reality* was reissued with an introduction written by the respected commentator Edward Mead Earle.' Brian W. Blouet, 'Halford Mackinder and the Pivotal Heartland', in Blouet, ed., *Global Geostrategy: Mackinder and the Defence of the West* (Abingdon: Frank Cass, 2005), 6. Earle was not friendly as a contemporary assessor of the other giant of geopolitical theory at the time, Nicholas John Spykman. See Spykman, *America's Strategy in World Politics: The United States and the Balance of Power* (1942; New Brunswick, NJ: Transaction Publishers, 2007); and Edward Mead Earle, 'Power Politics and American World Policy', *Political Science Quarterly*, 58 (March 1943), 94–106.
6. See Holger H. Herwig, '*Geopolitik*: Haushofer, Hitler, and Lebensraum', in Colin S. Gray and Geoffrey Sloan, eds., *Geopolitics, Geography, and Strategy* (London: Frank Cass, 1999), 218–41. Period piece analyses include: Derwent Whittlesey, 'Haushofer: The Geopolitician', in Edward Mead Earle, ed., *Makers of Modern Strategy: Military Thought from Machiavelli to Hitler* (Princeton: Princeton University Press, 1941), 388–411; id., *German Strategy of World Conquest* (London: Robinson, 1942); and Robert Strausz-Hupé, *Geopolitics: The Struggle for Space and Power* (1942; New York: Arno, 1972).
7. See Adolf Hitler, *Mein Kampf* (New York: Fredonia Classics, 2003), esp. 606–7, 610, 612, 622.
8. See Herwig, '*Geopolitik*'.
9. Geoffrey Parker, *Geopolitics: Past, Present and Future* (London: Pinter, 1998) is helpful, as is Jeremy Black, *Geopolitics* (London: The Social Affairs Unit, 2009). Colin Flint, *Introduction to Geopolitics* (Abingdon: Routledge, 2007), delivers on its title and is good of its kind. John O'Loughlin, ed., *Dictionary of Geopolitics* (Westport, CT: Greenwood Press, 1994), is a goldmine of useful information. For

geopolitically framed history, see Brian W. Blouet, *Geopolitics and Globalization in the Twentieth Century* (London: Reaktion Books, 2001) and Jakub J. Griegiel, *Great Powers and Geopolitical Change* (Baltimore: Johns Hopkins University Press, 2006).

10. See Everett C. Dolman, *Astropolitik: Classical Geopolitics in the Space Age* (London: Frank Cass, 2002).

11. Geographer Saul B. Cohen offers an acceptable alternative definition when he claims that '[t]he essence of geopolitical analysis is the relation of international political power to the geographical setting'. *Geography and Politics in a Divided World* (London: Methuen, 1964), 24. My definition is preferred because I deem it undesirable and gratuitous to include the qualifier 'international' to the wording.

12. I register this argument in my essay, 'Inescapable Geography', in Gray and Sloan, eds., *Geopolitics, Geography and Strategy*, 161–77.

13. Carl von Clausewitz, *On War*, trans. Michael Howard and Peter Paret (1832–4; Princeton, NJ: Princeton University Press, 1976), 132.

14. Clausewitz, *On War*, 605.

15. Justice Oliver Wendell Holmes, Jr., quoted in Robert J. McMahon, *Dean Acheson and the Creation of an American World Order* (Washington, DC: Potomac Books, 2009), 14.

16. See Christian Reus-Smith and Duncan Snidal, eds., *The Oxford Handbook of International Relations* (Oxford: Oxford University Press, 2008). This ambitious, massive, and potently inclusive monument to academic scholarship manages to have no explicitly geographical/geopolitical essay, while its subject index contains no entry for geography. These are extraordinary exclusions.

17. The sharp 'cultural turn' in recent strategic studies is examined closely and found seriously wanting in Patrick Porter, *Military Orientalism: Eastern War Through Western Eyes* (London: C. Hurst, 2009).

18. John Keegan, *A History of Warfare* (London: Hutchinson, 1993), is guilty of conceptual imperialism in favour of an unwise expansion of the domain allowed to culture.

19. Clausewitz, *On War*, 566.

20. Judy Pearsall and Bill Trumble, eds., *The Oxford English Reference Dictionary*, 2nd edn. (Oxford: Oxford University Press, 1996), 581.

21. See the fine, densely granular military geographical study by Harold Winters, *Battling the Elements: Weather and Terrain in the Conduct of War* (Baltimore: Johns Hopkins University Press, 1998).

22. The idea of a 'loss of strength gradient' (LSG) is fundamental to Clausewitz's argument on 'the diminishing force of the attack'. *On War*, 527–8. Modern social scientific explanation of the LSG is provided by economist Kenneth Boulding in his *Conflict and Defense: A General Theory* (New York: Harper and Brothers, 1962), 79, 245–7, 268–70.

23. Strategic theory seeking to explain cyberspace and cyber warfare remains thin, but is growing rapidly. Studies meriting honourable mention include: John Arquilla and David Ronfeldt, eds., *In Athena's Camp: Preparing for Conflict in the Information Age* (Santa Monica, CA: RAND, 1997); David J. Lonsdale, *The Nature of War in the Information Age: Clausewitzian Future* (London: Frank Cass, 2004);

Martin C. Libicki, *Conquest in Cyberspace: National Security and Information Warfare* (Cambridge: Cambridge University Press, 2007); id., *Cyberdeterrence and Cyberwar* (Santa Monica, CA: RAND, 2009; and Franklin D. Kramer, Stuart H. Starr, and Larry K. Wentz, eds., *Cyberpower and National Security* (Washington, DC: Potomac Books, 2009). The more academic works are complemented usefully by two popular works: Richard A. Clarke and Robert K. Knake, *Cyber War: The Next Threat to National Security and What To Do About It* (New York: Ecco, 2010); and James Gleick, *The Information: A History, A Theory, A Flood* (London: Fourth Estate, 2011). David J. Betz and Tim Stevens, *Cyberspace and the State: Toward a Strategy for Cyber-power* (Abingdon: Routledge for The International Institute for Strategic Studies, 2011), succeeds in being scholarly yet accessible. A dictionary definition advises that cyberspace is '[t]he three-dimensional environment, or space, of virtual reality, generated by computer'. Also, it is '[t]he notional space in which electronic communication takes place over computer networks'. John Lackie, ed., *Chambers Dictionary of Science and Technology* (Edinburgh: Chambers, 2007), 307.

24. The now fairly authoritative, though in the opinion of this theorist, contestable, proposition that deterrence can be either, or both, of a 'general' or an 'immediate' kind, is advanced in Patrick M. Morgan, *Deterrence: A Conceptual Analysis* (Beverly Hills, CA: Sage Publications, 1977), ch. 2. In addition, there is much to recommend Morgan's later book, *Deterrence Now* (Cambridge: Cambridge University Press, 2003) and also Lawrence Freedman, *Deterrence* (Cambridge: Polity Press, 2004).

25. Hitler's Aryan *völkisch* state required more soil that could be tilled by sturdy *Völk* who would be healthy, racially superior soldier-farmers. Somewhat prematurely, Nazi Germany began the process of moving 30 million 'volkisch' colonists eastwards into the conquered Slavic lands before the necessary military victory in the East was secure. Max Hastings, *All Hell Let Loose: The World at War, 1939–1945* (London: Harper Press, 2011), 154. *Mein Kampf* is admirably explicit. Klaus P. Fischer, *Nazi Germany: A New History* (London: Constable, 1995), 163–74, is a brief commentary on Nazi ideology as it was presented in *Mein Kampf.*

26. See Felix Driver, *Geography Militant: Cultures of Exploration and Empire* (Oxford: Blackwell, 2001).

27. Alfred Thayer Mahan, *The Influence of Sea Power upon History, 1660–1783* (1890; London: Methuen, 1965), ch. 1.

28. Mackinder, *Democratic Ideals and Reality*, 62.

29. Porter, *Military Orientalism*, warns effectively against the 'Orientalist' fallacy of assuming that those who are different are exotic and incomprehensible in Western terms, but in common with many such warnings, it can be taken too seriously.

30. See Gray, *The Strategy Bridge* and Harry R. Yarger, *Strategy and the National Security Professional: Strategic Thinking in the 21st Century* (Westport, CT: Praeger Security International, 2009).

31. Ken Booth, *Strategy and Ethnocentrism* (London: Croom Helm, 1979), is excellent.

32. For a grand narrative of grand theory, see the ambitious study by Ian Morris, *Why the West Rules—For Now: The Patterns of History and What They Reveal About the Future* (London: Profile Books, 2010).

33. The growth in the literature on the security implications of climate change is almost as alarming as is the now fashionable subject itself. Two samples from the emerging library are Carolyn Pumphrey, ed., *Global Climate Change: National Security Implications* (Carlisle, PA: Strategic Studies Institute, US Army War College, May 2008) and Jeffrey Mazo, *Climate Conflict: How Global Warming Threatens Security and What To Do About It* (Abingdon: Routledge for The International Institute for Strategic Studies, March 2010).

34. For the best of recent scholarship, see Chris Bellamy, *Absolute War: Soviet Russia in the Second World War* (London: Pan Macmillan, 2007) and David Stahel, *Operation Barbarossa and Germany's Defeat in the East* (Cambridge: Cambridge University Press, 2009). Also see Winters, *Battling the Elements*, ch. 4, esp. 86–96, 'Invading Another Climate as Seasons Change', and 185–7.

35. I. B. Holley, Jr., 'Reflections on the Search for Airpower Theory', in Phillip S. Meilinger, ed., *The Paths of Heaven: The Evolution of Airpower Theory* (Maxwell AFB, AL: Air University Press, 1997), 580.

36. Jeremy Black, *Great Powers and the Quest for Hegemony: The World Order since 1500* (New York: Routledge, 2008), 231.

37. See John Lewis Gaddis, *Russia, The Soviet Union, and the United States: An Interpretive History* (New York: John Wiley, 1978), 176, for an especially clear statement of the contrast.

38. Thucydides, *The Landmark Thucydides: A Comprehensive Guide to The Peloponnesian War*, ed. Robert B. Strassler, rev. trans. Richard Crawley (*c*.400 BC; New York: Free Press, 1996), 43.

39. Good examples of journalistic geopolitical argument include: Robert D. Kaplan, *The Revenge of Geography: What the Map Tells Us About Coming Conflicts and the Battle Against Fate* (New York: Random House, 2012); id., 'The Geography of Chinese Power'; and Parag Khanna, 'Remapping the World', *Time* (22 March 2010), 36–7.

40. See Mackinder, *Democratic Ideals and Reality*; Spykman, *America's Strategy in World Politics* and id., *The Geography of the Peace* (1944; Hamden, CT: Archon Books, 1969).

41. For Alfred Thayer Mahan the geopolitician, see his study, *The Problem of Asia and Its Effect upon International Policies* (Boston: Little Brown, 1905).

42. See Sun Tzu, *The Art of* War, trans. Samuel B. Griffith (*c*.490 BC; Oxford: Clarendon Press, 1963), 124–40; Clausewitz, *On War*, 348–51, 494; and Gray, *The Strategy Bridge*, 70–2.

43. Halford J. Mackinder's life and work are assessed in W. H. Parker, *Mackinder: Geography as an Aid to Statecraft* (Oxford: Clarendon Press, 1982); Brian W. Blouet, *Halford Mackinder: A Biography* (College Station, TX: A and M University Press, 1987); and id., ed., *Global Geostrategy*.

44. Nicholas J. Spykman's geopolitical theory has been remarkably under-assessed by scholars. For a lonely first-rate exception, see David Wilkinson, 'Spykman and Geopolitics', in Ciro E. Zoppo and Charles Zorgbibe, eds., *On Geopolitics: Classic and Nuclear* (Dordrecht: Martinus Nijhoff, 1985), 77–129. Spykman is long overdue for a serious intellectual biography.

45. See Colin S. Gray, 'Harry S. Truman and the Forming of American Grand Strategy in the Cold War, 1945–1953', in Williamson Murray, Richard Hart Sinnreich, and

James Lacey, eds., *The Shaping of Grand Strategy: Policy, Diplomacy, and War* (Cambridge: Cambridge University Press, 2011), 210–53.

46. Spykman, *The Geography of the Peace*, ch. 4, explains the rival geopolitical and geostrategic perspectives.
47. Nicholas J. Spykman quoted in Weigert, *Generals and Geographers*, 23.
48. See the relevant debate: Martin C. Libicki, 'The Emerging Primacy of Information', *Orbis*, 40 (Spring 1996), 261–74, and Colin S. Gray, 'The Continued Primacy of Geography', *Orbis*, 40 (Spring 1996), 247–59.
49. Betz and Stevens, *Cyberspace and the State*, ch. 1, is exceptionally helpful in explaining the meaning of cyberspace.
50. Herman Kahn, *On Thermonuclear War* (1960; New York: Free Press, 1969), 126.
51. Kahn, *On Thermonuclear War*, 126.
52. Kahn, *On Thermonuclear War*, 126.
53. Clausewitz, *On War*, 605.
54. Clausewitz, *On War*, 89.
55. A strategy of dissuasion is one intended to discourage an actual or potential rival from threatening action that would need to be deterred. Such a strategy strives to prevent the need for deterrence. Since the demise of the Soviet Union, the United States explicitly has sought to discourage the appearance of rivals who would require deterring. The concept of dissuasion is a close relative of Morgan's idea of 'general deterrence'. See n. 24, this chapter.
56. Kahn, *On Thermonuclear War*, 287.
57. The intellectually dazzling theoretical writings of Harvard economist Thomas C. Schelling were especially creative on the subject of political commitment and the coercive use of force. See his books: *The Strategy of Conflict* (Cambridge, MA: Harvard University Press, 1960) and *Arms and Influence* (New Haven, CT: Yale University Press, 1966). Intellectual brilliance and wisdom are not necessarily synonymous. Some of Schelling's ideas should have come with national security health warnings as suitable education for policy and strategic practice, so dangerous could they be if interpreted by less than brilliant or sufficiently prudent minds commanded by unstable personalities. Also see Lawrence Freedman, ed., *Strategic Coercion: Concepts and Cases* (Oxford: Oxford University Press, 1998) and Stephen J. Cimbala, *Coercive Military Strategy* (College Station, TX: Texas A and M University Press, 1998). Coercion was in season in the late 1990s.
58. Schelling, *Arms and Influence*, 36.
59. Schelling, *Arms and Influence*, 61, offers the felicitous concept emphasized.
60. See Hans Speier, 'Magic Geography', *Social Research* (September 1941), 310–30, and Spykman, *The Geography of the Peace*, ch. 2, 'Mapping the World'. Margaret MacMillan draws attention to the cynical use of map forgeries to provide (spurious) evidence in support of controversial territorial claims at the Paris Peace Conference of 1919 in *Peacemakers*, 131.
61. Black, *Geopolitics*, 200.
62. Black, *Geopolitics*, 200–1.
63. See Robert D. Kaplan, *Balkan Ghosts: A Journey Through History* (New York: Vintage Books, 1993). Kaplan overstates the murderous problems posed by ancient hatreds, real though the problems are.

64. See 'Moscow Embassy Telegram No. 511; "The Long Telegram", 22 February 1946', authored by George F. Kennan, reprinted in Thomas H. Etzold and John Lewis Gaddis, eds., *Containment: Documents on American Policy and Strategy, 1945–1950* (New York: Columbia University Press, 1978), 50–63.
65. See Edward J. Drea, *McNamara, Clifford, and the Burdens of Vietnam, 1965–1969*, Secretaries of Defense Historical Series, Vol. VI (Washington, DC: Historical Office, Office of the Secretary of Defense, 2011), 25, 43.
66. The classic 'possibilist' geopolitical study is Harold Sprout and Margaret Sprout, *The Ecological Perspective on Human Affairs: With Special Reference to International Politics* (Princeton, NJ: Princeton University Press, 1965).
67. Patrick Porter, 'A Matter of Choice: Strategy and Discretion in the Shadow of World War II', *The Journal of Strategic Studies*, 35 (2012), 317–43, is a useful revisionist challenge to standard views.
68. Eliot A. Cohen, *Supreme Command: Soldiers, Statesmen, and Leadership in Wartime* (New York: Free Press, 2002).

5

Technology: Magic Bullets?

Historically, good men with poor ships are better than poor men with good ships.

Alfred Thayer Mahan[1]

Since technology and war operate on a logic which is not only different but actually opposed, nothing is less conducive to victory in war than to wage it on technological principles—an approach which, in the name of operations research, systems analysis or cost/benefit calculation (or obtaining the greatest bang for the buck), treats war merely as an extension of technology.

Martin van Creveld[2]

The new inventions of the last twenty years seem to threaten a great revolution in army organization, armament, and tactics. Strategy alone will remain unaltered, with its principles the same as under the Scipios and Caesars, Frederick and Napoleon, since they are independent of the nature of the arms and organization of the troops.

The means of destruction are approaching perfection with frightful rapidity.

Baron Antoine Henri de Jomini[3]

5.1 FULLER'S FOLLY AND THE QUEST FOR THE DOMINANT EXPLANATION

In 1919, J. F. C. Fuller advanced one of the more foolish arguments ever written about strategic affairs. With wording so clear as to leave no room for ambiguity, he claimed the following:

Tools, or weapons, if only the right ones can be discovered, form 99 per cent of victory . . . Strategy, command, leadership, courage, discipline, supply, organisation and all the moral and physical paraphernalia of war are nothing to a high superiority of weapons—at most they go to form the one per cent, which makes the whole possible . . . [W]ar is primarily a matter of weapons and . . . the side which can improve its weapons the more rapidly is the side which is going to win.[4]

It may seem unfair and unscholarly so to highlight a few fragments of thought from 1919, given the immensity of Fuller's total lifetime *oeuvre*.[5] Nonetheless, the theory in the words quoted is a candidate master narrative by any definition. Fuller was so taken with the idea of dominant and decisive weapons that he employed it with characteristic vigour as the conceptual engine powering his exciting and influential 1946 book, *Armament and History*. The proposition that some weapons could be strategically decisive was not for him simply a passing fancy of Great War vintage.

Few military theorists write as incisively and emphatically about weapons and war as did Fuller, but many share his belief that technology is key to success in strategic history. The challenge here is to explain how an obviously correct argument, that weapons are important, can be accorded due respect, yet be so disciplined and contextualized that it is allowed no more explanatory potency than it merits. This discussion of strategy in technological perspective therefore confronts generically the same task as have the analyses in the other chapters in this book. Those chapters address the conceptual, ethical, cultural, and geographical perspectives, each of which undoubtedly is important, but how important is that? Among my purposes are the ambition to explain strategic phenomena holistically rather than in a way that strongly favours reductionist arguments, while also helping save essentialist explanation from self-damaging causal overstretch. Whereas better theory tends to favour trinitarian categorization, controversy and robust debate inclines towards taking bipolar form.[6] Understanding of strategy is not much aided when: strategic theory is assigned to an opposed pairing with strategic practice; morality and necessity are contrasted; culture and circumstance are twinned in opposition; geography is contrasted with human discretion; and, indicated as error here, when technology is contrasted with the non-trivial remainder items comprising allegedly only the one per cent of influence that Fuller allows them.

In order to examine the technological perspective it is essential to deploy and use the general theory of strategy. No analysis and explanation of the relative importance of technology can be trusted if it focuses upon 'mechanical arts and applied sciences' out of strategic context.[7] While it is a necessary truth to describe all weapons as examples of technology, it would not be accurate to describe all technologies relevant to strategic affairs as weapons, strictly understood. Before one can talk sensibly about a weapon ready for use, science needs to be applied as technology to produce the technology that may or may not be an effective weapon. Weapons have to be considered as weapon systems, and their examination in strategic perspective requires consideration of their number as well as doctrinal beliefs about contemporary best practice for their use. The centre of gravity of this chapter is an inclusive focus upon technology, but the exercise is feasible only in the context of the conceptual, ethical, cultural, and geographical perspectives explored earlier. This study is a cumulative treatment of aspects of strategy and I must admit that Fuller's theoretical message is far more arresting than is mine. Whereas he declaims that 'technology rules (ninety-nine per cent)', my words, not Fuller's, the competing claim here is only that strategy is complicated and holistic.

The story arc of this chapter is designed to advance the thesis that strategy is a gestalt, an 'organized whole perceived to be greater than the sum of its parts'.[8] This examination of the technological perspective begins with an explanation of my argument, and is succeeded by an examination of the proposition that technology should command as the master narrative of strategic history. The analysis moves on cumulatively to explore the fungibility of technology for the strategist, and it closes by considering the relative potency of technological innovation.

5.2 ATTITUDE, ASSUMPTIONS, ARGUMENT

Throughout this book the challenge to understanding has not been to decide 'whether', but always to attempt to judge 'how much'. For immediate impact in debate, any of the perspectives on strategy examined here may find itself sidelined as allegedly all but irrelevant in a particular historical case. But, the seductive attractions of opportunistically expedient great exclusions enjoy no traction here. However, the price paid for inclusivity is a risk of appearing to declaim the obvious. A foundational claim that all strategy is technological, *inter alia*, though undeniably true, can only provide limited footing for the full examination needed. The technological perspective is as essential as it must be meaningless when considered narrowly and out of context. That said, it is also important that technology not be wholly subsumed by its context. There is a logic and a contemporary grammar to technology that those who would think and act strategically need to understand. An important interpretation of this points to the reciprocal relationship between tactical offence and defence, a dynamic nexus fuelled in notable part by technological innovation in weapons. A leading biographer of Fuller has written that 'Fuller judged the intimate relationship between the offensive and the defensive to be the constant tactical factor.'[9] Technology serves policy, strategy, and tactics, but it has a dynamic character of its own. This dynamism means that at any one time technology may not be of a kind, or be available in the needed quantity, such that it can serve its masters well enough for their current political and strategic purposes.

For example, in late 1940 airborne radar was not ready for prime-time to guide RAF interceptor aircraft for effective air defence against the night-time Blitz.[10] There are always practical physical limits to the performance of available weaponized technology.

The argument that all strategy has a technological dimension is obviously true, but ironically it can be fuel for poor scholarship. Some scholars have attitudes towards technology which feed assumptions, which in their under acknowledged turn promote unsound argument that leans unduly in the direction of technophilia or technophobia.[11] I admit to the belief that the brain is superior to muscle, that politics and its policies are master, while technology and its artefacts are servant tools. However, to assert this hierarchy of precedence is not to marginalize the significance of that which is subordinate by definition. By rough analogy, being few in number and hard to replace, leaders are assumed to be more important than are followers, but leaders without followers have no one to lead. A person, an activity, or an object, can be both subordinate as well as essential. Because technophilia (a generic liking for technology for its own sake) and technophobia (a generic dislike, literally fear, of technology) are personality traits, they need to be countered by the discipline of recognition that strategy is a gestalt. Of course, there are limits to the extent to which seriously afflicted technophiliacs and technophobes can be corrected by holistic theory in the prejudiced assumptions behind their malpractice of strategy, but education should effect some amelioration of the contrasting maladies.[12]

While recognizing that strategy is always in some measure technological, also it is necessary to probe just what that unexciting truism means. It is helpful to consider technology contextually in two different ways. On the one hand, the technology of pressing contemporary interest to a strategist is the product of many contexts, most directly and obviously, though not solely, the technological itself and its foundations in the physical and mathematical sciences. On the other hand, the technological perspective needs to be understood with reference to the contexts for its utilization. In other words, understanding the technological perspective can be approached metaphorically as an 'upstream' challenge (where does technology come from?), as a 'downstream' challenge (how useful will technology prove to be in action?), or as both. 'Upstream' and 'downstream' are really a unity in the unending stream of time, because tomorrow's technology must grow out of today's technology, which came from the technology of yesterday.[13] There is a biasing dynamic inherent in paths taken in technological development, as well as in an apparent logic in technology itself, pushing the envelope of performance for its own sake because it might be doable. The inherent dynamic of technology breeding ever more technology is true of conceptualization also. Theory begets yet more theory, much of which will be more elaborate than what it replaces, though not necessarily more useful.[14]

Because context logically is hostile to boundaries, the familiar problem of indeterminate, extensive, and complex provenance intrudes. The technological perspective on strategy is interested not only in the sources of technology, but also in the time, place, and tactical circumstances of technology's practical performance for strategy. There is a complex and contestable relationship between the strategist's demand for technology and its supply. Best practice in the use of weaponized technology is rarely appreciated instantly, just as the identification of strategically desirable weapons often is subject to intense disagreement. Strategically relevant technologies sometimes are developed regardless of an absence of military demand (the atomic bomb, for example), while that demand is rarely authoritative. Soldiers have been known not to understand what they should ask technologists to provide, just as they can be mistaken in the tactical uses to which new capabilities are put. This is unavoidable, though it can be minimized if military organizations are effective learning institutions. As Winston Churchill noted with much insight in a Memorandum of 9 November 1916 addressed to Britain's Minister of Munitions:

> A hiatus exists between inventors who know what they could invent, if they only knew what was wanted, and the soldiers who know, or ought to know, what they want, and would ask for it if they only knew how much science could do for them. You have never really bridged that gap yet.[15]

Those who read and take to heart what Clausewitz wrote about uncertainty in his brilliant diagnosis of the 'climate of war', will not be surprised to discover for themselves that strategy is effected by a great deal of tactical and operational trial and error; experience usually is the most conclusive persuader.[16] In order to tell the time, it is not necessary to be erudite on the subject of watchmaking. *Ab extensio*, most professional politicians after 1945 have understood little of the science and engineering in the technology weaponized in the nuclear arsenals, and which *in extremis* they are legally and politically authorized contingently to employ.

Two contextual issue-areas intrude aggressively upon this examination. First, the technologies relevant to the military strategist's duties include many that have dual use, military and civilian. Communications technologies of all kinds (e.g. railways, the electric telegraph, aircraft, radio, motor cars, computers) are only the tip of this metaphorical iceberg. In order to explore the technological dimension to grand strategy, the boundaries of pertinent skills, objects, and other assets must transcend the usual boundaries asserted for conceptual categorization. The grand strategist may employ any or all of the assets of the polity for grand-strategic purposes. What, if anything, does that exclude in theory or practice? There has to be much sense in what one could term a 'strategy and society' approach to the subject. This contextual recognition is borrowed with adaptation from the long familiar 'war and society' literature. But, one has to be aware that desirable social inclusivity should not be permitted so imperial a role that it swallows the intended focus of interest, which is strategy.

Second, although technology is essential in the generation of fighting power ultimately for strategic effect, it is only one player on the tactical team that produces that effect. This ought to be obvious, but often it is missed by commentators of a technophiliac persuasion who can forget that inert machines have to be operated by people who are able and willing to do so, often at extreme personal risk. Also, it is common to assume that tactically potent weaponized, certainly militarily useful, technologies have self-evident strategic meaning. The theory of strategy says that all weapons are tactical in use, but strategic in effect, be that effect great or small. When some weapons mistakenly are thought of and labelled as 'strategic', allegedly in contrast to other weapons that logically therefore have to be non-strategic or sub-strategic (for a bizarre British concept), the labelling discourages thought about strategy. A Fulleresque 'dominant weapon' proves to be nothing of the kind if it is unreliable in action, and though tactically formidable in willing and able hands, alas is acquired, maintained, and operated in too few numbers, or employed with high effectiveness but for strategically irrelevant purposes. And this is only the shortest list of reasons why technically advanced machines may disappoint in their combat value. The fact that there is always a technological dimension to strategy should not mislead one into endorsing the fallacy that we fight with weaponized technology as in a closed-end system. Instead, we fight not with technology, but rather with weapon systems, inclusively defined, in holistic tactical endeavour for operational purposes, under the guidance of strategy, for the ends of policy (which is politics)—all in competition with an enemy. This is a minimal exposition of the great chain of causation that connects technology with strategic effectiveness. People fascinated by military phenomena for their own sake are militarists. This fascination need not be a politically serious malady, indeed often as entertainment it displaces political interest altogether. But, militarism disconnects the military instrument from its political *raison d'être*. Absent interest in the utility of the technology as a contributor to the combat power needed for the strategic effectiveness required to support national security, attraction to the material artefacts of militarized technology is a form of pornography. As sex decontextualized of human relationships is pornography, so also is delighting in military hardware and software and their supporting machines, decontextualized of strategic and political reference. The technological perspective on strategy has as a vital part of its 'grammar' what often are disdainfully called 'boy's toys', but it is essential to attempt to grasp the tactical and strategic meaning of their 'toys'. This is why it would be difficult to exaggerate the importance of the 'so what?' question, as the North Star of an education in strategy. One may well be impressed, even seduced in aesthetic and intellectual appreciation, by the cunning and beauty of weaponized technology, but the strategist needs to know what it means.

A British historical example of technophilia is the generally uncontested (by Britons) claim that the Supermarine Spitfire was the most beautiful aircraft ever built. Indeed, I cannot recall a book or television documentary about the Spitfire that failed to re-register this long standard claim. For Britons of all ages, even today, more than seventy years on from the Battle of Britain, the Spitfire is the supreme romanticized icon of a heroic national 'strategic moment'. The visually arresting military technology appeals to the senses and captures the imagination. The problem is that this seduction can fill all of the limited space available for appreciation and comprehension, so that strategy is not 'tacticized', as frequently mistakenly is claimed, rather is it shorn of its humanity in favour of inert tools, no matter how technically interesting, tactically efficient, and in some cases even aesthetically appealing they are judged to be.[17] For example, the Wehrmacht's MG-42, with its rate of fire of 1,200 rpm, was a lethal marvel of German engineering and was the envy of less well-armed enemies.

Because the technology in weaponry is not tactics, just as tactics are not strategy, the technological perspective on strategy can only be one, certainly important, such perspective. Ironically, the technological fetishism so prevalent in some Western cultures undermines appreciation of the strategic value of its subjects. It appears gratuitously challenging to assess the strategic merit in technological possibilities if one is mentally (and possibly morally) arrested by a variant of technophilia or, to be balanced, technophobia.

As a team player in combat and combat-support systems, technology has the potential both to have substitution value when other team members are weak (e.g. soldiers whose numbers or morale are low), or to require substitution when it falls technically short of the needed performance in action. Because technology is only one element in fighting power, and indeed in the mix of factors contributing to strategic effect, its military and strategic value is always relative to that provided by other contributing elements. This claim has practical implications in the sovereign realm of political and strategic choice. Those alert to context who wish to know how important one kind of weapon system is likely to be relative to another that might be selected for acquisition, should recognize the significance of the cautionary words 'it all depends . . .' The owners of such a candidate 'dominant weapon' as, for example, the Panzer MkV Panther, discovered that the battlespace dominance of their excellent medium tank was considerably attenuated by the narrowness of its tracks and the unreliability of logistical support when deep in Russian geography. Circumstances have much to say for understanding the technological perspective on strategy.

5.3 TECHNOLOGY AS GRAND NARRATIVE:
RMAs AND MTRs

Strategic history lends itself to a grand narrative that privileges technology. One need not sign up to a high-octane version of Fuller's dominant weapon thesis in order to argue that technology is a candidate for pole position as a mover and shaker of the course of history. There is need to consider technology both as weaponry and as enabler of weapon effectiveness, while recognizing its vital role in helping generate the wealth that pays for weapons and their supporting infrastructure. There is an inescapable reason why strategy is best represented in theory geometrically by the Venn diagram of overlapping areas. However, as a caveat, one has to be careful lest in the artwork aesthetic values overwhelm empirical evidence, with the result that all perspectives on strategy appear to be accorded equal significance. What is true in general theory always has particular meaning specific to each historical case, and even at different times in each theatre of operations.

The general theory of strategy is and has to be indifferent to the details of technology. The theory should be refined and amended to reflect strategic epiphanies of universal and eternal merit, but it has no need to accommodate appreciation specific to new technologies. This is why the theory in the writings of Sun Tzu, Thucydides, and Clausewitz does not age seriously, even though their books assuredly bear the stamp of their time, place, and circumstance of authorship. The general theory does not change, but the way in which it is expressed certainly does. The theory is always open for amendment and redrafting. However, it can never be open season for the invention of theory that would invalidate the extant theory. If this were not so, the theory of strategy would have been in constant flux since the early nineteenth century, as science and technology produced an overlapping succession of revolutionary changes in the material artefacts of war. From steam and steel, through oil and electricity, to nuclear energy, plastics, and electronics, the technological dimension to modern strategic history has been persistently unstable.[18] But, as usual it is prudent to enquire, 'so what?' What of importance about the strategy function has changed? The answer is nothing. This is why those who announce alarmingly that 'the sky is falling' upon strategy as we thought we knew it, are mistaken. The error lies in the failure to distinguish between strategy as general theory in contrast to that theory's manifestation in strategies tailored to answer the political demands of policy in particular historical circumstances. The general theory has to register the fact that strategy has an essential technological dimension. For that theory it matters not how many of the five physical geographies of rivalry and war are actively in play as domains for competitive behaviour. The claim made by Sir Michael Howard in 2011, for a 'transformation of strategy' for political, social, cultural, economic, military, technological, or any other reasons, has to refer only to strategy's character, not to its nature.[19] The strategies pursued in the twenty-first century will reflect changes in all of the porous categories just named.

In order to understand strategy all that one needs to know about technology is that it is a permanent factor. This elementary understanding must be appreciated in the context of general theory, because only thus can one be educated adequately to cope with the reality of strategy in practice. For example, it should be impossible to consider the technological perspective on, for example, the Second World War in 1940, without being alerted by the general theory of strategy to the importance of the duelling dynamic of conflict and also to war's human dimension. Strategic scholarship focusing on technological achievements and limitations is ever prone to forget that the enemy is likely to be present on a common technological frontier. The human element to the strategic narrative means that the importance of technology often depends on the skill and determination of the people who must practise violence with it, or for a yet greater challenge, without it.

To borrow and adapt a familiar maxim: they cannot know strategy who do not know technology, but they do not know strategy who only technology know. Education in strategy's general theory minimizes the likelihood that technophilia will succeed in capturing strategy. Prominent among the more classic of mistakes in strategic historical commentary is the assumption that weapons win wars. This pathetic error is revealed when film makers and authors refer casually to 'the weapons that won the war', rather than the weapons with which the war was won. Allegedly technically superior and purportedly dominant weapons are thus held autonomously to have influenced the course of history. The truth, of course, is that weapons and other militarily useful technologies have a highly variable enabling potential for strategic behaviour. For an historical example, the strategically significant difference between RAF Fighter Command and the Luftwaffe in 1940 lay not in the technologies themselves, which essentially were common, but much rather in the ways in which they were organized and employed in combat. This was a case not of technological advantage and disadvantage, so much as one of technology both well and poorly used. Ideas expressed in organization and doctrine for best current military practice are not simply adding value to technology, rather are they usually the main contributors to weapon-system effectiveness.

Of recent decades, at least, Americans have tended to favour strongly an approach to warfare that seeks advantage in the exploitation of technology.[20] The inclination to exploit technology to the point of heavy reliance was manifested with unmistakable enthusiasm in the discovery, adoption, and elaboration of the concept of revolution in military affairs (RMA) by the US defence community in the 1990s.[21] The proposition was that new technologies could enable prosecution of an RMA that would transform the military establishment. The purpose of the 'transformation'—for a while a magically iconic concept—was never as clear as was its character, which was to be the full military exploitation of new digital technologies.[22] This was a major version of what theorists of defence preparation term 'capabilities planning'.[23] Armed forces technologically superior to, and technically dominant over, any and all rivals or enemies would be empowered by the revolution effected by military digitization to threaten or wage agile network-centric joint warfare, rapier-like, with awesome precision (and therefore with low, or no, collateral damage), globally, and with a small military footprint. This was a dazzling technical-tactical prospect, potentially with high strategic value.

The theorists and practitioners who debated and embraced the RMA and then the transformation concepts so enthusiastically, had an attractive narra-tive to pursue, even if the reasons for the pursuit left much of strategic importance to be desired.[24] What the theories of, and plans for, RMA and transformation did not appear to appreciate sufficiently was the limited domain for revolution and transformation. Just what would it be that could lend itself to revolution and transformation? The answer had to be that a US-led RMA, and even a substantial military transformation, would change radically the way in which America and a few of its allies fight their 'way in warfare'—no less, but also no more. This process of change should alter the character of the warfare in which Americans would engage, though not necessarily in a linear fashion, because enemies could respond asymmetrically to the American style of warfare, and impose discipline, limitations, and course correction on it. Since war is a competitive endeavour as well as a violent one, it is unusual for a belligerent to be able conclusively to impose its preferred character of fighting upon its enemies. When such stylistic domin-ance is achieved, the conflict loses much of its nature as a duel, with the combat narrative more resembling a victory parade than a war. However, even when the enemy confidently is anticipated to be reducible to the status of strategically inert victim, there is much to be said in favour of remembering Clausewitz's prudent words on the subject of war being the realm of chance.[25] Not only can over-trumpeted triumphal marches up country to the enemy's capital have been not quite the victory parade as subsequently was briefly celebrated, but the warfare after the supposedly successful short war is apt to prove strategically and politically embarrassing: Afghanistan and Iraq in the 2000s are obvious cases in point.

There is little doubt that technology dependent RMAs and transformation can be effected, but when one asks the vital 'so what?' question, disturbing doubts arise. Even if the United States carries through a revolution and fields notably transformed armed forces, how do those facts relate to the strategic effectiveness of US military power, how significant are they? The answer is not as obvious as was assumed by many of the American debaters in the 1990s and early 2000s who enthused about RMA.[26] The reason why a technology-led

RMA is not self-evidently and necessarily strategically transformational, is the one flagged throughout this book. Specifically, the United States, *inter alia*, may be able to revolutionize and transform its military instrument, and in hindsight that may or may not be judged to have been desirable, it may well have been close to unavoidable—some broad and deep technological changes simply cannot be resisted—but what it cannot revolutionize and transform is the nature of war and of strategy. A country can alter markedly the kind of weaponized technologies in its order of battle, in good part as a consequence of changing radically its concepts of operation and its tactical doctrine. Also, that country can choose strategies different from those that would have matched better the erstwhile means in its military establishment prior to transformation. But, the general theory of strategy cannot be evaded or revolutionized and transformed as a consequence of radical changes that are subject to its dominion. When strategic reformer-revolutionaries talk excitedly and hubristically about 'game-changing' military ideas and technologies, or both, they are not usually clear as to the identity of the 'game' in question. Typically, such expansive expressions translate plausibly as meaning that we will or could fight in a different way, usually with some different military equipment, and that success inexorably should follow such bold innovation as the just reward for our modernity.

Unknowingly, many contributors to the rolling RMA-cum-transformation debate of the 1990s and early 2000s could not make sense enough of their exciting theses and counter-theses, because they were theoretically lost strategic souls who in addition often were short of empirical understanding. The latter misfortune can be attributed to the presentist and future speculative bias that blights strategic studies. A profession of would-be strategists actually populated mainly by social and physical scientists performing as defence analysts, innocent of more than a passing familiarity even with strategic, let alone other history, is not likely to stumble upon the deeper reasons for the fragility of much of its claimed wisdom.[27] This is a heavy charge, but it has distinguished provenance. It was advanced by the leading American strategic thinker of the early and middle years of the Cold War, Bernard Brodie. He was explicit in his disdain for former colleagues whose knowledge and understanding of history was decidedly limited, not to say cursory.[28] The argument here adds to Brodie's critique the charge that lack of understanding of strategic theory has severe practical consequences for efforts to comprehend the strategic significance of technological innovations.

The RMA concept taken over by American defence analysts from its Soviet homeland and adopted and adapted to its new American conceptual ownership, bore an important and exciting message. In the words of leading and well respected American defence theorist Andrew F. Krepinevich:

What is a military revolution? It is what occurs when the application of new technologies into a significant number of military systems combines with innovative operational concepts and organizational adoption in a way that fundamentally alters the character and conduct of conflict. It does so by producing a dramatic increase—often an order of magnitude or greater—in the combat potential and military effectiveness of armed forces.[29]

Krepinevich and others altered the wording of their preferred definition of an RMA, as was inevitable and indeed was to be expected, as study and debate proceeded apace through the 1990s. However, the core meaning, the centre of conceptual gravity one might say, of the RMA concept was not in doubt or much dispute. No matter whether the role played by technology in military revolution is believed to be great or small, close inspection reveals a significant fragility in RMA theory. It is tempting to claim that this fragility can be described more accurately as a fatal flaw. The problem lies in the assumption that appears to underpin Krepinevich's claim that military revolution 'fundamentally alters the character and conduct of conflict . . .' While this formula is superior to those that seek to insist that military revolution changes the nature of conflict, nonetheless it is empirically unsound and therefore unsafe as theory. The error lies in the claim that military revolution alters the nature of conflict—conceived as a simple military phenomenon. As written with the words quoted, RMAs are asserted to make a profound difference ('fundamentally alters') to conflict, as expressed logically meaning all conflict. The explanatory ambition in RMA theory is clearly conveyed in the wording of the foundational American report on the subject which, at the time of its writing in July 1992, was understood in Washington as military-technical revolution (MTR), a concept borrowed from Soviet military science. RMA was a broadening American adaptation. The 1992 report offered the following conceptual guidance:

What is revolutionary is not the speed with which the change takes place, but rather the magnitude of the change itself. At some point the cumulative effects of technological advances and military innovations will invalidate former conceptual frameworks by bringing about a fundamental change in the nature of warfare and, thus, in our definitions and measurement of military effectiveness.[30]

The 1994 article, for which understandably Andrew F. Krepinevich drew heavily upon his 1992 report, asserted prudently only that an RMA achieves a fundamental alteration in the character and conduct of conflict, not a 'fundamental change in the nature of warfare', as the report from two years earlier claimed heroically. However, it is troubling that the original study could make the impossible and therefore absurd claim at all, even if it was early in the American study cycle for the RMA concept. It is more troubling still that the authors and sponsors of the 1992 report remained sufficiently proud of it as to reissue it unaltered in 2002. In his 'Introduction' to the reissued report, the author endorses the judgement that this 1992 study has 'held up well over time'.[31] While there is much of value in the report, the entire conceptual project of RMA theory, which had potentially profound practical implications for military posture, was constructed on a shaky foundation of theory. Since the leading American scholars of the RMA idea plainly were somewhat confused as to whether changes in warfare's nature or character were the subject under discussion, it is scarcely surprising that less expert commentators floundered.

It is not correct to anticipate change in the nature of warfare, as even a cursory check on past and present military challenges readily reveals. The strategic effectiveness of a considerably transformed military instrument is always substantially contextually determined. No military revolution, past, present, or future has the contextually independent ability to drive the course and outcome of strategic history. High modernity in a transformed or transforming army need not correlate with strategic success (e.g. America's wars in Vietnam). The reason is because RMA theory is seriously weak in its indebtedness to, and accommodation of, the theory of war. The latter theory recognizes what Clausewitz judiciously noted to be either the objective (unchanging) or subjective (changing) nature—meaning character in this case—of war.[32] The military and strategic utility of a revolutionized army will, with reference to the value of its allegedly revolutionary qualities, depend considerably upon the circumstances of individual conflicts. The general theory of conflict must treat its included phenomena as consisting parts of a single body of experience. But, strategic history has to apply the general theory of conflict, war, and strategy to individual historical episodes that are always more or less distinctive. This is not to assert absurdly that by definitional necessity a single army cannot cope reasonably well enough with a range of conflicts posing disparate challenges. However, it is to argue that an army will not find that its transformed character yields anything close to a stable and predictable quality of strategic return across a range of different strategic contexts.

Armies transformed by military revolutions, whatever the catalysts of change (e.g. technological or social), can be undone militarily and hence strategically by what Edward N. Luttwak has termed 'the paradoxical logic of conflict'. This is better understood as the ironical logic of conflict.[33] Transformed armies may well fail to deliver what their political owners require. The reason is because it is rare for one side in a war to be able to anticipate accurately and then impose, in brutal validation of the favoured prediction, a style in warfare that flatters the capabilities that it secured by transformation. It is all too easy to theorize speculatively about military capabilities, but forgetting that war is a duel wherein the effectiveness of one's capabilities must be decided through competition and not unilaterally.[34] Strategic effectiveness is a concept of net achievement. Theories of military revolution, including revolution fuelled principally by technological innovation, must be assayed in the conceptual context of strategy's general theory. Often, this is not done. The result of such neglect is that the exciting promise of strategic advantage held to reside in RMA-shaped armed forces is not disciplined by consideration of what enemies might attempt to thwart them.

This discussion finds that much of the theorizing about military revolution has suffered from deep empirical and theoretical flaws. The following are common errors:

1. It is a mistake to assume that the conflicts of interest to current strategic practice can be treated as a single phenomenon. Conflicts are individual and therefore plural, even though they may be accommodated at a high level of generality under the umbrella of a unified general theory.

2. Since conflict is always of relevance to strategists in the forms taken by particular conflicts, it follows that general military capabilities are likely to find their effectiveness varying from case to case. For example, air power will be more effective when the enemy's soldiers are deployed obligingly apart from civilians, and in such simple terrain as desert.

3. Understanding of the enemy often is more lazily expedient than it should be or even could be. Strategy frequently is ironical, not strictly paradoxical (contradictory), when the nexus of cause and effect between belligerents is apparently non-linear. This non-linearity appears, for example, as countervailing efforts intended to evade and thereby offset the military effectiveness of a technology-led RMA. When seeking to understand how effective a revolutionized and transformed military instrument will be in action, one needs to remember that the enemy always has a vote on the answer to that question.

4. The general theory of strategy alerts the strategist to the context within which his military tools must function. Suitably alerted and educated, the strategist will not neglect the authority of political purpose that legitimizes his endeavours, the limited but still real strategic sovereignty of the enemy, the certainty of friction, and all the other elements that compose his complex domain.

Technology is not the only causal element identified in theories of military revolution; others include political and social change, as well as military organization and doctrine. However, technological innovation enjoys a deserved senior status in theories seeking to explain both the general course of history, and certainly the paths of strategic history. Scholars have argued convincingly that the subject of military revolution should not be approached by way of, or reduced to, consideration of technological change alone. To quote Andrew Krepinevich again from his influential article published in 1994:

Military revolutions comprise four elements: technological change, systems development, operational innovation, and organizational adoption.[35]

He proceeded to argue that

Each of these elements is in itself a necessity, but not a sufficient condition for realizing large gains in military effectiveness that characterize military revolutions. In particular, while advances in technology typically underwrite a military revolution, they alone do not constitute the revolution. The phenomenon is much broader in scope and consequence than technological innovation, however dramatic.[36]

Krepinevich is convincing in the words just quoted. That granted, it is important to recognize a significant risk of circularity in his argument. If military revolution is detectable because of the evidence provided by high combat effectiveness, one might be misled into assuming that military success is the product of RMA. When an identified RMA is believed to have been effected significantly by technological change, the logical error is likely to be compounded if strategic achievement is assumed to be the product of RMA: it might seem logical to seek evidence of RMA when and where strategic success is registered in historians' claims. The problem, however, is that strategic success can have a wide variety of parents beyond military revolution, let alone revolution achieved as a result of technological change.

This examination of the technological perspective on strategy is not hostile to its subject. The criticism and scepticism shown here is addressed only to mistaken beliefs about the role and relative importance of technology. Technology per se is not a suitable subject for an inherently critical examination. The technological dimension to statecraft, war, and strategy is as necessary as it is unavoidable. This approach to technology in its relation to strategy is the same as the one taken in the chapters on concepts, ethics, culture, and geography. In each case criticism was found appropriate when the perspective under examination is overvalued in a hypothetical strategic universe wherein monocausality rules supreme. In each chapter it has been necessary to save proper appreciation of the particular subject from the ill repute that follows upon excessively inclusive theorizing on its behalf. In similar vein, it is necessary to rescue prudent appreciation of the technological dimension from its more parochial cheerleaders, because, ironically, uncritical enthusiasm breeds unjustifiable scepticism.

5.4 TECHNOLOGY, STRATEGY, AND TACTICS

It is important to allow technology no more than its due as a dimension to strategic history, but also it is essential to accord it no less. Because this is a book of social and not of physical science, it is necessary to be satisfied with theory that occasionally is ignored by a roguish empirical exception. It is my thesis that technology drives military tactics, but that the weaponized technologies used in warfare cannot be treated as an example of technical supply thoroughly independent of military (and strategic) demand. If one enquires as to the provenance of weapons and their supporting systems, the answer has to include recognition of the variable authority of military demand. And that demand can be triggered by many stimulants, notably including current and anticipated practical challenges, as well as ambitions for improvement in combat power. It is useful to advance the following propositions, by way of explanation of the structure of the relationship between technology and strategy:

1. Technology drives tactics, shapes operations, and enables strategies; but that driver, shaper, and enabler is not created independent of demand from user communities.

2. Technology drives warfare directly, and war indirectly.

3. Technology is a team player in the gestalt that is strategy.

Phrased thus tersely the interconnectedness within points one and two may pass under-recognized. It should be heuristically helpful to pose the questions, what does technology do for the strategist, what role does it play? The obvious answer is that technology enables the strategist to practise strategy. This formulation reveals the limitations and practical hazards of an approach to the meeting of strategic challenges that seeks advantage through the exploitation of technology. Specifically, technology is not alone as a strategic enabler, while logic and historical experience reveal that technology potentially is vulnerable to many constraints upon its enabling potential. Not least, because if weaponized or otherwise weapon relevant technology can be a great enabler for us, then so might it be for our enemies.

A major difficulty for theory is the need to treat technology as a sufficiently discrete contributor to strategic enterprise as to be examinable as a distinctive subject warranting address as a perspective. This is the result of viewing strategy as a gestalt, a system of systems, wherein all elements have some variable impact upon everything else all the time. Explanation of the role and relative significance of any single element in a system of systems can appear analytically impossible. All that one can do is recognize the complexity, acknowledge the fact of multiple contexts, and then proceed carefully to see what authority attends the character of technology at a specific time and place.

If the technological dimension, in effect, is not to be swallowed by its contexts, it requires protection for some discrete examination. For the perspective to have analytical integrity, its subject must not be permitted to disappear, squeezed between its enabling causes and its consequences, allocated no influence of its own. In order to illuminate the strategic history of a particular event, episode, or period in the light of the technological perspective, one can pose a set of pertinent questions. The following should yield answers with some authority for particular times, places, and strategic actors.

1. What is the contemporary state of technological achievement?

2. Which technologies on the menu extant are mature and ready to be weaponized, or are believed to be close to readiness?

3. Which technologies are chosen for military adoption as weapons or direct contributors to weapons—by type, capability (performance data), numbers?

4. To which military tasks are extant technologies applied, and how are these assignments expressed in military doctrine (conveying current belief about best practice)?

5. How flexible and adaptable are current technologies in the face of changing military and strategic challenges?

This listing can be shrunk or expanded as desired, but it illustrates the eternal and universal fact that there is existentially an objective reality to the technological dimension to statecraft, war, strategy, and tactics. Scholars can be so assiduous in their endeavours to explain and thereby unwrap the complexities of weapon gestation, development, official adoption, and production that they forget to assign proper weight to the historical context. Of particular importance since the 1830s—to risk being somewhat arbitrary—what has been termed 'the invention of invention' through the dynamics of the modern scientific and implementing industrial revolution(s), has meant that the historical perspective on technology for strategy is highly significant.[37] Timing has been crucially important: the date of innovation and the lead-time required for its exploitations in weapons and their supporting systems ready enough for use. Consider, for example, the strategic worth of radar in the Battle of Britain in 1940. The feasibility of radar was demonstrated unarguably only in 26 February 1935. For another example from the same era, it was only in January 1939 that it was demonstrated that uranium atoms (235U) could be split by neutron bombardment (radioactivity had been discovered back in 1896, neutron particles in 1932). Radar was not ready for military action in 1935, neither was atomic fission in 1939. But the historical perspective on strategy is deeply interested in the facts that these scientific achievements of 1939 and 1935 happened to permit the time needed to weaponize them for the grim events that were anticipated, but could not be predicted reliably. It is worth noting that in 1939 it was not obvious that the splitting of uranium atoms would enable a militarily practicable weapon.

At any and every moment in history there is extant a particular technological dimension to strategy. That dimension will be more or less permissive of alternative choices for tactical exploitation and it will vary in detail from place to place, but nonetheless the technologies that technically are sufficiently up for the fights chosen by politicians in one year or another, were what they were: they were existential. Mind over muscle is a sound precept, but even superior brains are obliged to practise their strategic skills with the material artefacts engineered with the technology then current. The weapons ready enough for action today will need to have been the technologies of yesterday, ready then for development for weaponization so that they could be in action today (e.g. radar, 1935–40, atomic bomb, 1942–5).[38] There is always a lead-time story governing the generation of military power, one pertaining especially to the research, development, and acquisition process for new weapon systems. Any pre-war crisis or wartime combat can only be waged with the ready weaponized technologies of the day, and that day usually is historically definite and researchable by scholars. The integrity of the technological perspective can be obscured by its multiple contexts of politics, economics, culture, military doctrine and others, but the machines of and for war are what they are, by and large specifically so, at particular times, places, and with particular owners. Some of the apparent truths of strategic theory, certainly some of the more appealing items of strategic logic, can come to grief on the rocks of technological impossibility. This strategic theorist has long been frustrated by the apparent inability of ballistic missile defence (BMD) technologies to be able to perform as his preferred theory of deterrence by considerable defensive denial required.[39] The history of what is called strategic bombing in the Second World War is replete with examples of technological limitation constraining military and therefore strategic accomplishment.[40] This is not to deny that in exceptionally skilful hands and steady nerves, even poor technology may be coaxed to over-perform; for this reason the concept of the weapon system needs to include the motivation and ability of its human users. While noting the complexity of context and of causal chains that often are untraceable with confidence, it should be beyond reasonable dispute that the practice of strategy in history always must have a researchable technological dimension that warrants examination for the informing of a distinct perspective.

Having argued for the scholarly integrity of the technological perspective on strategy, now it is necessary to examine points stated boldly above on the whole subject of the structure of the relationship between technology and strategy. The first admittedly imperial claim is that technology drives tactics, shapes operations, and enables strategy. This trinitarian view could be protected and augmented by a large bodyguard of qualifications and caveats. Nonetheless, before one rushes to qualify an interesting proposition, it is essential to ensure that the idea intended to be the centre of conceptual gravity is suitably highlighted.

The first point registers the material reality that what one can use in warfare is restricted to the military tools available (home manufacture, purchase or lend-lease from abroad, capture from the enemy and reuse) by whatever means. There is often some range of tactical choice over particular weapons, but the selection is likely to be restricted by the details of weapon performance. Even if tactical choice is made that fails to privilege what could and should be done with accessible technology, the fact remains that men can only fight with the weapons available and working on the day.

To illustrate the complexity of cause and effect in strategic history, consider Allied strategic bombing in the Second World War in technological perspective. The USAAC (later USAAF) developed and acquired the B-17 four-engine heavy bomber in the belief that flying with rigorous tactical discipline in tight combat formation, and with as many as thirteen heavy (0.50 calibre) machine guns on board (the B-17G of 1943), it would be able to fight its way to and from enemy targets without fighter escort. This belief in self-defending bomber formations was the doctrinal product of service political interest, as well as of assumptions firmly anchored in the technological actualities of the early 1930s.[41] Because the assumptions, interests, and beliefs dominant in the USAAF were as just described when the force was built, deployed to operate from England, and sent into battle initially in 1942 and then in ever larger number in 1943, the American bomber force of that brief period suffered an operationally unacceptable loss rate. The immediate answer was to change tactical doctrine and escort the B-17s (and B-24s) with single-seat fighters flying close or distant escort. The response to the fact of defeat was deployment of the re-engined (with the Rolls Royce Merlin) P-51B Mustang, which with fuel drop-tanks had a combat radius of 600 miles.[42] Drop-tank technology was resisted for plausible, but unsound, reasons and it proved not to be an especially challenging technical fix to a severe tactical problem. But the fact that range extending drop-tanks were not a show-stopping technical problem was of no great relevance to the air crew who could only benefit from the engineered technology actually in the aircraft at the time. Long-range Mustangs did not fly from England until December 1943. The fact that they could have been ready much earlier is interesting, but unhistorical.

The tactical effectiveness of weaponized technology depends not only on its technical military performance as a weapon, but also on the quantity in which it is procured. There will be a critical mass of numbers, weight of firepower and so forth, that has qualitative consequences. A few weapons in the super category of relative performance metrics are typically far less than super in tactical effectiveness when too few of them are deployed. Quality can substitute for quantity, but belligerents driven to seek compensation for relatively low numbers in better individual weapons, often are undone by the limited return to such a strategy. Particularly is this true when the decision to pursue quality rather than quantity compels a wartime shortening of the prudent development and testing cycle. This was the story of German tank design and procurement in the Second World War.

The second element in the claims about technology's relationship with tactics, operations, and strategy, focuses on the influence of the technological dimension to warfare upon military campaign conception, design, and practicability in attempted execution. Extant technologies shape beliefs about what should be achievable, while they cast more than a token vote on the prudence of the plans. Good historical examples abound, but the great German offensive adventures of 1914 and 1918 in the West, and 1941–2 in the East, are close to being in a class of their own as exemplars of operational ideas impacted, in these cases negatively, by the state of the technologies available in relation to what was demanded of them. The modern marvel of an excellent railway network, superbly orchestrated for military purposes by expert professionals on the General Staff, allowed Germany to wage a two(plus)-front war on interior lines to outstanding defensive effect, but ironically with the ability to create unresolvable operational and strategic dilemmas for itself. Because railways must aid the defence more than the offence, as a retreating army falls back along its lines of communication destroying rail track as it goes, the railway that enables rapid mobilization cannot itself enable and sustain a rapid advance beyond the national frontiers.[43] The defending polity, in contrast, falls back upon and with its own railway network and often can shift the weight of defence expeditiously by lateral rail mobility parallel to the fighting front.[44] Of course, there is much more to nineteenth- and early twentieth-century warfare than this. However, this example shows how a modern technology could enable a grand operational concept and plan to be set in motion, but could not enable it to succeed in execution. By 1918 the German army was only modestly motorized, was not mechanized, and lacked more than token armoured forces. An important reason why the five Offensives of March–June 1918 all failed to achieve sustainable breakthroughs and breakouts was because the soldiers lacked access to the machines that they required in adequate numbers if they were to advance as swiftly as they needed with adequate combat power.[45] German technologies and tactics for infantry assault and combined arms combat orchestration were both state-of-the-art. But, the warriors could not move fast enough, they were short of the artillery support that was essential (the heavier guns were left far behind, and close-support aircraft could not compensate adequately), and their higher operational direction by military command was an expression of less than stellar generalship.

The fate of Nazi Germany's Operation Barbarossa in the Soviet Union in 1941, and its continuation and geostrategic extension, meaning logistical overextension to the Volga and the Caucasus in 1942 (Operation *Blau*), is a variant of the same narrative as that for 1914 and 1918. In their operational history of the Second World War, Williamson Murray and Alan R. Millett place suitable emphasis upon the deadly consequences of the logistical strains that Hitler's overly expansive operational grand design placed upon the

Wehrmacht in Russia. For example, with reference to the situation and condition of Friedrich von Paulus' Sixth Army in the summer of 1942, they record that:

> In mid-July Hitler was still focusing on encircling Soviet forces near Rostov and capturing that city. To do so, he provided a three- to four-day hiatus to the Soviets, who escaped across the Don in droves, as the German Sixth Army remained immobilized for lack of supplies north of the Don bend. Paulus's logistical situation depended on a single low-capacity rail line from which trucks had to haul supplies over ever-lengthening distances.[46]

With a military establishment hastily expanded and rearmed, and equipped for the relatively short-range warfare most agreeably befitting a polity located in the centre of Europe, Nazi Germany paradoxically chose to wage warfare at a range far beyond its logistical comfort zone. Regarded in technological perspective, German war-making in the Second World War was attempted at and fatally beyond the reach and range of its ability to supply reliably and move its military assets with the necessary speed and sustainable, or renewable, combat power. Invading a country that itself occupied space with continental scale distances and had few all-weather metalled roads, the Wehrmacht suffered enervation leading time after time to paralysis as a consequence of its severe technological shortfalls. Germany's tanks had tracks that were too narrow for the soft surfaces they must traverse, its aircraft had too short a range, its mechanization was too modest in scale, and its army was, in part therefore, far too dependent upon a few, a very few, long railway lines that were highly vulnerable to sabotage by partisans behind the front lines (and Rommel's logistical nightmare in North Africa in good part was the direct result of Germany's inability to sustain a campaign overseas in 1942–3). These were but a few of the larger technological shortfalls. Nazi Germany's world war was very much a railway war. While modern warfare certainly was motorized and ran on oil, the German (war) economy ran on coal and its army moved principally by train. The core logistical reality of German war-making has been summarized pithily as follows by Evan Mawdsley: 'The German railways were the logistical pivot of Hitler's war system.'[47] Mawdsley noted the military operational advantage of railways to '[t]he Germans, [who] with a central position could move ground and air forces rapidly from direction to direction using land transport to project their power'.[48] The problem was that the German army deep in Russia was much too far removed from the Reichsbahn's hub at home.

Nazi Germany's performance in operational level warfare was shaped and in some, ultimately fatal, cases its military performance was decided negatively by the country's technological deficiencies. This is not to claim that Germany could not invent, develop, and procure what history was to demonstrate would be needed for victory. But it is to claim that Germany did not make the technological choices that might have obviated or largely offset the strategic-ally debilitating limitations consequential upon the choices that it did make.

The third element in my trinity of propositions on the meaning of technol-ogy for strategy holds that it is an enabler. This claim is not particularly novel or intellectually exciting, but nonetheless it is necessary that it be registered as a vital structural reality for the whole house of strategy.[49] In theory, technology per se simply enables more or less well whatever the strategist decides to attempt. However, in practice the combination of the objective limitations on the effectiveness of near-term achievable technologies, and the subjective limitations imposed by executive discretion in the choices made, mean that explaining technology as an enabler is an unduly simple theory. Nonetheless, it is valuable not to forget the overall enabling function of technology, because the warm glow of admiration for cunning operational plans, and pride in the anticipated combat prowess of soldiers, can lead even experts astray towards a willingness to tolerate or ignore technical shortfalls that should discipline strategic ambition.

The second and third of the structural claims explaining the relationship between technology and strategy are in little need of supporting argumenta-tion. My thesis is that technology influences warfare directly, indeed it can be said to be the principal driver of the contemporary character of warfare. This is not to forget that weapon systems express tactical choices that may be anchored upon fragile assumptions about anticipated combat. The propos-ition that technology is moved on by its own dynamic of technical improve-ment has considerable merit, but it only muddies the waters of explanation needlessly at this stage in the argument. Both the concept and the historical reality of war are too inclusive in reasonable meaning to lend themselves usefully to examination for detection of direct evidence of the contribution of technology to the course of events. Technology is everywhere, all of the time, but it does not directly move history onwards. War is a political, legal, social, cultural, military, *inter alia*, multidimensional phenomenon, to which technology is only one contributor among many. And that contribution is directly only tactical, though indirectly its influence is felt through the military agencies of operations and strategy as well the other domains of grand strategy.

It can be difficult to avoid appraising strategic history with analysis that appears to swing excessively towards one of the two extremes cited earlier as technophilia or technophobia. My third and last structural claim is that technology is and can only be a team player in the strategist's whole domain, but the emphasis needs to be upon the noun, 'team player', not the limiting qualifier, 'only'. Technology is not a team of one for strategy, but nonetheless it is vital.

5.5 STRATEGIC FUNGIBILITY: SHORTFALLS AND COMPENSATION

Exploration of strategy's technological perspective has to be a study of context. Technology is a collective noun referring to the mechanical arts and applied sciences. But, neither collectively nor individually do those strategically essential technological enablers wage war. Rather, technology fights only when it appears as a tool for use in or to a weapon system. Typically, weapons need to be employed in substantial numbers. Also they usually perform better when employed synergistically with other kinds of weapons in a style of warfare known as combined arms. Technology works for strategy as weapon and weapon support systems that function more or less well, fit enough for purpose, for reasons that exceed the frontiers of their technological content. And those weapons, or tools, operate more or less cooperatively in shifting combinations to different kinds of effects depending upon the level of conflict. While every level ultimately has meaning for policy (politics), each does have a 'grammatical' integrity according to its unique nature.[50] The need to knit it all together purposefully is the challenge to the strategist.

Ironically perhaps, it is the very complexity of strategy that in principle allows the strategist to cope well enough with the limitations of the technology that he commands. All security communities have both strengths and weaknesses relative to the assets of their competitors. When the rivalry of peacetime competition escalates into war and its warfare, the respective strengths and weaknesses of the belligerents become a severe test for grand and military strategists. Although it is convenient to refer collectively to technology as if it is a single unified competence reflected in material artefacts, in reality it consists of scientific and engineering education for the solving of physical problems, as applied or certainly applicable by manufacturing industry. The products of that industry are the military and other tools with which warfare is waged. A country can invest in technology inclusively by supporting education for future technologists that is broad rather than narrow. Technology is what it is at any point in time, but when regarded in historical perspective it becomes clear that through their political systems societies exercise some choice over the quality and quantity of technology and its material products that they will be able to produce. In contrast to geography, which is physically near constant even though its strategic meaning alters, technology is always in motion. The technological perspective on modern strategy is highly sensitive to time. The pace of innovation varies widely among technologies, as do the rates of progress among the sciences on which technology must rest. This means that the contribution of technology to military effectiveness changes over time. However, an important reason why ever more capable weapons do not approach a perfection that should enable dazzling military victories lies in the

inherently competitive context of war and strategy. A rising tide of technological sophistication raises all boats at home and abroad.

For a contemporary example, digital technology and the skill to employ it is
relatively cheap and easy to acquire today. Stateless insurgents cannot afford
aircraft carriers or satellite systems, but they can use computers with a
sophistication that may seem disproportionate to the modesty of their physical
resource assets. Full-service armed forces able and equipped to compete for
dominance in each of strategic geography's five domains, most probably
constitute the first preference for many state competitors, were that option
practicable. But, in its mature industrial-age forms, high military potency was
not an option for most polities; they could not afford it and they were
fortunate if their national security did not need it. In the twenty-first century,
however, expert access to, and even combat in one of the world's great
commons, the electromagnetic spectrum (EMS) known rather casually as
cyberspace, appears to be a considerable leveller of capabilities between otherwise grossly asymmetric security communities.

The principle of strategic fungibility recognizes in theory the possibility of
compensation with particular strengths for identified weaknesses. Because
of its multiple contextualization, technology is exceptionally accommodating
of substitution. However, the general theory of strategic fungibility, in company with all other general theory in strategy, advises only with respect to what
can happen, not to what will occur at a specific time and place. Fungibility in
action as substitution is not quite the alchemical solution to the strategist's
dilemmas that an incautious celebration of its theoretical possibilities may
mislead the credulous to believe.

Because strategic fungibility is so easy to ridicule when excessive expectations are held of it, the sound logic in the theory can be underappreciated.
The theory explains logically that:

- Many, probably most, security challenges can be met by alternative
  strategies, each of which would be enabled by a different combination
  of military, *inter alia*, means.

- Even if there is a dominant grand-strategic solution, which is not always
  the case, it is likely that one or two other solutions would prove good
  enough. Excellence is desirable, but usually is not essential in statecraft
  and war; this is fortunate given the ubiquity and permanence of friction
  and error.

- In selecting a grand strategy, a prudent polity will choose one that
  privileges what it believes to be its relative strengths, thereby minimizing
  the potentially ill consequences of relying too heavily on, say, a demoral-
  ized army, or a technically obsolescent air force. The Byzantines survived
  for a thousand years by favouring brains over military muscle, leveraging

diplomacy, espionage, and cunning plans at the operational and tactical levels of warfare.[51]

- Technology, viewed collectively as well as specifically, usually offers both alternatives within its boundary and even categorically generic alternatives (e.g. substitution of quantity for quality, morale and sacrifice for firepower, and determination for skill).

There are several major reasons why general fungibility theory needs to be regarded sceptically, or at least should be applied only with caution in particular strategic contexts. Although there is much commonality in the technology deployed and employed in different geographical domains, there is not, and does not seem likely to be, much truly all-purpose technology for all domains manned by universal soldiers. Notwithstanding the rising tide of 'jointness' which requires close cooperation between, though not actual integration of, armies, navies, air forces, space forces, and possibly cyber forces, the distinctive physical geography of each domain translates into characteristic military behaviours. Obviously, given the global access in principle allowed by the EMS, cyberspace recognizes no geographical frontiers.[52] The strategic and sometimes the military purposes will be the same for each geographically specialized military instrument, but the ways by which, and the means with which, the military effect for strategic effect is achieved will differ—and the differences may well matter profoundly.

When a needed technology is lacking, one has a choice among: finding a non-technological makeweight for the technical shortfall; employing technology of the kind, but not the quality, needed; or using technology alternative to that which is missing. There is little general wisdom to be sought on this subject, beyond understanding the structure of the challenge. Of recent years the concept of asymmetrical warfare has attracted most of the analysis that addresses the broad fungibility question. Each historical case has to be examined individually. Fungibility should be approached not as desperate remedies for desperate and probably 'wicked' problems (with no good solutions), but rather as a permanent challenge. The challenge to the strategist does not so much lie in having to seek compensation for missing quality, quantity, or both, but rather in identifying the prudent bounds to his intended attempts at substitution. The whole strategic historical experience of defence planning at all levels of detail, eternally and universally, has required the exercising of choice among different kinds of military power (land, sea, and so forth); different elements within each kind (army: e.g. infantry, cavalry, artillery); and of different forms of armament within and supporting each branch of every kind of military force. In other words, combined joint arms inherently entail calculated balancing that is in a sense fungibility, for the purpose of maximizing the synergistic effect of different military contributions.

The difficulty resides in the necessity to recognize the practicable prudent limits of substitution. For example, if an enemy's armoured force cannot be opposed reliably by extant anti-tank technologies in the form of anti-tank artillery or our tanks, then one needs to find an asymmetrical answer. The range of possibilities is not wide and it may not include highly reliable options. One such option is to wage warfare of a kind wherein the enemy's armour cannot be employed effectively. This translates as combat in urban areas, mountains, swamps, and forests. Alas, the geopolitics and geostrategy of a particular conflict may not oblige by being unaccommodating to the large-scale employment of heavy armour. Another option, again in principle, is to wage a style of warfare that does not privilege the military utility of tanks. This option may condemn one to the conduct of an insurgency using guerrilla methods, which in practice may not be an option at all. To succeed in evading the enemy's strengths is not necessarily synonymous with a strategy for victory.

All strategic behaviour accumulates transaction costs. Technology can be a great enabler as a force multiplier. Considered tactically, technology does of course solve problems. Unfortunately, assuming that the enemy is likely to share much if not all of our technological prowess, our lethality in offence and defence is near certain to be matched in quality (i.e. military effectiveness) of method by his offence and defence. Strategic history appears to reveal that technological advantage is fleeting among political communities that enjoy a mainly common state of scientific achievement. In the two greatest wars of the twentieth century the losing side did not lose because it was unduly challenged technologically and failed to find compensation for that fact.[53] Indeed, in the Second World War in Europe German armament on balance was technologically superior to that of the Allies. The German shortfall was far more in the quantity, not the quality, of its arms (and soldiers).[54] In the First World War, more than four years of intense competitive innovative effort did not produce a technological edge of decisive strategic significance. Instead, the belligerents kept pace with each other in material means and military skills, which meant that the politically better led, better resourced, and socially more resilient alliance won. Throughout the war, though, particular substitutions had to be made in the attempt to compensate for demonstrated military weaknesses that were essentially technical.

In the First World War two systemic technological shortfalls demanded compensation, but the demand could not be met at the time.[55] First, infantry in the assault were in desperate need of the quality of command that could be provided only by real-time communication by radio. Easily man-portable reliable radio communication was not available. Second, an army on the offensive required reliable mechanized mobility to traverse rough and shot-over terrain and then to exploit a tactical breakthrough speedily so as to outrun the enemy's ability to rush reserves to plug the gaps achieved tactically in his front. The technical means to provide this necessary mobility were not on hand between 1914 and 1918.

Every period in history is an existential technological context for strategy and warfare. That context is always shifting with innovation and cultural borrowing, at some times much more rapidly than at others. But, the dynamism of technology should not be permitted to conceal the frequent fact of technological shortfall and the problems that it poses. Most such gaps can be worked around, met with compensatory equipment, tactics, or even strategy. The trouble is that some technological shortfalls admit of no plausible and available immediate solution. An obvious example of such unanswerable challenge in recent decades is the continuing unavailability of thoroughly reliable active defences to intercept ballistic missiles. The Cold War was about geopolitics, ideology, and personality, not nuclear-armed weaponry.[56] The nuclear arms competition was extant because of the politics, not the arms, but nonetheless there was a strategic deadlock imposed by a technological shortfall in the technical means of defence as contrasted with the prospective effectiveness of the offence. And, unusually in strategic history, unless one of the superpowers struck a conclusively effective early blow, truly a disarming first strike worthy of the name, even an excellent offence would not function as an adequate defence. This was the technologically mandated conundrum that promoted *de facto* the authority of the concept of a mutual deterrence hopefully rendered stable by the reciprocal unavoidable menace of nuclear retaliation. Strategic stability of this character was highly unsatisfactory, not to say dangerous, because for stability thus achieved to be sustained it required the human actors and their institutions not to make a fatal error or two for a future of indefinite duration.[57] Also, mistakes aside, there are always the perilous consequences of Clausewitz's 'friction' waiting to surprise those who are unlucky or simply hubristically overconfident.[58]

By way of a generic precedent for the technological peace claimed for the nuclear standoff, one can cite the long-lasting tactical crisis for the offence in land warfare that was triggered and sustained by the technical advances in the nineteenth and early twentieth centuries.[59] In that era armaments in most circumstances strongly favoured defence over offence. The crisis was revealed in the Crimea, matured unresolved in the American Civil War, and eventually was unmistakably chronic in the First World War until late in 1917. Unfortunately for the soldiers of this lengthy period, wars were waged on a large scale despite the tactical superiority of the defence.[60] The principal work-around to this technological military problem was to seek to win by operational manoeuvre, though for that to succeed an army requires open space for cunning movement, and—need one say—a foolish, inept, or unluckily inadvertently cooperative enemy: the French in 1870 were a prime example.[61] They sought to repeat their blunders of 1870 in the opening campaign of war in August 1914, but ironically a combination of German defensive firepower and operational errors rescued France from strategically decisive defeat.[62]

In the Cold War of 1947–89, policy and strategy responded to the techno-logical shortfalls of active missile defence by settling uneasily, and in the Soviet case unofficially, upon the technically mandated default non-choice of an aspirationally stable deterrence resting on the reciprocal menace of assured destruction. A majority of Western defence experts not only recognized the technological problem at issue, in addition they celebrated its apparent tech-nical intractability. Mutual assured destruction was widely believed to under-pin, even all but guarantee, a technological peace. This notion was and remains as fallacious as it is perilous to prudent statecraft. It is essential to register the point with the utmost clarity that peace, by any definition, should never be understood to be a consequence of technology. Peace and war are political conditions that always have a technological dimension. Of course, particular technologies will be believed to privilege styles in warfare that appear to offer great, or little, strategic benefit as enablers of swift success in combat. Polities do not fight because they are armed, even potentially de-cisively well-armed; rather do they fight for political reasons. Wars are not waged for the purpose of demonstrating tactical prowess as an end in itself.

The 'tactical crisis' in the nineteenth and early twentieth centuries that rendered the taking of ground either exorbitantly expensive in casualties or literally impossible, could be alleviated and possibly resolved only by an answer that in large part had to be technological. Scientific 'predicted' gunnery to suppress the defence and protect the infantry in the advance was the 'magic bullet' that cracked open even the sophisticated German zonal defences in-depth on the Western Front in the late summer and autumn of 1918. In vital addition, the tactics and armament of the infantry themselves had improved by a generation or more from those of 1914.[63] Infantry advanced to occupy ground effectively already 'taken' by precise and ample artillery fire. The infantry moved forward cautiously, assisted by tanks and aircraft in close support. This was classic combined-arms warfare, but it was not cheap in human cost. This historical illustration emphasizes the importance of a recur-ring fact in strategic history. From time to time a tactical problem deriving from a technological shortfall frustrates operational ingenuity, thwarts stra-tegic designs, and defeats policy and its politics. From 1914 until 1918 there were only two kinds of answer to the military problems revealed in the land warfare on the Western Front. With operational artistry and military strategy helpless, the answers had to be either political or military-technological and tactical. Because there is a great chain of cause and effect connecting tactical performance with the achievement or not of the political goals of policy, technical weakness that is tactically paralysing has a long and lethal reach through strategy to the political heights beyond. In the context of rival nuclear arsenals that could not be defeated in battle, meaning defeated because reliably shorn of their retaliatory sting, the superpowers in the Cold War decided that mutual deterrence would have to suffice in defining the central terms of their strategic relationship. The strategic choice had not been so easy to make in 1914–18, because politicians on both sides believed that they had serious prospects for the achievement of military, strategic, and as a consequence political victory. They may have been wrong, but hindsight is always superior as a guide to prudent behaviour than is the guesswork of prediction, though it is far more beneficial if it can appear earlier as foresight and, of course, had it been recognized as such, believed, and acted upon.

5.6 TECHNOLOGY: SERVANT AND MASTER

Although there should be no dispute as to the seniority of policy over its military instrument, or the weight in value of human brainpower over machines, nonetheless the technological perspective reveals clearly that its subject has to be respected as both servant and master of strategy. Technology quintessentially is servant in the form of tools ultimately for enabling what politicians demand of their strategists. But, regarded tactically, extant technology is always somewhat masterful. The technology available at a particular time to the tactician, and therefore in its tactical effect to be exploited by the strategist, influences and may even command what can and cannot be done. Even when there are technical work-arounds for the practical limits of current technology, those choices and the acceptance of their costs and risks will have been determined by the state of the technology that could not perform the needed tasks as soldiers would prefer. For example, in the absence of good enough anti-tank artillery, heroic German infantrymen could earn the tank destroyer medal by personally affixing a 'sticky' armour-piercing explosive to a vulnerable part of an enemy tank. Usually there are alternative solutions to a tactical problem, but it can be a challenge to find sufficiently skilful, brave, and lucky individuals to exercise them, let alone exercise them repeatedly.

In the accepting spirit of *faute de mieux*, soldiers will do what they are commanded to do, even when their technology, their military tools, are not fit enough for purpose. RAF Bomber Command could not survive bombing Germany in daylight, so it did what it could do and switched to bombing at night. Alas, it could not bomb precisely by night, with the result that it bombed imprecisely. In fact, the Command could not bomb precisely by our contemporary standard either by day or by night, though it could perform in late 1944 and 1945 with a quality of targeting accuracy in delivery that was a generation-plus in advance of its capability in 1941–2. The technical advances in British bombing in the Second World War are analogous to the improvement in quality and quantity of British artillery between August 1914 and the

Armistice in November 1918. As for the USAAF's performance in the some-what loosely combined, better expressed as coordinated, Combined Bomber Offensive (CBO), by early 1945 it was reduced to engaging (with airborne radar assisted bomb-aiming navigation) in the precision bombing of urban area targets, in the hope that 'confusion bombing' would promote such chaos that the German will or ability to fight on would collapse.[64] It is useful to recognize the enduring historical reality that there is a law of the instrument. The technology of the time, any time, sets parameters to military achievement, even to technical achievement secured as if it were turbo-charged by unusual human skill and extraordinary will. Radar-bombing through cloud cover could not be a precise exercise. But, the Allied bomber force was what it was by late 1944 and early 1945; a superb state-of-the-art high-technology military instrument that had been so expensive to build that it had to be used, imprecisely if necessary, all the while fighting was proceeding on the ground. It was politically, not to say morally, inconceivable not to allow a mighty force of heavy bombers to sit idly by when our soldiers were dying in combat. The probable fact that continuation of the bombing until the last days of the war was not strategically useful is beside the point of political and moral imperatives.

On the other end of the scale of destruction from inadequate navigation for accurate high altitude industrial-age bombing in the Second World War, lay the challenge of improvised explosive devices (IEDs) in Iraq and Afghanistan in the 2000s. These devices posed a technological challenge that could not be worked around wholly reliably by tactical avoidance. Intelligence on their location was rarely perfect, while adaptive methods to disable them could not be guaranteed to work. Experience in IED disposal was essential, but expensively bought in casualties. There were technological answers which worked well (e.g. robotic vehicles to destroy the devices), but they were not always available or tactically appropriate. The armoured vehicles sufficiently protected to resist blast effects, also limited troop mobility over soft ground, through narrow urban roadways, and prohibited attempted transit of weak bridges. In addition, the manned and unmanned vehicles that provided some technical part of the tactical answer to IEDs were expensive, slow to develop and procure, and therefore were vulnerable to budget cutting exercises at home. Furthermore, often it was argued that although a particular item of expensive equipment undoubtedly would be valuable for today and just possibly tomorrow, future military requirements for the conflicts of the days after tomorrow may well see no need for it. Therefore, the army has to soldier on without it through a current crisis because its legacy value is judged too low to be worth its budgetary costs.

To a degree all warfare is technological. But, warfare in some geographical environments is more technological than it is in others. However, even if warfare were to evolve to a condition characterized by combat waged wholly by technically autonomous machines (robots), those robotic machines would have needed to be invented, constructed, and electronically programmed in their ability to function autonomously.[65] This admittedly extreme example noted, it is significant that physical geography commands that warfare in its five environments must vary in its capital dependency and intensity. Once one grants the near banality that technology always matters for the strategist, regardless of the geographical domain, one needs hastily to advise that it matters far more for cyberspace, Earth-orbital space, the air, and at sea than it does for warfare on land. The reason is uncontroversial. On the ground in land warfare the human element in the military instrument has more discretion in its choice of behaviour than is true for combatants in other environments. In theory, individual soldiers and small units can hide, run, pursue, and exploit the wide variety of different terrain in which they might find themselves. Similarly, the variety of weapons and their supporting systems that may be accessible and available for their use is much broader than is the array of options available to warriors at sea in the air, for orbital space, or in cyberspace. These generalities are only that, general claims. In historical practice local details must be sovereign. Combat in any environment can be deadly, or as with cyber combat, have lethal consequences, but on land the human element is relatively more important than it is in the other geographies. The personal qualities as well as the professional skills of soldiers on the ground are likely to count for more in the equation that explains fighting power than would be true of the geographically specialized armed forces that 'man' ships, aircraft, or who control stand-off missiles and other vehicles, let alone those who only direct electrons to fight in the EMS; these are enduring geophysically mandated differences.[66]

The strategic history of modern times has recorded a cascade of temporally overlapping technological marvels. A succession of technologies overlap in time and then endure even though more recent technologies appear; they are weaponized and have merit as partial replacements for machines of earlier vintage. Although steam power has been replaced by oil and electricity, railways and ships persist and adapt technically as essential enablers of grand and military strategic projects. Motorization and mechanization in all their forms were characteristic, indeed defining, late industrial-age tools of military effort, yet they persist as essential today. The technology that permits heavier-than-air manned flight is still with us, even if in all but technically unrecognizable detail from its fragile beginnings a century ago. Manned flight, civilian and military, may be technically ageing for piloted (on-board or remotely) aircraft towards the zone wherein it is challengeable for many purposes, but the need for aircraft, air power sensibly understood inclusively, is not open to reasonable scepticism. This is not to deny that there is scope for controversy over the forms that air power should take.[67] The stream, episodically the torrent, of evolutionary and revolutionary technological innovations, has become a given for strategists to try and understand, exploit if they can, at least cope well enough with if they cannot, and in some cases counter when enemies threaten or employ them. But, still it would be difficult to vote decisively in favour either of continuity or change in a strategist's professional universe misunderstood as presenting such a falsely binary set of over-simple alternatives.

Material and intellectual change in strategic affairs has been characteristic of modern times, with the porous categories of continuity and change having a complex relationship. Technology and ideas about its meaning and therefore about its use are inalienably bound together. But, because strategy is adversarial the ever perfecting technology that always must help enable it typically is reduced in its potency for competitive advantage by the fact of intended counteraction. Muscle-powered missile weapons did not abolish war, but neither did gunpowder, the machine gun, nor even atomic fission and then fusion. In character, statecraft, war, and strategy have altered radically over the centuries, but in their nature they have been eternal. Some technologies claimed to be game-changing for warfare have proved to be rightly so labelled. Gunpowder weapons, the railway, motorization, aircraft, nuclear weapons, spacecraft, and computers, to cite but a handful of major technological innovations, have changed the ways in which war could be, actually needed to be, fought. But, have war, strategy, and warfare ceased to be what once they were? This question could be posed of the strategic history for any period anywhere on Earth. The answer has to be a resounding 'no'. This negative judgement must be recorded despite the fact of cumulatively revolutionary change in the technological artefacts that are tools for the strategist.

What have been revolutionized are the tactical means for armed conflict, with some lesser but still significant changes in preferred and arguably feasible strategic ways. The policy ends of strategy that are decided as ever by politics vary widely in detail from historical case to case, but they have yet to be transformed by any influence, direct or indirect, traceable to technology. This claim should be refutable by reference to nuclear weapons, but unfortunately it is not, at least not yet.

NOTES

1. Alfred Thayer Mahan, *The Influence of Sea Power upon the French Revolution and Empire, 1793–1812*, Vol. I (Boston: Little, Brown, 1898), 102.
2. Martin van Creveld, *Technology and War: From 2000 B.C. to the Present* (New York: Free Press, 1989), 319.
3. Baron Antoine Henri de Jomini, *The Art of War* (1838; London: Greenhill Books, 1992), 48.

4. J. F. C. Fuller, *Armament and History: A Study of the Influence of Armament on History from the Dawn of Classical Warfare to the Second World War* (London: Eyre and Spottiswoode, 1946), 31–2.

5. Fuller's 'most important writings' are listed in Brian Holden Reid's fine intellectual biography, *J. F. C. Fuller: Military Thinker* (New York: St. Martin's Press, 1987), esp. 259–64. Also, see Reid's *Studies in British Military Thought: Debates with Fuller and Liddell Hart* (Lincoln, NE: University of Nebraska Press, 1998).

6. See Colin S. Gray, *The Strategy Bridge: Theory for Practice* (Oxford: Oxford University Press, 2010), 278–83.

7. Judy Pearsall and Bill Trumble, eds., *The Oxford English Reference Dictionary (OERD)*, 2nd edn. (Oxford: Oxford University Press, 1996), 1480.

8. Pearsall and Trumble, eds., *OERD*, 584. There is no single concept word in English that conveys the meaning of the important idea conveyed in German by gestalt.

9. Reid, *Studies in British Military Thought*, 16.

10. See David Zimmerman, *Britain's Shield: The Story of Radar from War to Peace* (Stroud: Sutton Publishing, 2001), ch. 13.

11. This distinction is deployed effectively in Eliot Cohen, 'Technology and Warfare', in John Baylis, James J. Wirtz, and Colin S. Gray, eds., *Strategy in the Contemporary World*, 3rd edn. (Oxford: Oxford University Press, 2010), 141.

12. I seek to explain the reasonable goals for, but also the practical limits upon, education in strategy, in my *Schools for Strategy: Teaching Strategy for 21st Century Conflict* (Carlisle, PA: Strategic Studies Institute, US Army War College, November 2009).

13. J. F. C. Fuller's 'constant tactical factor' of offence/defence interaction, and Edward N. Luttwak's 'paradoxical logic of conflict', both capture this enduring competitive dynamic of technology in its role in strategic history. In Fuller's timeless words: 'From this law [the 'law of military development'] may be deduced a principle I will call the Constant Tactical Factor, which is: every improvement in weapon-power has aimed at lessening the danger on one side by increasing it on the other. Therefore every improvement in weapons has eventually been met by a counter-improvement which has rendered the improvement obsolete' (*Armament and History*, 33). In addition, see Edward N. Luttwak, *Strategy: The Logic of War and Peace*, rev. edn. (1987; Cambridge, MA: Harvard University Press, 2001), xii.

14. I pursue this somewhat controversial idea in my *Categorical Confusion: The Strategic Implications of Recognizing Challenges Either as Irregular or Traditional* (Carlisle, PA: Strategic Studies Institute, US Army War College, February 2012).

15. Winston S. Churchill, *The World Crisis, 1911–1918*, Vol. II [of 2] (London: Odhams Press, 1938), 1442 (and additionally 1177–9).

16. Carl von Clausewitz, *On War*, trans. Michael Howard and Peter Paret (1832–4; Princeton, NJ: Princeton University Press, 1976), 104.

17. Michael I. Handel, *Masters of War: Classical Strategic Thought*, 3rd edn. (London: Frank Cass, 2001), 353–60. The thesis that strategy can be tacticized is a popular but nonetheless categorical impossibility, as is the proposition that one can have a strategy of tactics. A belligerent may not function in a purposefully strategic way—both Germany and Japan in the last two years of the Second World War, for examples—but although its tactical military performance must have strategic

effect, tactics do not magically become strategy, though they may stand in for them.

18. John Terraine, 'The Substance of the War', in Hugh Cecil and Peter H. Liddle, eds., *Facing Armageddon: The First World War Experience* (London: Leo Cooper, 1996), 3–15.

19. Michael Howard, 'The Transformation of Strategy', *The RUSI Journal*, 156 (August/September 2011), 12–16.

20. For some persuasive historical perspective that insists we should not overemphasize the technological in appraising the American way(s) in warfare, see Brian McAllister Linn, *The Echo of Battle: The Army's Way of War* (Cambridge, MA: Harvard University Press, 2007) and Eliot A. Cohen, *Conquered into Liberty: Two Centuries of Battles Along the Great Warpath That Made the American Way of War* (New York: Free Press, 2011).

21. The literature on RMA is now huge. The following are a small selection of useful books and report-length studies: Barry D. Watts, *The Maturing Revolution in Military Affairs* (Washington, DC: Center for Strategic and Budgetary Assessments, 2011); Dima Adamsky, *The Culture of Military Innovation: The Impact of Cultural Factors on the Revolution in Military Affairs in Russia, the US, and Israel* (Stanford, CA: Stanford University Press, 2010); Tim Benbow, *The Magic Bullet? Understanding the Revolution in Military Affairs* (London: Brassey's, 2004); Colin S. Gray, *Strategy for Chaos: Revolutions in Military Affairs and the Evidence of History* (London: Frank Cass, 2002); Andrew F. Krepinevich, *The Military–Technical Revolution: A Preliminary Assessment* (July 1992; Washington, DC: Center for Strategic and Budgetary Assessments, 2002); Michael J. Mazarr, *The Military Technical Revolution: A Structural Framework* (Washington, DC: Center for Strategic and International Studies, March 1993); MacGregor Knox and Williamson Murray, eds., *The Dynamics of Military Revolution, 1300–2050* (Cambridge: Cambridge University Press, 2001); William A. Owens, *Lifting the Fog of War* (New York: Farrar, Straus & Giroux, 2000); Elinor C. Sloan, *The Revolution in Military Affairs: Implications for Canada and NATO* (Montreal and Kingston: McGill-Queens University Press, 2002); and Keith Thomas, ed., *The Revolution in Military Affairs: Warfare in the Information Age* (Canberra: Australian Defence Studies Centre, 1997).

22. See Robert L. Bateman III, ed., *Digital War: A View from the Front Lines* (Novato, CA: Presidio Press, 1999); David J. Lonsdale, *The Nature of War in the Information Age: Clausewitzian Future* (London: Frank Cass, 2004); and, for an excellent synoptic view, Paul K. Davis, 'Military Transformation? Which Transformation and What Lies Ahead?', in Stephen J. Cimbala, ed., *The George W. Bush Defense Program: Policy, Strategy and War* (Dulles, VA: Potomac Books, 2011), 11–41.

23. For expert professional studies, see Paul K. Davis, *Analytic Architecture for Capabilities-Based Planning, Mission-System Analysis, and Transformation*, MR-1513-OSD (Santa Monica, CA: RAND, 2002) and for a more recent treatment, Davis and Peter A. Wilson, *Looming Discontinuities in U.S. Military Strategy and Defense Planning: Colliding RMAs Necessitate a New Strategy*, Occasional Paper (Santa Monica, CA: RAND, 2011).

24. See two insightful period-piece studies by Lawrence Freedman: *The Revolution in Strategic Affairs*, Adelphi Paper 318 (London: International Institute for Strategic Studies, April 1998); and *The Transformation of Strategic Affairs*, Adelphi Paper 379 (London: International Institute for Strategic Studies, March 2006).
25. Clausewitz, *On War*, 85.
26. See some writings by Max Boot: 'The New American Way of War', *Foreign Affairs*, 82 (July/August 2003), 41–58; 'The Struggle to Transform the Military', *Foreign Affairs*, 84 (March/April 2005), 103–11; and, for the full story, *War Made New: Technology, Warfare and the Course of History, 1500 to Today* (New York: Gotham Books, 2006).
27. I confess to promotion of the contestable concept of strategic history. See Colin S. Gray, *War, Peace, and International Relations: An Introduction to Strategic History*, 2nd edn. (Abingdon: Routledge, 2011).
28. Bernard Brodie, *War and Politics* (New York: Macmillan, 1973), 474–5.
29. Andrew F. Krepinevich, 'Cavalry to Computer: The Pattern of Military Revolutions', *The National Interest*, 37 (Fall 1994), 30.
30. Krepinevich, *The Military–Technical Revolution*, 3.
31. Krepinevich, *The Military–Technical Revolution*, iv.
32. Clausewitz, *On War*, 85.
33. Luttwak, *Strategy*, xii. But, see Antulio J. Echevarria II, *Preparing for One War and Getting Another* (Carlisle, PA: Strategic Studies Institute, US Army War College, September 2010).
34. I am grateful to my colleague, Patrick Porter, for the clarity and persuasiveness with which he makes this crucial point in his *Military Orientalism: Eastern War Through Western Eyes* (London: C. Hurst, 2009), 65, 170.
35. Krepinevich, 'Cavalry to Computer', 30.
36. Krepinevich, 'Cavalry to Computer', 30. RAF Fighter Command in summer 1940 illustrates clearly that technology as weapon systems and their supporting structures constitutes only a part of the strategic story. Weapons only approach their potential for military and strategic effectiveness when they are employed by appropriate doctrine in realization of a situationally suitable concept of operations.
37. Van Creveld, *Technology and War*, ch. 15. Maurice Pearton, *Diplomacy, War and Technology since 1830* (Lawrence, KS: University Press of Kansas, 1984) and Merritt Roe Smith, ed., *Military Enterprise and Technological Change: Perspectives on the American Experience* (Cambridge, MA: MIT Press, 1987) also are helpful.
38. On radar, see Alan Beyerchen, 'From Radio to Radar: Interwar Military Adaptation to Technological Change in Germany, the United Kingdom, and the United States', in Williamson Murray and Alan R. Millett, eds., *Military Innovation in the Interwar Period* (Cambridge: Cambridge University Press, 1996), 265–99; Zimmerman, *Britain's Shield* and Robert Budieri, *The Invention that Changed the World: The Story of Radar from War to Peace* (London: Abacus, 1998). On nuclear weapons, see Gerald DeGroot, *The Bomb: A Life* (London: Jonathan Cape, 2004) and Jeremy Bernstein, *Nuclear Weapons: What You Need to Know* (Cambridge: Cambridge University Press, 2008).

39. For example, see the conceptually powerful article by Donald G. Brennan, 'The Case for Missile Defense', *Foreign Affairs*, 43 (April 1969), 81–8, to which one could well respond, 'if only!'

40. The technologies necessary for strategic bombing have to be understood in their full context for use. With that caveat in mind, see Max Hastings, *Bomber Command* (New York: Dial Press, 1979); Kenneth P. Werrell, *Blankets of Fire: US Bombers over Japan during World War II* (Washington, DC: Smithsonian Institution Press, 1996); and Tami Davis Biddle, *Rhetoric and Reality in Air Warfare: The Evolution of British and American Ideas about Strategic Bombing, 1914–1945* (Princeton, NJ: Princeton University Press, 2002).

41. Peter R. Faber, 'Interwar US Army Aviation and the Air Corps Tactical School: Incubators of American Airpower', in Phillip S. Meilinger, ed., *The Paths of Heaven: The Evolution of Airpower Theory* (Maxwell AFB, AL: Air University Press, 1997), 183–238, and David E. Johnson, *Fast Tanks and Heavy Bombers: Innovation in the U.S. Army, 1917–1945* (Ithaca, NY: Cornell University Press, 1998), ch. 11, are outstanding.

42. Stephen L. MacFarland and Wesley Phillips Newton, *To Command the Sky: The Battle for Air Superiority over Germany, 1942–1944* (Washington, DC: Smithsonian Institution Press, 1991), esp. fig. 4, 105.

43. See Annika Mumbauer, 'German War Plans', in Richard F. Hamilton and Holger H. Herwig, eds., *War Planning, 1914* (Cambridge: Cambridge University Press, 2010), 48. On the implications of railways for strategy and operations in the nineteenth century, see Dennis E. Showalter, *Railroads and Rifles: Soldiers, Technology, and the Unification of Germany* (Hamden, CT: Archon Books, 1986) and Keir A. Lieber, *War and the Engineers: The Primacy of Politics over Technology* (Ithaca, NY: Cornell University Press, 2005), ch. 2.

44. In late August and early September 1914, the French Army demonstrated conclusively the potency of lateral railway communications for the defending side. See Holger H. Herwig, *The Marne, 1914: The Opening of World War I and the Battle That Changed the World* (New York: Random House, 2009).

45. David T. Zabecki, *The German 1918 Offensives: A Case Study in the Operational Level of War* (Abingdon: Routledge, 2006).

46. Williamson Murray and Allan R. Millett, *A War To Be Won: Fighting the Second World War* (Cambridge, MA: Harvard University Press, 2000), 280–1.

47. Evan Mawdsley, *World War II: A New History* (Cambridge: Cambridge University Press, 2009), 250.

48. Mawdsley, *World War II*, 250.

49. T. E. Lawrence, *Seven Pillars of Wisdom: A Triumph* (New York: Anchor Books, 1991), 191. I comment on this useful metaphor in my book *The Strategy Bridge*, 47 n17.

50. With thanks, and possibly an apology, to Clausewitz, *On War*, 605.

51. See John Halidon, *Warfare, State and Society in the Byzantine World, 565–1204* (London: UCL Press, 1999); id., *The Byzantine Wars: Battles and Campaigns of the Byzantine Era* (Stroud: Tempus, 2001); and Edward N. Luttwak, *The Grand Strategy of the Byzantine Empire* (Cambridge, MA: The Belknap Press of Harvard University Press, 2009). Principal original sources include three translations by

Father George T. Dennis, S.J.: Maurice (Emperor), *Maurice's Strategikon: Handbook of Byzantine Military Strategy*, trans. George T. Dennis (*c*.600; Philadelphia, PA: University of Pennsylvania Press, 1984); Anon., *Three Byzantine Military Treatises*, trans. George T. Dennis (Emperor Justinian I, r. 527–65; Washington, DC: Dumbarton Oaks, 1985); and (Emperor) Leo VI, *The Taktika of Leo VI*, trans. George T. Dennis (r. 886–912; Washington, DC: Dumbarton Oaks, 2010).

52. This geophysical reality and its military and strategic implications are well explained in Elinor L. Sloan, *Modern Military Strategy: An Introduction* (Abingdon: Routledge, 2012), ch. 6.

53. The literature is immense, but two very different books shed bright light: Richard J. Overy, *Why the Allies Won* (London: Jonathan Cape, 1995) and Adam Tooze, *Wages of Destruction: The Making and Breaking of the Nazi Economy* (London: Allen Lane, 2006).

54. See Terraine, 'The Substance of the War', which is a short masterpiece; while Jeremy Black, *The Great War and the Making of the Modern World* (London: Continuum, 2011) is a superior narrative in a crowded field.

55. Showalter believes that '[s]oldiers and scholars agree that even in the wars of industrial societies, anything more than marginal technical advantages are rare. What is loosely described as technological superiority usually means either greater skill at employing roughly equivalent means, or simply greater numbers. When it does exist, superiority in the quality of weapons and equipment in land warfare is marginal and ephemeral, seldom remaining long with any army.' *Railroads and Rifles*, 13. I am strongly in agreement with Showalter.

56. I have addressed this subject in some detail in two recent studies: Colin S. Gray, 'Mission Improbable, Fear, Culture, and Interest: Peace Making, 1943–1949', in Williamson Murray and Jim Lacey, eds., *The Making of Peace: Rulers, States, and the Aftermath of War* (Cambridge: Cambridge University Press, 2009), 265–91, and id., 'The Nuclear Age and the Cold War', in John Andreas Olsen and Gray, eds., *The Practice of Strategy: From Alexander the Great to the Present* (Oxford: Oxford University Press, 2011), 237–59.

57. This troubling thought was well articulated in a notable article in 1973 by Fred Charles Ikle: 'Can Nuclear Deterrence Last Out the Century?' *Foreign Affairs*, 51 (January 1973), 267–85. Ikle revisited the subject in his essay, 'Nuclear Strategy: Can There Be a Happy Ending?' *Foreign Affairs*, 63 (Spring 1985), 810–26. Despite the period-piece flavour of these articles, they address an enduring cause for serious concern.

58. Clausewitz, *On War*, 119–21.

59. The finest study of the 'tactical crisis' and efforts to resolve it is Antulio J. Echevarria II, *After Clausewitz: German Military Thinkers Before the Great War* (Lawrence, KS: University Press of Kansas, 2000).

60. Brent Nosworthy, *The Bloody Crucible of Courage: Fighting Methods and Combat Experience of the Civil War* (New York: Carroll and Graf Publishers, 2005) is an expert analysis of mid-nineteenth-century combat.

61. See Michael Howard, *The Franco-Prussian War: The German Invasion of France, 1870–1871* (London: Methuen, 1981) and Geoffrey Wawro, *The Franco-Prussian*

War: The German Conquest of France in 1870–1871 (Cambridge: Cambridge University Press, 2003).

62. The opening weeks of the warfare in the West are analysed in Terence Zuber, *The Battle of the Frontiers: Ardennes 1914* (Stroud: Tempus Publishing, 2007).

63. Outstanding studies include: Gary Sheffield, *Forgotten Victory: The First World War: Myths and Realities* (London: Headline, 2001); David T. Zabecki, *Steel Wind: Colonel Georg Bruchmuller and the Birth of Modern Artillery* (Westport, CT: Praeger, 1994); Jonathan B. A. Bailey, 'The First World War and the Birth of Modern Warfare', in Knox and Murray, eds., *The Dynamics of Military Revolution, 1300–2050*, 132–53; and David Stevenson, *With Our Backs to the Wall: Victory and Defeat in 1918* (London: Allen Lane, 2011), ch. 3.

64. See Donald L. Miller, *Eighth Air Force: The American Bomber Crews in Britain* (London: Aurum Press, 2008), ch. 16. For valuable context, see Robert S. Ehlers, Jr., *Targeting the Reich: Air Intelligence and the Allied Bombing Campaigns* (Lawrence, KS: University of Kansas Press, 2009).

65. It is hard to remove the human dimension from robotic styles in warfare, but see P. W. Singer, *Wired for War: The Robotics Revolution and Conflict in the 21st Century* (New York: Penguin Press, 2009).

66. On the concept of fighting power, see the pioneering study by Martin van Creveld, *Fighting Power: German and U.S. Army Performances, 1939–1945* (Westport, CT: Greenwood Press, 1982).

67. Recent writings on air power that bear directly on the discussion in the text include Martin van Creveld, *The Age of Air Power* (New York: Public Affairs, 2011) and Colin S. Gray, *Airpower for Strategic Effect* (Maxwell AFB, AL: Air University Press, 2012). Thomas P. Ehrhard, 'Unmanned Aircraft: 50 Years of Innovation and Frustration', unpub. PhD diss. (Washington, DC: Johns Hopkins University, 2004) tells the (largely American) story of UAVs, or remotely piloted aircraft as air professionals prefer to call them. An authoritative contemporary British view is to be found in Development, Concepts and Doctrine Centre (DCDC), *The UK Approach to Unmanned Aircraft Systems*, Joint Doctrine Note 2/11 (Shrivenham: Ministry of Defence, 2011).

6

Conclusion: The Whole House of Strategy, Perilous Dualism

When it grew too hot for dreamless dozing, I picked up my tangle again, and went on ravelling it out, considering now the whole house of war in its structural aspect which was strategy, in its arrangements, which were tactics, and in the sentiment to its inhabitants which was psychology; for my personal duty was command, and the commander, like the master architect, was responsible for all.

The first confusion was the false antithesis between strategy, the aim in war, the synoptic regard seeing each part relative for the whole, and tactics, the means towards a strategic level, the particular steps of its staircase. They seemed only points of view from which to ponder the elements of war, the Algebraical element of things, a Biological element of lives, and the Psychological element of ideas.

T. E. Lawrence[1]

Any use of the word 'power' with an environmental modifier like 'cyber' can only be a subjective one; it does not illuminate the core nature of power, except to connote that power operates in 'cyber' environments, as it does anywhere else where social relations occur.

David J. Betz and Tim Stevens[2]

6.1 STRATEGY IN VENN GEOMETRY

The epigraphs above share the virtue of a common unified and unifying view of the subjects of war and power. Each performs excellently in the theory function as it was explained by Carl von Clausewitz. They sort out what is most in need of sorting: the partial from the whole, the subjective and transient from the objective and enduring. Lawrence sees a whole house of war, which I adapt as a whole house of strategy. Betz and Stevens argue for a single understanding of power, which holds logically for a no less properly imperial comprehension of strategy. When Lawrence was writing brilliantly about strategy for the conduct of guerrilla warfare in the Arab Revolt against the much decayed but still quite formidable Ottoman Empire, he was talking about the same subject of strategy as are Betz and Stevens in their examination of the strategic meaning and values of cyber operations. Strategy is strategy and its general theory has authority over any and every historical case of attempts at its practical application.[3]

In its organization and argument this text reflects a perilous duality flagged in this chapter's title. It is ironic, not paradoxical, that although *Perspectives on Strategy* argues for a holistic understanding of strategy and lays emphasis upon a general theory whose tenets unite the field, it is committed to exploring the single subject of strategy from different perspectives. The contradiction between unity and division is only apparent, because it is the robust inclusivity of the general theory of strategy that enables particular perspectives to be explored safely. When the general theory is regarded properly as being conceptually sovereign, the danger is greatly reduced that strategic practice will be in thrall to some reductionist views (e.g. strategy regarded as applied intellect, morality, culture, geography, or technology). It is only possible to allow the distinctive perspectives on the whole house of strategy their due when that edifice is standing whole and well-constructed. Conceptually, this text can be represented as a Venn diagram of intersecting data sets for elements partial to the entire project of strategy (see Figure 6.1). There is no correct number of perspectives in which strategy can be viewed. As a social scientist this author is intellectually comfortable with a subject that does not yield to research and analysis in quest of a Higgs boson-like most fundamental particle of truth. As a fairly devout Clausewitzian I would like to claim that politics is the God particle for strategy, but such an assertion could not be entirely satisfactory.[4] When one starts down the path of fundamental enquiry into causality there is unlikely to be a happy epiphany, because the journey can have no attainable end. Behind and fuelling politics one finds human nature, but a nature that probably requires circumstantial placement to be translatable for a meaningful perspective on strategy. The early chapters here sought to explain the difficulty in coming to grips analytically with moral and other authority. As context always itself must have context, so moral authority can only derive in its turn from yet higher moral authority, and so on, rather unhelpfully for useful understanding. Ironically, to gain understanding need not mean to secure much enlightenment. After all, how helpful is it to understand why strategy is so difficult to do well?

The intersection, which is to say the overlapping, of the distinctive partial perspectives on strategy which Venn geometry indicates, is a phenomenon of porosity essential for intellectual grasp of the wholeness of the house of strategy. The Venn educated strategist is disciplined in analysis and judgement

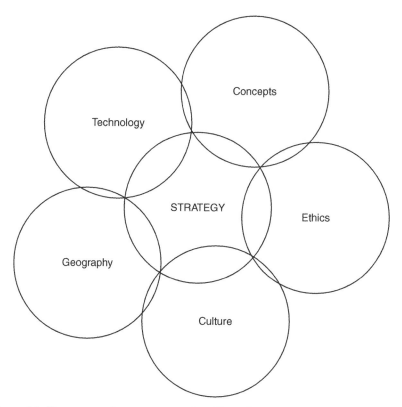

Figure 6.1 Five perspectives on strategy in a Venn diagram

by appreciation of the important distinction between necessary and sufficient causal factors. Many a sufficient political ambition has been frustrated by a contemporary lack of the necessary means or circumstances to realize it. Venn's concept that translates here as overlapping elements, dimensions, or factors that in practice need to be viewed as porous categories, may be a stylized mathematician's conceit, but it presents a tolerable, if much simplified, representation of the complexity of the strategist's realm.

Unlike strategy's general theory, which should by definition be complete, if ever unfinished in the possibility of its improvement in form, perspectives on strategy can always be augmented or reduced according to intellectual taste and fashion concerning desirable inclusivity and exclusivity. The 'perilous dualism' to which the chapter title here refers is that of scholarly mission creep. To explain, studies of the Second World War respectively in conceptual, moral, cultural, geographical, or technological perspective may slip the leash of conceptual and empirical discipline and 'go native' by producing a moral, or cultural history of the war. The partial perspective intentionally privileged from the outset, in effect is permitted to swallow the rest. This is a familiar malady. Library shelves groan with the weight of worthy books on such partial subjects as 'the war at sea', 'the war in the air', and so forth.

In his command performance the strategist strives to cope well enough with multi-layered complexity. Each perspective examined here, in addition to the super ones of politics and human nature that deliberately were eschewed, are always in play and have some relevance for strategy. This can be analytically frustrating to the scholar who seeks unwisely a measure of certain understanding that history, let alone contemporary or future contexts, cannot provide, no matter how elegant the equations or powerful data analysing machines may be. Notwithstanding claims to the contrary, it is not accurate to conceive of strategic studies as a scholarly discipline. What is unhelpful is effort to maintain the 'stovepipes' of alleged purity for historical, social scientific, or hard physical scientific methodologies. Social science without history can be likened to driving in the dark without a rear-view mirror to reveal whence you have come and what is behind you.[5] History with little or no social science worthy of the name is likely to teeter on the brink of explanation that under-reaches in the meaning to events that it can supply. Indeed, so powerfully can the specific contextuality of history impose a respect for (yesterday's) presentism, that the historian is likely to be unable to answer, if he even understands, the social scientific strategist's question that has been deployed often in these pages, 'so what?'

While the general theory of strategy educates about the permanent structure and functioning of the whole of its subject, it aspires to achieve no more than that. The theory educates its students to help enable them to cope with the specific strategic challenges of their day. My theme of a perilous dualism is intended to capture two realities: that of a united subject, but also that of a subject manifesting itself in ever changing forms. The architectural endurance of the whole house of strategy might mislead the unwary into believing that the weight of relative influence of the five perspectives examined here either is permanent or is equal among all of them. Just as maps can be designed to advance political claims because of their magically deceitful distorting cartography, so the geometry of a tidy Venn diagram has the potential to obscure as well as enlighten. In historical practice, every perspective yields a contributing sub-narrative to the gestalt of the grand narrative of strategy. But, those sub-narratives, confusingly interdependent though they are, reveal a course of events and suggest an explanation wherein some factors would seem to carry more weight than others.

Elsewhere, I have offered the dual-track argument that while, on the one hand, strategy is difficult to do well enough because of the complexity of its domain, on the other hand that complexity provides options to help work around problems. Each chapter here privileges a particular perspective on strategy, though recognizes porosity and interdependence among them. The challenge to clarity of understanding posed by the complexity of the whole house of strategy is easily illustrated. Wherever one looks in strategic history, the competition for pole position as most significant perspective is apt to be intense; if it is not, the reason probably is because scholars have not examined the case in sufficient width, depth, and context.[6]

To illustrate: what might a 'perspectives' study choose to register about Nazi Germany's desperate last gamble in the West with its Ardennes Offensive, launched on 16 December 1944? Historical circumstance explains much of German motivation; the geographical perspective helps explain (mis)perceived opportunity, with weather being a significant arbiter of military effectiveness; in conceptual perspective the organizing operational idea had positive resonance and the boldness of the military stroke appealed to the personality of the Führer, as well as seeming to meet the need of Germany's strategic situation. This gross simplification is offered in order to indicate how problematic it must be to attempt to unpack the complexity inherent in a strategic history with its many dimensions. For any strategic historical case, there will be human decisionmakers behaving with variable discretion in a context of political, bureaucratical, cultural, moral, and other contexts. Histories that favour the conceptual, the ethical, or the geographical perspective, *inter alia*, can hardly help but give an unbalanced interpretation of events. And yet, each perspective is in some measure true. The general theory of strategy should be able to advise on what to look for, but it can never be mobilized itself to explain how the perspectives it accommodates should be rank-ordered for their relative potency. Geography (e.g. distance, terrain, weather) usually explains a lot, but the specific reasons why it is relevant to historical strategies have to be sought in human personality, circumstance, and beliefs.

The attractions of monocausality ('strategy is really all about . . .') are as obvious and substantial as they are lethal to balanced understanding. Having said that, nonetheless the scholar would be well advised not to be so tolerant in his or her recognition of complexity and multi-causality that meaningful explanation is impossible. One can adapt Gresham's Law—that bad money tends to drive out good—to read that a proliferation of strategic explanations with lower value tends to obscure and diminish the worth attached to explanations with higher value. Although all coins in circulation have some value, the fact that those of lower worth circulate more rapidly—Gresham's point— should not be allowed to obscure the intrinsic worth of higher denomination coins. To convert this illustration: although strategic history is a drama played by a cast comprising every perspective, however organized conceptually by category, at most times, in most places, and in most circumstances some perspectives, perhaps just one or two such, can plausibly be judged dominant (e.g. the political spirit is willing, the purpose is morally imperative, but alas the helicopters cannot fly in fog).

The strategic theorist can be thought of as a maker of conceptual tools for the practising strategist. In his harrowing moral memoir of his combat tour in Vietnam as a young Marine officer, Karl Marlantes offers the thought that

> Weapons are tools. Tools are an extension of ourselves. Tools make you more effective. They are ego enhancing. Ask any good carpenter how he feels about a really good tool. We enhance our feelings of self-worth if we have good tools.[7]

When strategic theorists discuss the relationship in strategic history between mind and muscle, brain and brawn, they are apt to commit the same kind of error as do politicians and soldiers, though from a different point of view. Of course, there is an objective empirical difference between thought and behaviour. But, in historical reality this seemingly unambiguous distinction is blurred. Behaviour is thought in action. Not all concepts are converted into action and applied in strategic performance in the field, but it is a fair generalization to claim that there has to be some fusion of thought and deed. Orders, commands, may be obviously exterior to the directed behaviour, but there is a sense in which, once committed to action, the military instrument will have internalized the relevant part of the conceptual contribution to fighting power. The soldiers commanded will attempt to play out the roles that the conceptual script demands, while the troops' armament and elements of supporting infrastructure reflect and express recent conceptual preferences. The distinction between the theory and the practice of strategy is both objective and subjective; it is real, yet it is also artificial. The mind and its conceptual constructions is not set aside, parked for the duration, when soldiers go to war or when inert materials are converted and assembled into weapons.

The essential unity in the apparent duality that is strategic thought and strategic practice is a major source of misunderstanding and confusion in strategic studies, but so also is what one can identify as the yearning for ever more fundamental truth. By analogy, the God particle malady has lurked close to this text throughout. The laudable desire to penetrate ever deeper into the complex mystery that is strategy has the unfortunate and undeserved consequence of fuelling scholars in a futile quest. Expeditionary effort to discover the true source of the metaphorical Nile for strategy, diverts endeavour from grasping that which is attainable and is both good enough for its purpose and incapable of major improvement. In truth, the source of the Nile for the understanding of strategy already exists and is readily accessible in the canon of strategic classics written over the course of two and a half millennia. The nature of strategy, including good enough explanation of why strategy in general must assume different characters for historically unique situations, is laid bare for all time by the 'classical' theorists.[8] Nonetheless, it is human to strive to improve, and as a consequence ill-fated ventures are launched to unearth that which is not there. While it should be useful to practising strategists for them to identify and test their assumptions, it is a fallacy to believe that inattention to assumptions constitutes a potentially correctible fatal flaw in strategy-making. The reason is that many influences that may misdirect a polity's strategic performance are certain to be more than ready to impair a navel-gazing exercise in assumption spotting and evaluation. As-sumptions by their nature tend to be more deeply rooted and less well evidenced than are opinions; they cannot miraculously be sanitized by a strategy-making process able mysteriously and abruptly to be wondrously objective about such subjective tenets.

As well as the hope that the specification and testing of assumptions will serve a panacea filtering duty, a reductionist urge can seduce scholars and commentators into the error of the big game hunt for the factor that could be the prime mover of strategic phenomena. Among its many virtues, the general theory of strategy serves to discourage monocausal explanation. For example, while there is support in the theory for the claim that strategy must be technological, in plentiful addition the theory asserts also that strategy is political, human, ethical, and geographical, *inter alia*. But, because strategy is so complex in its working parts, and causes and effects are inherently so problematic, there is always some empirical basis upon which an overreaching partial theory can rest. It is a prime duty of strategic education so well to explain the enduring structure and functioning of strategy that the limitations of partial theory are identified. Just as there is no single master cause of war that might be expunged from history as a result of dedicated assault, though politics and human nature (or human behaviour in society) would be prime candidates were causal cleansing practicable, so also there is no golden key to the understanding of strategy in theory and for practice. The closest that scholars can come to securing a reliable, comprehensive, eternal, and universal grip on the subject is by allowing themselves to be educated by the general theory. The theory, sufficiently absorbed intellectually, should enable the practising strategist to understand not what he needs to do, but rather how he can proceed to try to solve his problems.

Because the strategist always must attend to the balancing of political ends with available means, orchestrated in appropriate ways, there is a simple structure to any strategic project. On the one hand, the subject is formidably complex and encompasses a cast of thousands that can prevent success. But, on the other hand, there is an elegant simplicity to the triadic structure of the strategy function that almost begs for duty in service of effective practical performance. Strategic tasks exist at every level of human effort, from grand strategy or national security, to a small-scale operation by a company of soldiers. Emphasis repeatedly has been placed here upon the empirical fact of porosity between apparently distinctive conceptual categories. Ends, ways, and means—and assumptions also, notwithstanding the sceptical comments offered in their regard—are as unarguably different in meaning from each other as they are interdependent. Historical contextual detail is known to contemporaries as it may be to later scholars, in as much fine granular detail as they need or are able to discover. But, in principle at least the elegant simplicity of the ends, ways, and means trinitarian formula provides so potent an organizing concept that the complexity, confusion, and even the chaos of messy interdependent behaviours and events are manageable. The competent strategist copes with complexity, confusion, and impending chaos, he does not seek the fool's goal of a winning formula that rests upon a severely reductionist prioritization of what matters more, and less. Even when pursuing a strategy that privileges a particular operational concept, military capability, or even a contextually powerful weapon system, the well-educated strategist makes specific decisions and acts in particular ways in the light of his grasp of the architecture of the whole house of strategy.

6.2 PERSPECTIVES ON STRATEGY

This book offers no prescriptions for policy, strategy, or tactics; my purpose here is strictly educational. The world is awash with political and strategic advice purporting to be remedies for current and anticipated ills. Rather less abundant, though, are works that seek to render thought about strategic problems more robust. To that end this work has examined strategic phenomena from five perspectives, each of which is seriously under-theorized for the explanation necessary as a basis for understanding. Despite the familiar character of these perspectives—there are no eccentric outliers here—and their intrinsic significance, comprehension of their meaning for strategy in general and for their relative importance in particular historical cases, has been seriously weak. Every perspective considered either is or should be the subject of lively debate. It is worth mentioning that strategic education has been ill-served by paucity of cooperation between the somewhat rival 'stovepipe' professionalisms of military history and strategic studies. Tribal members of the latter persuasion incline professionally to take a negative view of 'mere' historical narrative, while members of the former readily wax eloquent on the subject of strategists with an empirical historical knowledge so thin that their theorization inherently must be suspect. The social scientist as strategist frequently finds professional historian colleagues to be methodologically challenged, specifically in their neglect of the 'so what?' question that has populated these pages promiscuously.

Although the domain of this enquiry has been immense, the analytical goal has been distinctly modest. Specifically, the intention has been simply to explore the subject of strategy rigorously, which means at some length and in suitable depth, from perspectives with sufficient focus as hopefully to enhance understanding; each perspective is intellectually contested terrain. These pages have sought both to shed light on the particular through the agency of a holistic view with its general theory, and to enhance the value that can be squeezed out of particular perspectives for illumination of the whole house of strategy. I have no surprising conclusion with which to amaze the reader. This brief concluding chapter does not serve the function of the gathering at the close of a classic detective story where the master sleuth reveals who did what to whom, why, when and how. The plot of strategy is well known, though this familiarity does not seem to convert readily into the quality of understanding desirable for competent strategic practice. The pieces of the strategy puzzle are well known and have their alleged high importance touted by contending interest groups. But, what is not well known is how major elements that contribute to the making and execution of strategy interact and somehow produce a single team performance.

Each perspective exploited here encourages predatory theorizing by its scholar-advocates. Concepts, ethics, culture, geography, and technology: each has misled some scholarly devotees into asserting that it either does or should provide the master narrative. By this I mean that strategic history is purported to be really the story of concepts and theory, or morality and its ethics, or culture, or geography and its geopolitics and geostrategy, or of technology (pick one, or possibly two!). It is my conviction that if there is a master narrative to strategic history it is to be found in the ceaseless quest for power by human beings both individually and socially regarded. Power is sought as a value in and of itself, as well as for its instrumental worth in aid of interests that are ever open to subjective evaluation as being defensive or offensive, though usually are both. The relations of relative power, known as politics generically are eternal and universal because they derive from the biology of our speciation. Humans cooperate, combine, and compete for security that has survival value as well as more limited benefit. The master narrative is strategy itself, in all its complexity and with all its variability in character over time and in different places. I will not claim that performance of the strategy function is defining for the human species, but in no matter how simplified a form it is registered, the strategic formula summarized as ends, ways, and means is vitally relevant to the survival or the demise of all life. The dimensions of strategy explored in this book are not discretionary categorical qualities of strategic performance. Every security community has a strategic thread to its history. Furthermore, each such community, at all times and in all places, in principle can be examined in the perspectives deployed forensically here.

Intellectual dissection of a complex subject such as strategy is necessary for depth of particular understanding, but the unity of historical actuality is mistreated and may be misrepresented as a result. It would be unusual and may be impossible for strategists to focus narrowly upon only a single dimension of their contemporary challenges. In the world of the strategist everything is, or may be, connected to everything else. Recall that the very complexity of the strategist's world itself ironically can allow for considerable flexibility in behaviour. It would be satisfying to be able to claim at this terminal point in the book that all can now be revealed, and 'theory/concepts (morality/ethics, culture, geography, or technology—select only one) did it: the golden key to the understanding of strategy and strategic history is . . . ' Alas, such agreeable certainty and clarity is not possible. Instead, one must offer qualification, nuance, porous categories with their 'fuzziness' in border areas, and allow for occasional situational exceptions to what appear to be general truths. This highly qualitative social science is not to everyone's taste. What follows are summary reflections on the subjects that provided the distinctive perspectives explored and exploited here.

1. *Concepts*: Strategy cannot be understood and explained satisfactorily strictly with reference to ideas. Strategic theory and its expressive concepts are necessary, but not sufficient ingredients in the mix that is strategy. Mind is superior to human muscle and to the inert material of military tools, but exceptions great and small are fuelled mightily by material referents to perceptions and considerations, as well as by circumstances and memories. In addition, no matter its absolute or relative potency, the mind and its concepts may need muscular and other material enablers if they are to affect behaviour. How a weapon is employed is more significant than are the weapon's technical characteristics, but this claim has a significant potential to mislead. Superior concepts carry no guarantee of strategic success in the deeply ironic realm of strategy (unless, that is, one succumbs, innocently of course, to unintended tautology). Excellence in concepts always is decided in practice by a host of factors, most importantly including their situational relevance. Also, strategic history reveals that the strategic intellect often has fallen perilously far behind emerging material technical realities. The case of cyber power today and the pressing need for its strategic comprehension is but the latest example of conceptual lag. Strategic theory to inform and organize strategy of a changing character required to answer new specific questions is apt to be faint but pursuing, as the saying has it.

2. *Ethics*: The ethical perspective on strategy unarguably is important and essential; what is more, it is unavoidable for human beings. The reason why this is so is because we humans appear to be hard-wired to think in moral terms. It is a survival necessity for our species to reason morally. We need to distinguish right from wrong, permitted from forbidden behaviour. So far so

good, since it would seem that moral reasoning, applied in ethical codes, is inherent in our humanity. Unfortunately, there are two major factors which serve to complicate the picture. First, one needs to recognize that just because all people, except for deviant and dysfunctional individuals, think morally, it does not follow that they think morally in the same way. In other words, while it matters profoundly that my neighbours should have a clear sense of right and wrong, what matters no less strongly is the content of their moral beliefs. What do they believe to be rightful action? Culture rules over, transcends, and becomes ethics. The problem for the strategist is not an enemy who eccentrically is amoral, but rather one who is licensed in his behaviour by an ethical code that expresses moral beliefs I reject. Second, it is a universal and apparently eternal truth that strategic ethics are always more or less situationally determined, notwithstanding the sincerity of the moral beliefs that typically they reflect. Morality in action as strategic ethics frequently accepts the perceived necessity of circumstances as an excuse for what otherwise must be categorized as wrongful behaviour. Moral beliefs always need translation into an ethical code for applicability in the unforgiving world of perceived and often misperceived (expedient) necessity. Even if there were a truly universal morality, strategic situations are far from universal and place widely varying demands upon human consciences. And, to repeat, it is not the existential fact of a conscience that is the principal source of challenge, but rather the detail in its contents.

3. *Culture*: The cultural perspective examines a rather vaporous subject that is both exogenous and endogenous to strategy. Is there an American, Russian, Chinese, *inter alia* way of war, or way in strategy? Perhaps a shift from the singular to the plural is more appropriate, as also is serious entertainment of the idea that ways in war and strategy may change over time. If one is willing to grant the proposition that because a polity's military instrument is certain to be diverse in its complex character, it has to follow that it is likely to harbour a range of preferred 'ways'. The more closely one examines the idea of culture, and the more nuanced one's appreciation of its ever arguable complex domain, the more difficult it can be to find forensic merit in it as an aid to strategic understanding, let alone as a valuable predictive tool. Not only does culture inspire and sometimes demand an influence upon behaviour, but inconveniently for analytical discipline there is culture in, as well as on, behaviour. Culturally fuelled action itself can beget culture in many forms. Is there not a sense in which all strategic behaviour simply has to be culturally expressive? After all, such behaviour is performed by necessarily and unavoidably encultured people who are shaped in their thoughts and deeds by the interests of the organizations they represent, interests expressed in some cultural forms. The challenge is neither to find the lacunae in culturalist arguments, nor is it to seek to refute anti-culturalist assault. By and large, those necessary tasks have been completed. The mission now is to save what is

sensible in the arguments for cultural awareness about strategy from the claims in its praise that were excessive. Sensibly understood, culture is not the singular golden key to strategic understanding, but it can nonetheless provide vital clues and cues that have practical value. Culture is inescapable from Man's estate, and enculturation always is somewhat local in content to time, place, and as a consequence identity, much of which is socially inherited. It follows that culture merits attention as a factor that conditions thought and may contribute to choice of deeds. But, to claim that culture conditions means only that; it does not mean that culture determines.

4. *Geography*: As culture is perilously imperial for strategic understanding in its elusive ethereality, so geography menaces conceptual grip for reason of its physical ubiquity. While much if not all that matters for strategy has some often arguably cultural content, there is no room for dispute over the presence of the geographical wherever strategy is thought or done. The unique geo-physical properties of each of the five geographical domains of strategy—land, sea, air, Earth-orbital space, and cyberspace—dominate tactical feasibility and hence operational and strategic opportunity for political gain. The physical stage for the long-running drama of strategic history is indifferent to human strategic endeavours. The Russian winter does not itself magically, but impossibly purposefully, punish German invaders, but those invaders certainly suffer great harm when they campaign inadequately prepared for the local climate. Geography is neutral in human strategic history, but it is liable to be influential as security communities seek to exploit or offset geographically defined opportunities and limitations. Strategy must always be done in geography, while often essentially it is about geography. And geography is not only a physical matter of the natural realm. In addition, the geography coveted most is deemed sacred and is uniquely valued by a political community (or two such). The challenge is less to recognize the relevance of geography to strategy, than to be able to restrict its allotted scope for influence to some prudent distance short of the exciting assertion that geography is destiny. This claim has merit, but considered in isolation it falls a long way short of providing the whole grand narrative of strategic history. Geography, geopolitics, and geostrategy have been imprudently neglected by students of strategy for more than half a century. Scholars need to close up with the world of strategic practice in allowing geographical considerations their notable due, while being careful not to overreach.

5. *Technology*: Strategy is not about technology, though much of the popular media effort to exploit the largely male fascination with machines ('boy's toys'?) focuses on the military means in the strategy triad. As a consequence one might be excused the belief that technology's artefacts lie at the core of strategy. Whereas the moral impulses behind ethics and the values expressed in culture themselves yield motives that in political form serve as the ends of

strategy, concepts and technology are strictly enablers of strategic achievement; as tools disconnected from their strategic and political purposes they have no merit. There are a few strategic and military ideas that in their intellectual elegance attract praise, while some of the machines of war are widely held to be iconically beautiful (e.g. the Spitfire). However, neither strategic ideas nor weapon systems are discovered in order to be attractive to the intellect or to the emotions as ends in themselves. Particular intellectual and technical forms are preferred for the anticipated excellence of their fit as enablers for the realization of strategic and military intentions. The argument that we fight with, and not for, technology engineered as weapons, is so obvious as to be banal. And yet the whole political and societal effort to invent, pay for, produce, improve, and use with doctrinal best practice, weapons and their supporting systems, is so consuming of attention that the political ends and strategic ways often disappear from view. Money and physicality attract public attention. Weapons in action, photogenically often in motion at least, can be understood tactically, as can their monetary cost; hence they attract notice and controversy. Means are easier to grasp and debate than are strategic ways and political purposes. One might recall with advantage these immortal cognate words by Michael Howard: '... the complex problem of running an army at all is liable to occupy his [the commander's] mind so completely that it is very easy to forget what it is being run *for*'.[9] Expertise in tactical matters necessarily confers no like grasp of genuinely strategic concerns, but such expertise is essential if the strategist is to comprehend what his military instrument might be able to accomplish. Although strategy is ever superordinate in providing meaning for behaviour, it has to be done by tactics. When understanding of strategy is not grasped in the round as presented in the general theory, its particular military instruments, ranging from special operations forces, through long-range bomber fleets, to individually super-destructive weapons, commonly are confused with—are mistaken for—strategy. This prime conceptual error of miscategorization is found most frequently in the mistaken belief that there are some inherently strategic weapons, while other weapons allegedly are sub- (or non-)strategic. This conceptual confusion has harmful consequences for the quality of strategic understanding upon which national and international security relies. Technology matters greatly, but it is only one of the vital ingredients that generate fighting power, the others being the intellect and morale (or brain and spirit).

Strategy is a practical project that always is practised in particular times and places. Whatever the historical examples of strategy one elects to consider, they had temporal provenance and consequences as legacy value from past experience. The study and the practice of strategy has to deal with continuity and change as well as causes and consequences. The future is not foreseeable, but an historical perspective ensures that the great chain of contestable historical causation at least should be noticed and respected, even though it could not have been predicted in real-time, which is to say in advance. The ever imperfect wisdom of hindsight serves as a source of caveats potent for contemporary strategic practitioners. They may be seduced by the apparent novelty of current challenges into forgetting that the chain of causes and effects (e.g. first, second, and third order) is likely to be neither reliably predictable nor even capable of anticipation. The practising strategist is a risk taker of varying courage, wisdom, and luck who throws metaphorical dice. Clausewitz went to some pains to make this claim. Some historians are suspicious of social scientists who have been known to engage in professional poaching on their tribal terrain. Admittedly, the integrity of the past can be violated by later scholars who have cases to make that far transcend unimpeachable evidence. But, since the facts of the past tend to be silent unless they are explained, which means theorized, it is not obvious that the historian and the social scientist must differ for reason of their preferred methodologies. I believe that social scientific strategists should be deeply respectful of the past, which has to mean of the stories told by historians that collectively are termed history. In addition, indeed in parallel, I believe that historian strategists need all of the assistance in seeking understanding for plausible explanation they can extract from the writings of their strategist colleagues who are social scientists. Adoption of the elementary but elemental, triptych of ends, ways, and means, as a guide for strategic historical enquiry would be a useful step towards some enlightening fusion of scholarly realms.

The triadic skeleton of strategy can be employed to advantage in highlighting Air Chief Marshal Sir Hugh Dowding's strategic achievement in 1940.[10] He had a clear negative *end*—denying the Luftwaffe a credible (to the Führer) claim to have achieved air superiority over south-east England; an effective *way*—by maintaining a constant modest level of opposition in the air; and sufficiently effective *means* in the form of the world leading air defence capability of RAF Fighter Command. Dowding assumed and hoped that his *end* of victory denial would suffice to deter a German invasion. Fortune tends to favour the competent strategist. War is always a game of chance, but Dowding had loaded the dice strongly in Britain's favour.

This examination of strategy in perspective shows that the subject is a unity. When examined closely, every perspective employed in these pages is revealed both to be identifiably distinctive, yet also porous to influence from other perspectives. It has to follow that the subject of strategy cannot sensibly be regarded as offering alternative flavours in substantive interpretation. It is not sound to conceive of strategy as being essentially, or even primarily, a conceptual, moral, cultural, geographical, or technological project (*inter alia*): it is all of those combined, even fused, albeit in combinations with historically widely varying relative weights. Strategy is a single enterprise. Theory and practice have to be considered as one whole project, not merely as joint ventures that episodically are linked in a relationship of some interdependence; the nexus is far more organic than that. The unity of all strategic phenomena is expressed effectively in strategy's general theory. That theory provides the big tent of understanding that binds the whole entire subject together.

This work closes with a quotation from a book published in 1889 by Colonel (later General) Sir William F. Butler. His subject is 'Chinese' Gordon (of Khartoum), as an archetypal, and not implausibly even the iconic, Victorian Christian hero, a military engineer who saw much action in Asia and Africa. Colonel Butler's hagiographic words emphasize helpfully the sense in my basic thesis asserting the unity of the whole house of strategy.

> In England there has long been an idea prevalent in the minds of many persons that the soldier should be a species of man distinct from the rest of the community. He should be purely and simply a soldier, ready to knock down upon word of command being duly given for that purpose, but knowing nothing of the business of building up; leaving that important branch of life to Mr Civil Commissioner this and Mr Civil Administrator that. It is needless to say that Charles Gordon held a totally different view of the soldier's proper sphere of action, and with him the building part of the soldier's profession was far more important than the breaking part. The surgeon who could only cut off a leg or amputate an arm, but who knew nothing of binding up the wound or stopping an open artery, could not be of much account in any estimate of men. Gordon understood the fact that nations as well as individuals have pulses, that the leader who would lead to any definite end must know how to count these pulsations, and, in addition to his skill as a sword-cutter, must be able to do a good deal of the binding up of wounds, even though he had himself caused them. To say this is, of course, only to say that Gordon was great, in a sense greater than any merit of action in arms could aspire to. The nation that will insist upon drawing a broad line of demarcation between the fighting man and the thinking man is liable to find its fighting done by fools and its thinking by cowards.[11]

NOTES

1. T. E. Lawrence, *Seven Pillars of Wisdom: A Triumph* (New York: Anchor Books, 1991), 191–2.

2. David J. Betz and Tim Stevens, *Cyberspace and the State: Toward a Strategy for Cyber-Power* (Abingdon: Routledge for The International Institute for Strategic Studies, 2011), 43.

3. This proposition is a theme central to John Andreas Olsen and Colin S. Gray, eds., *The Practice of Strategy: From Alexander the Great to the Present* (Oxford: Oxford University Press, 2011) and is defended in my 'Conclusion', 286–300.

4. Apparently, although the elusive Higgs boson particle has had a divine quality flippantly attributed to it in journalistic usage, the God in 'God particle' is regarded, possibly unreliably, as an abbreviated mistaken corruption of 'goddammed'.

5. I am grateful to Richard Danzig for the inspired wording of the title to his monograph, *Driving in the Dark: Ten Propositions About Prediction and National Security* (Washington, DC: Center for a New American Security, October 2011).

6. Michael Howard, *The Causes of Wars and Other Essays* (London: Counterpoint, 1983), 215–17.

7. Karl Marlantes, *What It is Like to Go to War* (London: Corvus, 2011), 71.

8. See Colin S. Gray, *The Strategy Bridge: Theory for Practice* (Oxford: Oxford University Press, 2010), 264–6, Appendix B, 'General Strategic Theory: The Classical Canon'.

9. Howard, *The Causes of Wars*, 214 (emphasis in the original).

10. I offer strategic explanation of Air Chief Marshal Sir Hugh Dowding's victory in 1940 in my 'study', 'Dowding and the British Strategy of Air Defence, 1936–1940', (forthcoming). Outstanding analyses include John Ferris, 'Achieving Air Ascendancy: Challenge and Response in British Strategic Air Defence, 1915–40', in Sebastian Cox and Peter Gray, eds., *Air Power History: Turning Points from Kitty Hawk to Kosovo* (London: Frank Cass, 2002), 21–50; Stephen Bungay, *The Most Dangerous Enemy: A History of the Battle of Britain* (London: Aurum Press, 2001); and R. J. Overy, *The Battle of Britain: Myth and Reality* (London: Penguin Books, 2010).

11. William F. Butler, *Charles George Gordon* (London: Macmillan, 1889), 85. I am grateful to Frank G. Hoffman for locating these elusive words for me.

Bibliography

Adamsky, Dima, *The Culture of Military Innovation: The Impact of Cultural Factors on the Revolution in Military Affairs in Russia, the US, and Israel* (Stanford, CA: Stanford University Press, 2010).

Anon., *Three Byzantine Military Treatises*, trans. George T. Dennis, S. J. (Emperor Justinian I, r. 527–65; Washington, DC: Dumbarton Oaks, 1985).

Arbella, Alex, *Soldiers of Reason: The RAND Corporation and the Rise of the American Empire* (Orlando, FL: Harcourt, 2008).

Aron, Raymond, *Peace and War: A Theory of International Relations* (Garden City, NY: Doubleday, 1966).

Arquilla, John and David Ronfeldt, 'Cyberwar is Coming!', in Arquilla and Ronfeldt, eds., *In Athena's Camp: Preparing for Conflict in the Information Age* (Santa Monica, CA: RAND, 1997), 23–60.

————eds., *In Athena's Camp: Preparing for Conflict in the Information Age* (Santa Monica, CA: RAND, 1997).

Bailey, Jonathan B. A., 'The First World War and the Birth of Modern Warfare', in Macgregor Knox and Williamson Murray, eds., *The Dynamics of Military Revolution, 1300–2050* (Cambridge: Cambridge University Press, 2001), 132–53.

Barnett, Roger W., *Navy Culture: Why the Navy Thinks Differently* (Annapolis, MD: Naval Institute Press, 2009).

Barrass, Gordon S., *The Great Cold War: A Journey Through the Hall of Mirrors* (Stanford, CA: Stanford University Press, 2009).

Bateman, Robert L., III, ed., *Digital War: A View from the Front Lines* (Novato, CA: Presidio Press, 1999).

Bathurst, Robert B., *Intelligence and the Mirror: On Creating an Enemy* (London: Sage Publications, 1993).

Baylis, John and John Garnett, eds., *Makers of Nuclear Strategy* (New York: St. Martin's Press, 1991).

——James J. Wirtz, and Colin S. Gray, eds., *Strategy in the Contemporary World*, 3rd edn. (Oxford: Oxford University Press, 2010).

Beitz, David, 'Cyberwar is not Coming', *Infinity Journal*, 3 (Summer 2011), 21–4.

Bellamy, Chris, *Absolute War: Soviet Russia in the Second World War* (London: Pan Macmillan, 2007).

Benbow, Tim, *The Magic Bullet? Understanding the Revolution in Military Affairs* (London: Brassey's, 2004).

Bernstein, Jeremy, *Nuclear Weapons: What You Need to Know* (Cambridge: Cambridge University Press, 2008).

Betz, David J. and Tim Stevens, *Cyberspace and the State: Toward a Strategy for Cyber-Power* (Abingdon: Routledge for The International Institute for Strategic Studies, 2011).

Beyerchen, Alan, 'From Radio to Radar: Interwar Military Adaptation to Techno-
logical Change in Germany, the United Kingdom, and the United States', in
Williamson Murray and Alan R. Millett, eds., *Military Innovation in the Interwar
Period* (Cambridge: Cambridge University Press, 1996), 265–99.

Biddle, Tami Davis, *Rhetoric and Reality in Air Warfare: The Evolution of British and
American Ideas about Strategic Bombing, 1914–1945* (Princeton, NJ: Princeton
University Press, 2002).

Black, Jeremy, *Rethinking Military History* (Abingdon: Routledge, 2004).

—— *The Curse of History* (London: The Social Affairs Unit, 2008).

—— *Great Powers and the Quest for Hegemony: The World Order since 1500* (New
York: Routledge, 2008).

—— *Geopolitics* (London: The Social Affairs Unit, 2009).

—— *The Great War and the Making of the Modern World* (London: Continuum,
2011).

Blair, Tony, 'The Blair Doctrine', 22 April 1999 <http://www.pbs.org/newshour/bb/
international/jan-june99/blair_doctrine4-23.html> accessed 12 July 2011.

Blouet, Brian W., *Halford Mackinder: A Biography* (College Station, TX: Texas A and
M University Press, 1987).

—— *Geopolitics and Globalization in the Twentieth Century* (London: Reaktion Books,
2001).

—— ed., *Global Geostrategy: Mackinder and the Defence of the West* (Abingdon: Frank
Cass, 2005).

—— 'Halford Mackinder and the Pivotal Heartland', in Blouet, ed., *Global Geostrategy:
Mackinder and the Defence of the West* (Abingdon: Frank Cass, 2005), 1–16.

Boemke, Manfred F., Roger Chickering, and Stig Forster, eds., *Anticipating Total War:
The German and American Experiences* (Cambridge: Cambridge University Press,
1999).

Boorstin, Daniel J., *Gresham's Law: Knowledge or Information?* (Washington, DC:
Library of Congress, 1980).

Boot, Max, 'The New American Way of War', *Foreign Affairs*, 82 (July/August 2003),
41–58.

—— 'The Struggle to Transform the Military', *Foreign Affairs*, 84 (March/April 2005),
103–11.

—— *War Made New: Technology, Warfare and the Course of History, 1500 to Today*
(New York: Gotham Books, 2006).

Booth, Ken, *Strategy and Ethnocentrism* (London: Croom Helm, 1979).

—— *Theory of World Security* (Cambridge: Cambridge University Press, 2007).

Boulding, Kenneth, *Conflict and Defense: A General Theory* (New York: Harper and
Brothers, 1962).

Boyle, Joseph, 'Natural Law and International Ethics', in Terry Nardin and David
R. Mapel, eds., *Traditions of International Ethics* (Cambridge: Cambridge University Press, 1992), 112–35.

Brennan, Donald G., 'The Case for Missile Defense', *Foreign Affairs*, 43 (April 1969),
81–8.

Brodie, Bernard, ed., *The Absolute Weapon: Atomic Power and World Order* (New
York: Harcourt Brace, 1946).

—— *War and Politics* (New York: Macmillan, 1973).

Budiansky, Stephen, *Air Power: From Kitty Hawk to Gulf War II* (London: Penguin Books, 2004).

Budieri, Robert, *The Invention that Changed the World: The Story of Radar from War to Peace* (London: Abacus, 1998).

Builder, Carl H., *The Masks of War: American Military Styles in Strategy and Analysis* (Baltimore, MD: Johns Hopkins University Press, 1989).

Bungay, Stephen, *The Most Dangerous Enemy: A History of the Battle of Britain* (London: Aurum Press, 2001).

Burleigh, Michael, The *Third Reich: A New History* (London: Pan Macmillan, 2001).

—— *Sacred Causes: Politics and Religion from the European Dictators to Al Qaeda* (London: Harper Perennial, 2007).

—— *Moral Combat: A History of World War II* (London: Harper Press, 2010).

Butler, William F., *Charles George Gordon* (London: Macmillan, 1889).

Byers, Michael, *War Law: Understanding International Law and Armed Conflict* (New York: Grove Press, 2005).

Callwell, Charles E., *Small Wars: A Tactical Textbook for Imperial Soldiers*, 3rd edn. (1906; London: Greenhill Books, 1990).

Campbell, James, *The Ghost Mountain Boys* (New York: Crown Publishers, 2007).

Cecil, Hugh and Peter H. Liddle, eds., *Facing Armageddon: The First World War Experience* (London: Leo Cooper, 1996).

Chickering, Roger, 'Total War: The Use and Abuse of a Concept', in Manfred F. Boemke, Chickering, and Stig Forster, eds., *Anticipating Total War: The German and American Experiences* (Cambridge: Cambridge University Press, 1999), 13–28.

Chivers, C. J., *The Gun: The AK-47 and the Evolution of War* (London: Allen Lane, 2010).

Churchill, Winston S., *The World Crisis, 1911–1918*, 2 vols. (London: Odhams Press, 1938).

Cimbala, Stephen J., *Coercive Military Strategy* (College Station, TX: Texas A and M University Press, 1998).

—— ed., *The George W. Bush Defense Program: Policy, Strategy and War* (Dulles, VA: Potomac Books, 2011).

Clarke, Richard A. and Robert K. Knake, *Cyber War: The Next Threat to National Security and What to Do About It* (New York: Ecco, 2010).

Clausewitz, Carl von, *On War*, trans. Michael Howard and Peter Paret (1832–4; Princeton, NJ: Princeton University Press, 1976).

Coates, A. J., *The Ethics of War* (Manchester: Manchester University Press, 1997).

Cohen, Eliot A., *Supreme Command: Soldiers, Statesmen, and Leadership in Wartime* (New York: Free Press, 2002).

—— 'Technology and Warfare', in John Baylis, James J. Wirtz, and Colin S. Gray, eds., *Strategy in the Contemporary World*, 3rd edn. (Oxford: Oxford University Press, 2010), 141–60.

—— *Conquered into Liberty: Two Centuries of Battles Along the Great Warpath That Made the American Way of War* (New York: Free Press, 2011).

Cohen, Saul B., *Geography and Politics in a Divided World* (London: Methuen, 1964).

Coker, Christopher, *Ethics and War in the 21st Century* (Abingdon: Routledge, 2008).

Cox, Sebastian and Peter Gray, eds., *Air Power History: Turning Points from Kitty Hawk to Kosovo* (London: Frank Cass, 2002).

Creveld, Martin van, *Fighting Power: German and U.S. Army Performances, 1939–1945* (Westport, CT: Greenwood Press, 1982).

—— *Technology and War: From 2000 B.C. to the Present* (New York: Free Press, 1989).

—— *The Culture of War* (New York: Ballantine Books, 2008).

—— *The Age of Airpower* (New York: Public Affairs, 2011).

Daalder, Ivo and Michael O'Hanlon: *Winning Ugly: NATO's War to Save Kosovo* (Washington, DC: Brookings Institution Press, 2000).

Danzig, Richard, *Driving in the Dark: Ten Propositions About Prediction and National Security* (Washington, DC: Center for a New American Security, October 2011).

Davis, Paul K., *Analytic Architecture for Capabilities-Based Planning, Mission-System Analysis, and Transformation*, MR-1513-OSD (Santa Monica, CA: RAND, 2002).

—— 'Military Transformation? Which Transformation and What Lies Ahead?', in Stephen J. Cimbala, ed., *The George W. Bush Defense Program: Policy, Strategy and War* (Dulles, VA: Potomac Books, 2011), 11–41.

—— and Peter A. Wilson, *Looming Discontinuities in U.S. Military Strategy and Defense Planning: Colliding RMAs Necessitate a New Strategy*, Occasional Paper (Santa Monica, CA: RAND, 2011).

DeGroot, Gerard J., *The Bomb: A Life* (London: Jonathan Cape, 2004).

Demchak, Chris C. and Peter Dombrowski, 'Rise of a Cybered Westphalian Age', *Strategic Studies Quarterly*, 5 (Spring 2011), 32–61.

Desch, Michael C., 'Culture Clash: Assessing the Importance of Ideas in Security Studies', *International Security*, 23 (Summer 1998), 141–70.

Development, Concepts and Doctrine Centre (DCDC), *The UK Approach to Unmanned Aircraft Systems*, Joint Doctrine Note 2/11 (Shrivenham: Ministry of Defence, 2011).

Dolman, Everett C., *Astropolitik: Classical Geopolitics in the Space Age* (London: Frank Cass, 2002).

Drea, Edward J., *McNamara, Clifford, and the Burdens of Vietnam, 1965–1969*, Secretaries of Defense Historical Series, Vol. VI (Washington, DC: Historical Office, Office of the Secretary of Defense, 2011).

Driver, Felix, *Geography Militant: Cultures of Exploration and Empire* (Oxford: Blackwell, 2001).

Earle, Edward Mead, ed., *Makers of Modern Strategy: Military Thought from Machiavelli to Hitler* (Princeton, NJ: Princeton University Press, 1941).

—— 'Power Politics and American World Policy', *Political Science Quarterly*, 58 (March 1943), 94–106.

Echevarria Antulio J., II, *After Clausewitz: German Military Thinkers Before the Great War* (Lawrence, KS: University Press of Kansas, 2000).

—— *Preparing for One War and Getting Another* (Carlisle, PA: Strategic Studies Institute, US Army War College, September 2010).

—— 'American Strategic Culture: Problems and Prospects', in Hew Strachan and Sibylle Scheipers, eds., *The Changing Character of War* (Oxford: Oxford University Press, 2011), 431–45.

—— 'Reconsidering War's Logic and Grammar', *Infinity Journal*, 2 (Spring 2011), 4–7.

Ehlers, Robert S., Jr., *Targeting the Reich: Air Intelligence and the Allied Bombing Campaigns*, (Lawrence, KS: University of Kansas Press, 2009).

Ehrhard, Thomas P., 'Unmanned Aircraft: 50 Years of Innovation and Frustration', unpub. PhD diss. (Washington, DC: Johns Hopkins University, 2004).

Ellis, John, *The Social History of the Machine Gun* (Baltimore: Johns Hopkins University Press, 1986).

Etzold, Thomas H. and John Lewis Gaddis, eds., *Containment: Documents on American Policy and Strategy, 1945–1950* (New York: Columbia University Press, 1978).

Faber, Peter R., 'Interwar US Army Aviation and the Air Corps Tactical School: Incubators of American Airpower', in Phillip S. Meilinger, ed., *The Paths of Heaven: The Evolution of Airpower Theory* (Maxwell AFB, AL: Air University Press, 1997), 183–238.

Farwell, James P., and Rafal Rohozinski, 'Stuxnet and the Future of Cyber War', *Survival*, 53 (February–March 2011), 41–60.

Ferris, John, 'Achieving Air Ascendancy: Challenge and Response in British Strategic Air Defence, 1915–40', in Sebastian Cox and Peter Gray, eds., *Air Power History: Turning Points from Kitty Hawk to Kosovo* (London: Frank Cass, 2002), 21–50.

Fischer, Klaus P., *Nazi Germany: A New History* (London: Constable, 1995).

Fisher, David, *Morality and War: Can War be Just in the Twenty-First Century?* (Oxford: Oxford University Press, 2011).

Flint, Colin, *Introduction to Geopolitics* (Abingdon: Routledge, 2007).

France, John, *Perilous Glory: The Rise of Western Military Power* (New Haven, CT: Yale University Press, 2011).

Freedman, Lawrence, 'Has Strategy Reached a Dead-End?' *Futures*, 11 (April 1979), 122–31.

——*The Revolution in Strategic Affairs*, Adelphi Paper 318 (London: International Institute for Strategic Studies, April 1998).

——ed., *Strategic Coercion: Concepts and Cases* (Oxford: Oxford University Press, 1998).

——*The Evolution of Nuclear Strategy*, 3rd edn. (Basingstoke: Palgrave Macmillan, 2003).

——*Deterrence* (Cambridge: Polity Press, 2004).

——*The Transformation of Strategic Affairs*, Adelphi Paper 379 (London: International Institute for Strategic Studies, March 2006).

Frieser, Karl-Heinz, *The Blitzkrieg Legend: The 1940 Campaign in the West* (Annapolis, MD: Naval Institute Press, 2005).

Fuller, J. F. C., *Armament and History: A Study of the Influence of Armament on History from the Dawn of Classical Warfare to the Second World War* (London: Eyre and Spottiswoode, 1946).

Gaddis, John Lewis, *Russia, The Soviet Union, and the United States: An Interpretive History* (New York: John Wiley, 1978).

——*The Landscape of History: How Historians Map the Past* (New York: Oxford University Press, 2002).

Gat, Azar, *The Origins of Military Thought: from the Enlightenment to Clausewitz* (Oxford: Clarendon Press, 1989).

——*War in Human Civilization* (Oxford: Oxford University Press, 2006).

Gentile, Gian P., 'A Strategy of Tactics: Population-centric COIN and the Army', *Parameters*, 39 (Autumn 2009), 5–17.

Gleick, James, *The Information: A History, A Theory, A Flood* (London: Fourth Estate, 2011).

Goldhagen, Daniel Jonah, *Hitler's Willing Executioners: Ordinary Germans and the Holocaust* (London: Abacus, 1996).

—— *Worse Than War: Genocide, Eliminationism, and the Ongoing Assault on Humanity* (Boston: Little, Brown, 2009).

Graham, Dominick, *Against Odds: Reflections on the Experiences of the British Army, 1914–45* (Basingstoke: Macmillan, 1999).

Gray, Christine, *International Law and the Use of Force*, 3rd edn. (Oxford: Oxford University Press, 2008).

Gray, Colin S., 'Across the Nuclear Divide—Strategic Studies, Past and Present', *International Security*, 2 (Summer 1977), 24–46.

—— *Strategic Studies and Public Policy: The American Experience* (Lexington, KY: University Press of Kentucky, 1982).

—— *Nuclear Strategy and National Style* (Lanham, MD: University Press of America, 1986).

—— *House of Cards: Why Arms Control Must Fail* (Ithaca, NY: Cornell University Press, 1992).

—— 'The Continued Primacy of Geography', *Orbis*, 40 (Spring 1996), 247–59.

—— 'The Influence of Space Power upon History', *Comparative Strategy*, 15 (October–December 1996), 293–308.

—— 'Inescapable Geography', in Gray and Geoffrey Sloan, eds., *Geopolitics, Geography and Strategy* (London: Frank Cass, 1999), 161–77.

—— *Modern Strategy* (Oxford: Oxford University Press, 1999).

—— *Strategy for Chaos: Revolutions in Military Affairs and the Evidence of History* (London: Frank Cass, 2002).

—— 'Mission Improbable, Fear, Culture, and Interest: Peace Making, 1943–1949', in Williamson Murray and Jim Lacey, eds., *The Making of Peace: Rulers, States, and the Aftermath of War* (Cambridge: Cambridge University Press, 2009), 265–91.

—— *National Security Dilemmas: Challenges and Opportunities* (Washington, DC: Potomac Books, 2009).

—— *Schools for Strategy: Teaching Strategy for 21st Century Conflict* (Carlisle, PA: Strategic Studies Institute, US Army War College, 2009).

—— *Understanding Airpower: Bonfire of the Fallacies*, Research Paper 2009-3 (Maxwell AFB, AL: Air Force Research Institute, March 2009).

—— 'Moral Advantage, Strategic Advantage?' *The Journal of Strategic Studies*, 33 (June 2010), 333–65.

—— 'Strategic Thoughts for Defence Planners', *Survival*, 52 (June–July 2010), 159–78.

—— *The Strategy Bridge: Theory for Practice* (Oxford: Oxford University Press, 2010).

—— 'Conclusion', in John Andreas Olsen and Gray, eds., *The Practice of Strategy: From Alexander the Great to the Present* (Oxford: Oxford University Press, 2011), 287–300.

—— 'Harry S. Truman and the Forming of American Grand Strategy in the Cold War, 1945–1953', in Williamson Murray, Richard Hart Sinnreich, and James Lacey, eds.,

The Shaping of Grand Strategy: Policy, Diplomacy and War (Cambridge: Cambridge University Press, 2011), 210–53.

—— 'The Nuclear Age and the Cold War', in John Andreas Olsen and Gray, eds., *The Practice of Strategy: From Alexander the Great to the Present* (Oxford: Oxford University Press, 2011), 237–59.

—— *War, Peace, and International Relations: An Introduction to Strategic History*, 2nd edn. (Abingdon: Routledge, 2011).

—— *Airpower for Strategic Effect* (Maxwell AFB, AL: Air University Press, 2012).

—— *Categorical Confusion: The Strategic Implications of Recognizing Challenges Either as Irregular or Traditional* (Carlisle, PA: Strategic Studies Institute, US Army War College, February 2012).

—— and Geoffrey Sloan, eds., *Geopolitics, Geography and Strategy* (London: Frank Cass, 1999).

Gray, J. Glenn, *The Warriors: Reflections on Men in Battle* (New York: Harper Torchbooks, 1967).

Green, Leslie C., *The Contemporary Law of Armed Conflict*, 2nd edn. (Manchester: Manchester University Press, 2000).

Griegiel, Jakub J., *Great Powers and Geopolitical Change* (Baltimore: Johns Hopkins University Press, 2006).

Grossman, Dave, *On Killing: The Psychological Cost of Learning to Kill in War and Society* (Boston: Little, Brown, 1995).

Guthrie, Charles and Michael Quinlan, *Just War: The Just War Tradition: Ethics in Modern Warfare* (London: Bloomsbury Publishing, 2007).

Hagland, David G., 'What Good is Strategic Culture?', in Jeannie L. Johnson, Kerry M. Kartchner, and Jeffrey A. Larsen, eds., *Strategic Culture and Weapons of Mass Destruction: Culturally Based Insights into Comparative National Security Policymaking* (New York: Palgrave Macmillan, 2009), 15–31.

Halidon, John, *Warfare, State and Society in the Byzantine World, 565–1204* (London: UCL Press, 1999).

—— *The Byzantine Wars: Battles and Campaigns of the Byzantine* Era (Stroud: Tempus, 2001).

Halperin, Morton H., *Limited War in the Nuclear Age* (New York: Wiley, 1963).

Hamilton, Richard F. and Holger H. Herwig, eds., *War Planning, 1914* (Cambridge: Cambridge University Press, 2010).

Hammes, T. X. *The Sling and The Stone: On War in the 21st Century* (St. Paul, MN: Zenith Press, 2004).

—— 'Assumptions—A Fatal Oversight', *Infinity Journal*, 1 (Winter 2010), 4–6.

Handel, Michael I., ed., *Intelligence and Military Operations* (London: Frank Cass, 1990).

—— *Masters of War: Classical Strategic Thought*, 3rd edn. (London: Frank Cass, 2001).

Hanson, Neil, *First Blitz: The Secret German Plan to Raze London to the Ground in 1918* (London: Corgi Books, 2009).

Hanson, Victor Davis, *The Western Way of War: Infantry Battle in Classical Greece* (London: Hodder & Stoughton, 1989).

—— *Why the West Has Won: Carnage and Culture from Salamis to Vietnam* (London: Faber and Faber, 2001).

Hardin, Russell, et al., eds., *Nuclear Deterrence: Ethics and Strategy* (Chicago: University of Chicago Press, 1985).

Hastings, Max, *Bomber Command* (New York: Dial Press, 1979).

——*All Hell Let Loose: The World at War, 1939–1945* (London: Harper Press, 2011).

Henriksen, Rune, 'Warriors in Combat—What Makes People Actively Fight in Combat?' *The Journal of Strategic Studies*, 30 (April 2007), 187–223.

Herodotus, *The Landmark Herodotus: The Histories*, ed. Robert B. Strassler, trans. Andrea L. Purvis (*c.*450–20 BC; New York: Parthenon Books, 2007).

Herwig, Holger H., '*Geopolitik*: Haushofer, Hitler, and Lebensraum', in Colin S. Gray and Geoffrey Sloan, eds., *Geopolitics, Geography, and Strategy* (London: Frank Cass, 1999), 218–41.

——*The Marne, 1914: The Opening of World War I and the Battle That Changed the World* (New York: Random House, 2009).

Heuser, Beatrice, *The Evolution of Strategy: Thinking War from Antiquity to the Present* (Cambridge: Cambridge University Press, 2010).

——'Strategy Before the Word: Ancient Wisdom for the Modern World', *The RUSI Journal*, 155 (February/March 2010), 36–42.

——*The Strategy Makers: Thoughts on War and Society from Machiavelli to Clausewitz* (Santa Barbara, CA: Praeger, 2010).

Higham, Robin and Stephen J. Harris, 'Conclusion', in Higham and Harris, eds., *Why Air Forces Fail: The Anatomy of Defeat* (Lexington, KY: University Press of Kentucky, 2006), 341–55.

————eds., *Why Air Forces Fail: The Anatomy of Defeat* (Lexington, KY: University Press of Kentucky, 2006).

Hitler, Adolf, *Mein Kampf* (New York: Fredonia Classics, 2003).

Holland, Tom, *In the Shadow of the Sword: The Battle for Global Empire and the End of the Ancient World* (London: Little, Brown, 2012).

Holley, I. B., Jr., 'Reflections on the Search for Airpower Theory', in Phillip S. Meilinger, ed., *The Paths of Heaven: The Evolution of Airpower Theory* (Maxwell AFB, AL: Air University Press, 1997), 579–99.

Howard, Michael, *The Franco-Prussian War: The German Invasion of France, 1870–1871* (London: Methuen, 1981).

——*The Causes of Wars and Other Essays* (London: Counterpoint, 1983).

——*War and the Liberal Conscience* (London: C. Hurst, 2008).

——'The Transformation of Strategy', *The RUSI Journal*, 156 (August/September 2011), 12–16.

Ikle, Fred Charles, 'After Detection—What?' *Foreign Affairs*, 39 (January 1961), 208–20.

——'Can Nuclear Deterrence Last Out the Century?' *Foreign Affairs*, 51 (January 1973), 267–85.

——'Nuclear Strategy: Can There Be a Happy Ending?' *Foreign Affairs*, 63 (Spring 1985), 810–26.

Imlay, Talbot C., 'Total War', *The Journal of Strategic Studies*, 30 (June 2007), 547–70.

——and Monica Duffy Toft, eds., *The Fog of Peace and War Planning: Military and Strategic Planning under Uncertainty* (Abingdon: Routledge, 2006).

Irwin, Robert, *For Lust of Knowing: The Orientalists and their Enemies* (London: Penguin Books 2007).

Jenkins, Philip, *Jesus Wars: How Four Patriarchs, Three Queens, and Two Emperors Decided What Christians Would Believe for the Next 1,500 Years* (London: SPCK, 2010).

Johnson, David E., *Fast Tanks and Heavy Bombers: Innovation in the U.S. Army, 1917–1945* (Ithaca, NY: Cornell University Press, 1998).

—— *Learning Large Lessons: The Evolving Roles of Ground Power and Air Power in the Post-Cold War Era, MG-405-AF* (Santa Monica, CA: RAND, 2006).

Johnson, Jeannie L. and Matthew T. Berrett, 'Cultural Topography: A New Research Tool for Intelligence Analysis', *Studies in Intelligence*, 55 (Extracts, June 2011), 1–22.

—— Kerry M. Kartchner, and Jeffrey A. Larsen, eds., *Strategic Culture and Weapons of Mass Destruction: Culturally Based Insights into Comparative National Security Policymaking* (Abingdon: Routledge, 2009).

Johnson, Rob, *The Afghan Way of War: Culture and Pragmatism: A Critical History* (London: C. Hurst, 2011).

Johnston, Alastair Iain, *Cultural Realism: Strategic Culture and Grand Strategy in Chinese History* (Ithaca, NY: Cornell University Press, 1995).

—— Thinking about Strategic Culture', *International Security*, 19 (Spring 1995), 32–64.

Jomini, Baron Antoine Henri de, *The Art of War* (1838; London: Greenhill Books, 1992).

Kahn, Herman, *Thinking About the Unthinkable* (New York: Horizon Press, 1964).

—— *On Thermonuclear War* (1960; New York: Free Press, 1969).

Kaplan, Fred, *The Wizards of Armageddon* (New York: Simon & Schuster, 1983).

Kaplan, Robert D., *Balkan Ghosts: A Journey Through History* (New York: Vintage Books, 1993).

—— *The Revenge of Geography: What the Map Tells Us About Coming Conflicts and the Battle Against Fate* (New York: Random House, 2012).

—— 'The Geography of Chinese Power', *Foreign Affairs*, 89 (May/June 2010), 22–41.

Katzenstein, Peter J., ed., *The Culture of National Security: Norms and Identity in World Politics* (New York: Columbia University Press, 1996).

Kavka, Gregory S., *Moral Paradoxes of Nuclear Deterrence* (Cambridge: Cambridge University Press, 1987).

Keegan, John, *The Face of Battle* (London: Jonathan Cape, 1976).

—— *The Mask of Command* (New York: Viking Penguin, 1987).

—— *A History of Warfare* (London: Hutchinson, 1993).

Kennan, George F., 'Moscow Embassy Telegram No. 511; "The Long Telegram", February 22, 1946', reprinted in Thomas H. Etzold and John Lewis Gaddis, eds., *Containment: Documents on American Policy and Strategy, 1945–1950* (New York: Columbia University Press, 1978), 50–63.

Kennedy, David, *Of War and Law* (Princeton, NJ: Princeton University Press, 2006).

Khanna, Parag, 'Remapping the World', *Time* (22 March 2010), 36–7.

Kilcullen, David, *The Accidental Guerrilla: Fighting Small Wars in the Midst of a Big One* (London: C. Hurst, 2009).

Knox, MacGregor and Williamson Murray, eds., *The Dynamics of Military Revolution, 1300–2050* (Cambridge: Cambridge University Press, 2001).

Kramer, Franklin D., Stuart H. Starr, and Larry K. Wentz, eds., *Cyberpower and National Security* (Dulles, VA: Potomac Books, 2009).

Krepinevich, Andrew F., 'Cavalry to Computer: The Pattern of Military Revolutions', *The National Interest*, 37 (Fall 1994), 30–42.

——*The Military–Technical Revolution: A Preliminary Assessment* (July 1992; Washington, DC: Center for Strategic and Budgetary Assessments, 2002).

Lackie, John, ed., *Chambers Dictionary of Science and Technology* (Edinburgh: Chambers, 2007), 307.

Lambeth, Benjamin S., *NATO's Air War for Kosovo: A Strategic and Operational Assessment* (Santa Monica, CA: RAND, 2001).

Lasswell, Harold D., *Politics: Who Gets What, When, How* (New York: Peter Smith, 1950).

Lawrence, T. E., *Seven Pillars of Wisdom: A Triumph* (New York: Anchor Books, 1991).

Lebow, Richard Ned, *A Cultural Theory of International Relations* (Cambridge: Cambridge University Press, 2008).

Leffler, Melvyn P. and Odd Arne Westad, eds., *The Cambridge History of the Cold War*, 3 vols. (Cambridge: Cambridge University Press, 2010).

Leo VI (Emperor), *The Taktika of Leo VI*, trans. George T. Dennis, S.J. (r. 886–912; Washington, DC: Dumbarton Oaks, 2010).

Libicki, Martin C., 'The Emerging Primacy of Information', *Orbis*, 40 (Spring 1996), 261–74.

——*Conquest in Cyberspace: National Security and Information Warfare* (Cambridge: Cambridge University Press, 2007).

——*Cyberdeterrence and Cyberwar* (Santa Monica, CA: RAND, 2009).

Lieber, Keir A., *War and the Engineers: The Primacy of Politics over Technology* (Ithaca, NY: Cornell University Press, 2005).

Linn, Brian McAllister., *The Echo of Battle: The Army's Way of War* (Cambridge, MA: Harvard University Press, 2007).

Lonsdale, David J., *The Nature of War in the Information Age: Clausewitzian Future* (London: Frank Cass, 2004).

Lutes, Charles D. and Peter L. Hays, eds., *Toward a Theory of Spacepower: Selected Essays* (Washington, DC: National Defense University Press, 2011).

Luttwak, Edward N., *Strategy: The Logic of War and Peace*, rev. edn. (1987; Cambridge, MA: Harvard University Press, 2001).

——*The Grand Strategy of the Byzantine Empire* (Cambridge, MA: The Belknap Press of Harvard University Press, 2009).

Lynn, John A., *Battle: A History of Combat and Culture* (Boulder, CO: Westview Press, 2003).

MacFarland, Stephen L. and Wesley Phillips Newton, *To Command the Sky: The Battle for Air Superiority over Germany, 1942–1944* (Washington, DC: Smithsonian Institution Press, 1991).

McFate, Montgomery, 'Culture', in Thomas Rid and Thomas Keaney, eds., *Understanding Counterinsurgency: Doctrine, Operations, and Challenges* (Abingdon: Routledge, 2010), 189–204.

Mackinder, Halford J., *Democratic Ideals and Reality* (1919, 1942; New Brunswick, NJ: Transaction Publishers, 2007).

McMahan, Jeff, 'Deterrence and Deontology', in Russell Hardin et al., eds., *Nuclear Deterrence, Ethics, and Strategy* (Chicago: University of Chicago Press, 1985), 141–60.

——*Killing in War* (Oxford: Clarendon Press, 2009).

McMahon, Robert J., *Dean Acheson and the Creation of an American World Order* (Washington, DC: Potomac Books, 2009).

MacMillan, Margaret, *Peacemakers: The Paris Conference of 1919 and its Attempt to End War* (London: John Murray, 2001), 132.

Mahan, Alfred Thayer, *The Influence of Sea Power upon the French Revolution and Empire, 1793–1812*, 2 vols. (Boston: Little, Brown, 1898).

——*The Problem of Asia and Its Effect upon International Policies* (Boston: Little, Brown, 1905).

——*The Influence of Sea Power upon History, 1660–1783* (1890; London: Methuen, 1965).

Mahnken, Thomas G., *Technology and the American Way of War since 1945* (New York: Columbia University Press, 2008).

——'U.S. Strategic and Organizational Subcultures', in Jeannie L. Johnson, Kerry M. Kartchner, and Jeffrey A. Larsen, eds., *Strategic Culture and Weapons of Mass Destruction: Culturally Based Insights into Comparative National Security Policy-making* (New York: Palgrave Macmillan, 2009), 69–84.

——*Understanding Dominant Features of Chinese Strategic Culture*, IDA Paper P-4614 (Washington, DC: Institute for Defense Analyses, August 2010).

Markham, Ian S., *Do Morals Matter? A Guide to Contemporary Religious Ethics* (Oxford: Blackwell Publishing, 2007).

Marlantes, Karl, *What It Is Like to Go to War* (London: Corvus, 2011).

Marston, Daniel and Carter Malkesian, eds., *Counterinsurgency in Modern Warfare* (Botley: Osprey Publishing, 2008).

Mastry, Vojtech, *The Cold War and Soviet Insecurity: The Stalin Years* (New York: Oxford University Press, 1996).

Marx, Karl, *The Eighteenth Brumaire of Louis Napoleon*, in Marx and Friedrich Engels, *Selected Works in Two Volumes*, Vol. 1 (1852; Moscow: Foreign Languages Publishing House, 1962).

Maurice, (Emperor), *Maurice's Strategikon: Handbook of Byzantine Military Strategy*, trans. George T. Dennis, S.J. (*c.* 600 AD; Philadelphia, PA: University of Pennsylvania Press, 1984).

Mawdsley, Evan, *World War II: A New History* (Cambridge: Cambridge University Press, 2009).

Mazarr, Michael J., *The Military Technical Revolution: A Structural Framework* (Washington, DC: Center for Strategic and International Studies, March 1993).

Mazo, Jeffrey, *Climate Conflict: How Global Warming Threatens Security and What To Do About It* (Abingdon: Routledge for The International Institute for Strategic Studies, March 2010).

Megargee, Geoffrey P., *War of Annihilation: Combat and Genocide on the Eastern Front, 1941* (Lanham, MD: Rowman & Littlefield, 2006).

Meilinger, Phillip S., ed., *The Paths of Heaven: The Evolution of Airpower Theory* (Maxwell AFB, AL: Air University Press, 1997).

Miller, Donald L., *Eighth Air Force: The American Bomber Crews in Britain* (London: Aurum Press, 2008).

Morgan, Forrest E., *Compellence and the Strategic Culture of Imperial Japan: Implications for Coercive Diplomacy in the Twenty-First Century* (Westport, CT: Praeger Publishers, 2003).

Morgan, Patrick M., *Deterrence: A Conceptual Analysis* (Beverly Hills, CA: Sage Publications, 1977).

——*Deterrence Now* (Cambridge: Cambridge University Press, 2003).

Morris, Ian, *Why the West Rules—For Now: The Patterns of History and What They Reveal About the Future* (London: Profile Books, 2010).

Mumbauer, Annika, 'German War Plans', in Richard F. Hamilton and Holger H. Herwig, eds., *War Planning, 1914* (Cambridge: Cambridge University Press, 2010), 48–79.

Murray, Williamson, *The Change in the European Balance of Power, 1938–1939: The Path to Ruin* (Princeton, NJ: Princeton University Press, 1984).

——*Luftwaffe* (Baltimore, MD: The Nautical and Aviation Publishing Company of America, 1985).

——*German Military Effectiveness* (Baltimore: The Nautical and Aviation Publishing Company of America, 1992).

——'Net Assessment in Nazi Germany in the 1930s', in Murray and Allan R. Millett, eds., *Calculations: Net Assessment and the Coming of World War II* (New York: Free Press, 1992), 60–97.

—— and Mark Grimsley, 'Introduction: On Strategy', in Murray, MacGregor Knox, and Alvin Bernstein, eds., *The Making of Strategy: Rulers, States, and War* (Cambridge: Cambridge University Press, 1994), 1–23.

—— and Jim Lacey, eds., *The Making of Peace: Rulers, States, and the Aftermath of War* (Cambridge: Cambridge University Press, 2009).

—— and Allan R. Millett, eds., *Calculations: Net Assessment and the Coming of World War II* (New York: Free Press, 1992).

—— —— eds., *Military Innovation in the Interwar Period* (Cambridge: Cambridge University Press, 1996).

—— —— *A War To Be Won: Fighting the Second World War* (Cambridge, MA: Harvard University Press, 2000).

——MacGregor Knox, and Alvin Bernstein, eds., *The Making of Strategy: Rulers, States, and War* (Cambridge: Cambridge University Press, 1994).

—— Richard Hart Sinnreich, and James Lacey, eds., *The Shaping of Grand Strategy: Policy, Diplomacy, and War* (Cambridge: Cambridge University Press, 2011).

Nardin, Terry and David R. Mapel, eds., *Traditions of International Ethics* (Cambridge: Cambridge University Press, 1992).

Newmyer, Jacqueline, 'The Revolution in Military Affairs with Chinese Characteristics', *The Journal of Strategic Studies*, 33 (August 2010), 483–504.

Norris, Robert S. and Hans M. Kristensen, 'Global Nuclear Weapon Inventories, 1945–2010', *Bulletin of the Atomic Scientists*, 66 (July/August 2010), 77–83.

Nosworthy, Brent, *The Bloody Crucible of Courage: Fighting Methods and Combat Experience of the Civil War* (New York: Carroll and Graf Publishers, 2005).

Nye, Joseph S., Jr., *Nuclear Ethics* (New York: Free Press, 1986).

Oberg, Jim, *Space Power Theory* (Washington, DC: Government Printing Office, 1999).

Ogilvie-White, Tanya, ed., *On Nuclear Deterrence: The Correspondence of Sir Michael Quinlan* (Abingdon: Routledge for The International Institute for Strategic Studies, 2011).

O'Loughlin, John, ed., *Dictionary of Geopolitics* (Westport, CT: Greenwood Press, 1994).

Olsen, John Andreas, ed., *A History of Air Warfare* (Dulles, VA: Potomac Books, 2010).

—— and Colin S. Gray, eds., *The Practice of Strategy: From Alexander the Great to the Present* (Oxford: Oxford University Press, 2011).

Overy, Richard J., *Why the Allies Won* (London: Jonathan Cape, 1995).

—— *The Battle of Britain: Myth and Reality* (London: Penguin Books, 2010).

Owens, William A., *Lifting the Fog of War* (New York: Farrar, Straus & Giroux, 2000).

Paine, Sally C. M., 'The Japanese Way of War', paper delivered to the Conference on Asian Strategic Studies, US Naval War College, Newport, RI, August 2011.

Paret, Peter, *Clausewitz and the State* (New York: Oxford University Press, 1976).

Parker, Geoffrey, *Geopolitics: Past, Present and Future* (London: Pinter, 1998).

Parker, W. H., *Mackinder: Geography as an Aid to Statecraft* (Oxford: Clarendon Press, 1982).

Payne, Keith B., *The Great American Gamble: The Theory and Practice of Deterrence from Cold War to the Twenty-First Century* (Fairfax, VA: National Institute Press, 2008).

Pearsall, Judy and Bill Trumble, eds., *The Oxford English Reference Dictionary*, 2nd edn. (Oxford: Oxford University Press, 1996).

Pearton, Maurice, *Diplomacy, War and Technology since 1830* (Lawrence, KS: University Press of Kansas, 1984).

Porter, Patrick, 'Good Anthropology, Bad History: The Cultural Turn in Studying War', *Parameters*, 37 (Summer 2007), 45–58.

—— *Military Orientalism: Eastern War Through Western Eyes* (London: C. Hurst, 2009).

—— 'A Matter of Choice: Strategy and Discretion in the Shadow of World War II', *The Journal of Strategic Studies*, 35 (2012), 317–43.

Posen, Barry R., 'Command of the Commons: The Military Foundation of U.S. Hegemony', *International Security*, 28 (Summer 2003), 5–46.

Pouncey, Peter R., *The Necessities of War: A Study of Thucydides' Pessimism* (New York: Columbia University Press, 1980).

Pumphrey, Carolyn, ed., *Global Climate Change: National Security Implications* (Carlisle, PA: Strategic Studies Institute, US Army War College, May 2008).

Quinlan, Michael, *Thinking About Nuclear Weapons; Principles, Problems, Prospects* (Oxford: Oxford University Press, 2009).

Rabkin, Jeremy, 'Can We Win a War If We Have to Fight By Cosmopolitan Rules?' *Orbis*, 55 (Fall 2011), 700–16.

Randall, Lisa, *Knocking on Heaven's Door: How Physics and Scientific Thinking Illuminate the Modern World* (London: Bodley Head, 2011).

Reid, Brian Holden, *J. F. C. Fuller: Military Thinker* (New York: St. Martin's Press, 1987).

——*Studies in British Military Thought: Debates with Fuller and Liddell Hart* (Lincoln, NE: University of Nebraska Press, 1998).

Reus-Smith, Christian and Duncan Snidal, eds., *The Oxford Handbook of International Relations* (Oxford: Oxford University Press, 2008).

Rid, Thomas and Thomas Keaney, eds., *Understanding Counterinsurgency: Doctrine, Operations, and Challenges* (Abingdon: Routledge, 2010).

Roberts, Adam, 'The Civilian in Modern War', in Hew Strachan and Sybille Scheipers, eds., *The Changing Character of War* (Oxford: Oxford University Press, 2011), 357–80.

——and Richard Guelff, eds., *Documents on the Laws of War*, 3rd edn. (Oxford: Oxford University Press, 2000).

Roberts, J. M., *The New Penguin History of the World*, 5th edn. (London: Penguin Books, 2007).

Rosen, Stephen Peter, *War and Human Nature* (Princeton, NJ: Princeton University Press, 2005).

Rosenberg, David Alan, 'The Origins of Overkill: Nuclear Weapons and American Strategy', *International Security*, 7 (Spring 1983), 3–71.

Ross, Stephen T., *American War Plans, 1945–1950* (London: Frank Cass, 1996).

Schelling, Thomas C., *The Strategy of Conflict* (New York: Oxford University Press, 1960).

——*Arms and Influence* (New Haven, CT: Yale University Press, 1966).

Schroeder, Paul W., 'Napoleon's Foreign Policy: A Criminal Enterprise', *The Journal of Military History*, 54 (April 1990), 147–61.

Shaw, Malcolm N., *International Law*, 6th edn. (Cambridge: Cambridge University Press, 2008).

Shaw, Martin, *War and Genocide: Organized Killing in Modern Society* (Cambridge: Polity Press, 2003).

Sheffield, Gary, *Forgotten Victory: The First World War: Myths and Realities* (London: Headline, 2001).

Sheldon, John B., 'Deciphering Cyberpower: Strategic Purpose in Peace and War', *Strategic Studies Quarterly*, 5 (Summer 2011), 95–112.

Showalter, Dennis E. *Railroads and Rifles: Soldiers, Technology, and the Unification of Germany* (Hamden, CT: Archon Books, 1986).

Shue, Henry, ed., *Nuclear Deterrence and Moral Restraint: Critical Choices for American Strategy* (Cambridge: Cambridge University Press, 1989).

Singer, P. W., *Wired for War: The Robotics Revolution and Conflict in the 21st Century* (New York: Penguin Press, 2009).

Sloan, Elinor C., *The Revolution in Military Affairs: Implications for Canada and NATO* (Montreal and Kingston: McGill-Queens University Press, 2002).

——*Modern Military Strategy: An Introduction* (Abingdon: Routledge, 2012).

Smith, Anthony, *Machine Gun: The Story of the Men and the Weapons that Changed the Face of War* (London: Judy Piatkus, 2002).

Smith, Merritt Roe, *Military Enterprise and Technological Change: Perspectives on the American Experience* (Cambridge, MA: MIT Press, 1987).

Smith, Michael V., 'Ten Propositions Regarding Spacepower', thesis (Maxwell AFB, AL: School of Advanced Air and Space Studies, Air University, June 2001).

Smith, Rupert, *The Utility of Force: The Art of War in the Modern World* (London: Allen Lane, 2005).

Snyder, Jack L., *The Soviet Strategic Culture: Implications for Limited Nuclear Operations, R-2154-AF* (Santa Monica, CA: RAND, September 1977).

Sondhaus, Lawrence, *Strategic Culture and Ways of War* (Abingdon: Routledge, 2006).

Speier, Hans, 'Magic Geography', *Social Research* (September 1941), 310–30.

Sprout, Harold and Margaret Sprout, *The Ecological Perspective on Human Affairs with Special Reference to International Politics* (Princeton, NJ: Princeton University Press, 1965).

Spykman, Nicholas J. *The Geography of the Peace* (1944; Hamden, CT: Archon Books, 1969).

——*America's Strategy in World Politics: The United States and the Balance of Power* (1942; New Brunswick, NJ: Transaction Publishers, 2007).

Stahel, David, *Operation Barbarossa and Germany's Defeat in the East* (Cambridge: Cambridge University Press, 2009).

Stevenson, David, *With Our Backs to the Wall: Victory and Defeat in 1918* (London: Allen Lane, 2011).

Strachan, Hew, *Clausewitz's 'On War': A Biography* (New York: Atlantic Monthly Press, 2007).

—— 'Strategy in the Twenty-First Century', in Strachan and Sybille Scheipers, eds., *The Changing Character of War* (Oxford: Oxford University Press, 2011), 503–23.

—— and Sybille Scheipers, eds., *The Changing Character of War* (Oxford: Oxford University Press, 2011).

Strausz-Hupé, Robert, *Geopolitics: The Struggle for Space and Power* (1942; New York: Arno, 1972).

Taylor, A. J. P., *The Origins of the Second World War* (London: Hamish Hamilton, 1961).

Terraine, John, 'The Substance of the War', in Hugh Cecil and Peter H. Liddle, eds., *Facing Armageddon: The First World War Experience* (London: Leo Cooper, 1996), 3–15.

Thomas, Keith, ed., *The Revolution in Military Affairs: Warfare in the Information Age* (Canberra: Australian Defence Studies Centre, 1997).

Thucydides, *The Landmark Thucydides: A Comprehensive Guide to the Peloponnesian War*, ed. Robert B. Strassler, rev. trans. Richard Crawley (*c*.400 BC; New York: Free Press, 1996).

Till, Geoffrey, *Seapower: A Guide to the Twenty-First Century*, 2nd edn. (Abingdon: Routledge, 2009).

Tooze, Adam, *Wages of Destruction: The Making and Breaking of the Nazi Economy* (London: Allen Lane, 2006).

Tzu, Sun *The Art of War*, trans. Samuel B. Griffith (*c*.490 BC: Oxford: Clarendon Press, 1963).

US Army and Marine Corps, *Counterinsurgency Field Manual* (Chicago: University of Chicago Press, 2007).

US Joint Chiefs of Staff, *The U.S. Department of Defense Dictionary of Military Terms*, rev. edn. (London: Greenhill Books, 1990).

Walzer, Michael, *Just and Unjust Wars: A Moral Argument with Historical Illustrations*, 3rd edn. (New York: Basic Books, 1977).

Watts, Barry D., *The Maturing Revolution in Military Affairs* (Washington, DC: Center for Strategic and Budgetary Assessments, 2011).

Wawro, Geoffrey, *The Franco-Prussian War: The German Conquest of France in 1870–1871* (Cambridge: Cambridge University Press, 2003).

Weigert, Hans W., *Generals and Geographers: The Twilight of Geopolitics* (New York: Oxford University Press, 1942).

Werrell, Kenneth P., *Blankets of Fire: US Bombers over Japan during World War II* (Washington, DC: Smithsonian Institution Press, 1996).

Whittlesey, Derwent, 'Haushofer: The Geopolitician', in Edward Mead Earle, ed., *Makers of Modern Strategy: Military Thought from Machiavelli to Hitler* (Princeton, NJ: Princeton University Press, 1941), 388–411.

——*German Strategy of World Conquest* (London: Robinson, 1942).

Wilkinson, David, 'Spykman and Geopolitics', in Ciro E. Zoppo and Charles Zorgbibe, eds., *On Geopolitics: Classical and Nuclear* (Dordrecht: Martinus Nijhoff, 1985), 77–129.

Winters, Harold, *Battling the Elements: Weather and Terrain in the Conduct of War* (Baltimore: Johns Hopkins University Press, 1998).

Wylie, J. C., *Military Strategy: A General Theory of Power Control* (1967; Annapolis, MD: Naval Institute Press, 1989).

Yarger, Harry R., *Strategy and the National Security Professional: Strategic Thinking in the 21st Century* (Westport, CT: Praeger Security International, 2009).

Yoder, John Howard, *Christian Attitudes to War, Peace, and Revolution* (Grand Rapids, MI: Brazos Press, 2009).

Zabecki, David T., *Steel Wind: Colonel Georg Bruchmuller and the Birth of Modern Artillery* (Westport, CT: Praeger, 1994).

——*The German 1918 Offensives: A Case Study in the Operational Level of War* (Abingdon: Routledge, 2006).

Zimmerman, David, *Britain's Shield: Radar and the Defeat of the Luftwaffe* (Stroud: Sutton Publishing, 2001).

Zoppo, Ciro E. and Charles Zorgbibe, eds., *On Geopolitics: Classical and Nuclear* (Dordrecht: Martinus Nijhoff, 1985).

Zuber, Terence, *The Battle of the Frontiers: Ardennes 1914* (Stroud: Tempus Publishing, 2007).

Index

Note: Bold entries refer to figures or tables.

and regional hegemony 131
and Revolution in Military Affairs 161–5
and Second World War 146
and significance of location 126–7
and Vietnam War 140–1, 145
US Air Force (USAF) 24
US Army Air Corps (USAAC) 28
US Army Air Forces (USAAF), and strategic
    bombing 171, 182

Verdun 124
Vietnam War 140–1, 145
Vikings 143

Walzer, Michael 44, 61, 74n14
war:
  and categorical difference from law and
      morality 69–70
  and competitive nature of 165, 175–6
  and failure to agree on concept of 14
  and human face of 10–11
  and political purpose 14
  and politics 59–60
war convention 44, 59, 61, 62, 74n14
weapons:
  and Fuller on 153–4
  and weapon systems 154–5, 175
  see also technology
weapons development 20
Weigert, Hans W 116, 117
will 57
William of Occam 84
World Community 54
Wylie, J C 16, 98

Yoder, John Howard 39, 70

Printed and bound by CPI Group (UK) Ltd, Croydon, CR0 4YY